Essential Test Tips Video from Trivium Test Prep

Dear Customer,

Thank you for purchasing from Trivium Test Prep! Whether you're looking to join the military, get into college, or advance your career, we're honored to be a part of your journey.

To show our appreciation (and to help you relieve a little of that test-prep stress), we're offering a **FREE *PHR Essential Test Tips* Video** by Trivium Test Prep. Our video includes 35 test preparation strategies that will help keep you calm and collected before and during your big exam. All we ask is that you email us your feedback and describe your experience with our product. Amazing, awful, or just so-so: we want to hear what you have to say!

To receive your **FREE *PHR Essential Test Tips* Video**, please email us at 5star@ triviumtestprep.com. Include "Free 5 Star" in the subject line and the following information in your email:

1. The title of the product you purchased.
2. Your rating from 1 – 5 (with 5 being the best).
3. Your feedback about the product, including how our materials helped you meet your goals and ways in which we can improve our products.
4. Your full name and shipping address so we can send your **FREE *PHR Essential Test Tips* Video**.

If you have any questions or concerns please feel free to contact us directly at 5star@triviumtestprep.com.

Thank you, and good luck with your studies!

PHR Study Guide 2024-2025

3 Practice Tests and PHR Exam Prep for HRCI

[Aligned to the New Outline]

B. Hettinger

ISBN-13: 9781637986875

TABLE OF CONTENTS

ONLINE RESOURCES

Trivium includes online resources with the purchase of this study guide to help you fully prepare for the exam.

Practice Test #3

The 3rd practice test is provided online in an interactive format.

Review Questions

Need more practice? Our review questions use a variety of formats to help you memorize key terms and concepts.

From Stress to Success

Watch "From Stress to Success," a brief but insightful YouTube video that offers the tips, tricks, and secrets experts use to score higher on the exam.

Reviews

Leave a review, send us helpful feedback, or sign up for Trivium promotions—including free books!

Access these materials at: **triviumtestprep.com/phr-online-resources**

Introduction

Congratulations on choosing to take the Professional in Human Resources (PHR®) exam! By purchasing this book, you've taken the first step toward becoming a certified Professional in Human Resources.

This guide will provide you with a detailed overview of the PHR® so that you will know exactly what to expect on test day. We'll take you through all of the concepts covered on the exam and give you the opportunity to evaluate your knowledge with practice questions. Even if it's been awhile since you last took a major test, don't worry; we'll make sure you're more than ready!

The HR Certification Institute (HRCI)

The Professional in Human Resources (PHR®) exam is offered by the internationally recognized HR Certification Institute (HRCI), which has certified over 130,000 HR professionals around the world. Certification by the HRCI is a globally recognized demonstration of professional achievement.

PHR® Certification

PHR® certification is appropriate for department-oriented HR professionals who execute specific HR duties, implement HR programs, and report to more senior HR professionals. Certification requires knowledge of applicable employment laws and regulations as well as mastery of the technical aspects of HR.

HRCI designs the PHR based on knowledge determined by HR practitioners around the world. HR tasks—and the knowledge needed to perform them—are extensively researched and grouped into functional areas, which are described below.

Functional Area Name and Number	Percentage of Exam
Business Management (01)	14%
Workforce Planning and Talent Acquisition (02)	14%
Learning and Development (03)	10%
Total Rewards (04)	15%
Employee Engagement (05)*	17%
Employee and Labor Relations (06)	20%
HR Information Management (07)*	10%

*The Employee Engagement and HR Information Management functional areas are new to the exam as of March 2024.

Eligibility Requirements for the Exam

HRCI requires all PHR exam candidates to meet one of the following eligibility requirements:

- at least one year of professional experience in an HR role AND a master's degree (or higher)
- at least two years of professional experience in an HR role AND a bachelor's degree
- at least four years of professional experience in an HR role

College degrees do not have to be in an HR-related field.

All PHR candidates must apply to take the exam; this can be done through the HRCI website. Candidates have 180 days from the time of application approval to schedule their exams.

Please visit hrci.org for more information on professional requirements, including how these must be documented during the application process for the exam.

How is the PHR® Scored and Administered?

HRCI offers the PHR® as a computer-based exam through its partnership with Pearson Vue. The test can be taken at a Pearson Vue test center or it may be taken at home, through online proctoring. Test takers must present a valid, unexpired photo ID before sitting for the exam. Those taking the exam at home through remote proctoring must complete online check-in protocols as prompted. It is imperative that the name on the ID matches the name on the exam application. Expect to spend two hours and thirty minutes taking the exam:

- Test: **2 hours**
- Administrative Purposes: **30 minutes**

The exam consists of 115 multiple-choice questions. Ninety questions are scored, and twenty-five questions are pretest, unscored questions. Each question lists four possible answer options; only one option is correct.

You will receive a preliminary score immediately after you complete the computer-based exam. Within one week of taking the exam, HRCI will send a notice to let you know that your official results are available. Scores range from 100 – 700. You will need a scaled score of at least 500 to pass the exam.

About This Guide

This guide will help you master the most important test topics and develop critical test-taking skills. We have built features into our books to prepare you for your exam and increase your score. Along with a detailed summary of the test's format, content, and scoring, we offer an in-depth overview of the content knowledge required to pass the test. Throughout the guide, you'll find sidebars that provide interesting information, highlight key concepts, and review content so that you can solidify your understanding. You can also evaluate your knowledge with sample questions throughout the text as well as practice tests. We're pleased you've chosen Trivium to be a part of your journey!

Chapter 1 – Human Resources and the Business Environment

The Role of Human Resource Management in the Business Environment

Human resource management describes the activities that are essential to managing an organization's employees, or its **human capital**. HR professionals oversee compensation and benefits, training and development, recruitment and hiring, strategic management, and other functions.

HR departments recruit, retain, and motivate the best employees for the organization. To do so, they must keep the company competitive in terms of compensation, benefits, learning opportunities, career advancement, work-life balance, and other matters important to employees.

At the same time, HR plays an important business role in the organization. HR management strategizes how to allocate staff appropriately, maintain regulatory compliance, and prevent risks. Aligning "people needs" with business needs is essential to the organization's viability and attractiveness in the marketplace.

HR functions and areas of expertise include recruitment, health and safety, employee relations, compensation and benefits, and compliance. HR practitioners may perform tasks related to a combination of these functions or specialize in one (or a small few) of these areas. Small businesses that do not have a dedicated HR professional will sometimes outsource these functions or join a professional employer organization to get the same benefits that an internal HR team provides.

This chapter provides a brief overview of the role of the Human Resources professional in terms of recruitment, health and safety, employee relations, compliance, compensation and benefits, training and development, and policies and procedures. A description of the distinctions between HR generalists and HR specialists is also provided.

Differences between HR Generalists and HR Specialists

HR professionals typically fall into one of two categories: generalists or specialists. **HR generalists**, also called HR managers or HR business partners, have a broad range of responsibilities in one or more of the functional areas of human resources. Larger organizations usually employ **HR specialists**, who have technical knowledge and skills in specific areas.

There are different levels of generalists and specialists in an organization, depending on its size, budget, and other needs. Examples of specialist job titles are described in Table 1.1.

Table 1.1. Functional Areas of HR and Related Job Titles	
Functional Area	**Job Title Examples**
Recruiting	▪ Recruiter ▪ Recruiting Assistant; Recruiting Coordinator ▪ Talent Acquisition Specialist ▪ Staffing Manager
Training and Organizational Development	▪ Learning and Organizational Development Manager ▪ Organizational Development Specialist
Compensation and Benefits	▪ Compensation Analyst ▪ Benefits Specialist ▪ Total Rewards Manager
Employee and Labor Relations	▪ Performance Manager Specialist ▪ Employee Relations Manager ▪ Labor Relations Manager
Safety	▪ Risk Management Specialist ▪ Workers' Compensation Specialist
HR Information Systems	▪ HRIS Administrator ▪ HRIS Manager

Practice Question

1. Which of the following describes a practitioner with expertise in a specific area of human resources?

A) HR generalist
B) HR manager
C) HR specialist
D) HR expert

The Business Environment

Business Acumen

Business acumen refers to the following:

- speaking the language of business
- understanding the multiple functions of an organization
- being able to show the value of HR to the organization

In recent years, the tactical HR generalist role has changed into a business partnership with senior leadership to develop and execute personnel strategies. Still, the administrative and tactical aspects of HR remain necessary for business operations. To be influential, HR business partners must position themselves as tactical operators, strategic advisors, and champions for change.

Developing a strong understanding of the organization, its operations, and its external environment is essential for any HR business partner to become a strategic advisor to senior management. HR business partners must align themselves closely with the values of the organization and the vision of its leaders in order to be seen as valuable partners. To accomplish this they must

- develop in-depth knowledge about the business, including its operations, financials, and strategy;
- build key relationships in the organization to influence the strategic agenda;
- earn leaders' trust so that HR can contribute to business results;
- prioritize processes that deliver the most benefits;
- develop credibility through competence, honesty, and high standards;
- champion HR solutions that add to the bottom line today and for future needs; and
- act as a catalyst for continued business performance.

As business partners, HR practitioners share the responsibility for the business's success by executing HR strategies that lead to tangible results. HR partners quantify HR's contribution to business performance and staff effectiveness in all operations. HR business partners ensure that duties are assigned to those with appropriate qualifications, design meaningful career paths to motivate employees, actively manage talent, create staffing and succession plans, and foster an open work environment where ideas are shared.

Strategic Management

Over the past century, companies have grown larger and more complicated as the demands of consumers and the business environment have grown more complex and nuanced. Products are now created using elaborate processes with multiple workers and machines. Additionally, as the US economy has evolved from primarily manufacturing products to providing services, companies must accommodate demand and trends in order to stay competitive. Over time, companies have developed new processes, restructured their personnel, adopted new tools, and reevaluated management practices to ensure that their employees are able to achieve these overarching goals.

To stay competitive in a continually evolving global marketplace, business leaders must be able to quickly respond and adapt to change in the industry, economy, workforce, and regulatory environment. They must know their clients' needs and develop useful products and services to meet those needs. Successful business leaders continually scan the environment, make predictions, and develop business plans to stay competitive. This ongoing process of creation, research, reassessment, and development is called **strategic management**. Strategic management is important to human resource professionals because it affects how HR adds value to the organization through policies, procedures, and programs.

Strategic HR management is achieved when HR leaders and practitioners develop overall management strategies for the company. Since organizations are composed of people, the human resource professional's function must focus on those items that impact the people of the organization. When the organization must respond to changes in the marketplace, industry, or regulatory environment, HR practitioners are responsible for aligning the organization's people, policies, and processes with these changes. To be successful, they must collaborate with business leadership to stay aware of business goals, objectives, and strategic vision.

The Strategic Planning Process

In order to respond to changes in the marketplace and continue to grow, organizations periodically undergo **strategic planning**, which is a process of defining its overall purpose and goals and how these goals will be achieved. Through strategic planning, an organization determines its current status, direction, approach, and how it will measure its success. Strategic planning focuses on the organization as a whole rather than on a particular product or service. The process, which is generally carried out on a periodic basis, answers the following questions about the organization:

- Where are we now?
- Where do we want to be in ___ years?
- How will we get there?
- How will we know when we are there?

There are several approaches to strategic planning that may be tailored to the unique needs of the organization depending on its size, leadership, maturity level, and culture:

- Goals-based planning focuses on the organization's mission, vision, and values. Goals are set to achieve the mission; the steps needed to achieve the goals are determined.
- Issues-based planning focuses on the issues facing the organization and determines the steps needed to address those issues.
- Organic planning focuses on a common vision and values and identifying best practices and methodologies in the organization. The stakeholders focus on what is already working rather than fixing problems.

Regardless of the method, strategic plans are typically developed for a period of one year or more. Some plans may be in-depth, with step-by-step actions, while others are high-level plans with no steps. The strategic planning process typically has the following elements:

- **Plan the process:** Stakeholders decide on process, participants, and time frame. Preplanning reduces errors in the planning process and achieves commitment from leaders.

- **Study the environment:** Stakeholders use tools like statistical models, SWOT analysis, PESTLE analysis, and Porter's Five Forces to determine the organization's present state.
- **Formulate a strategy:** Stakeholders develop the organization's mission, vision, values, goals, and objectives; they focus on the future and the organization's direction or destination.
- **Implement the strategy:** Stakeholders articulate goals, develop budgets, create action plans, and execute plans.
- **Evaluate the strategy:** Stakeholders evaluate the strategy periodically and make adjustments.

The formal strategic plan, however, is not as important as the process itself, or as the execution of the plan. An organization gains many benefits through the strategic planning process:

- creating a sense of purpose
- helping leadership set goals
- enhancing communication with staff
- keeping staff involved
- enabling leadership to allocate resources appropriately
- creating accountability
- building consensus

Uniting stakeholders to discuss the future of the organization is a healthy process that will keep it adaptable to change and viable in the marketplace. Leveraging the existing organizational hierarchy to execute the plan and reviewing progress periodically are keys to successfully implementing the strategic plan.

Mission, Vision, and Values

During the strategic planning process, an organization typically reviews its mission, vision, and values statements:

- A **mission statement** defines the organization's purpose, what it offers, whom it serves, and where it operates.
- A **vision statement** outlines the organization's goals.
- An organization's **core values** frame its perspective and guide its actions.

If the organization has not already created these, or is doing so for the first time, it typically will develop these statements as part of the strategic planning process. Once these statements are formalized, the organization develops goals to support them. These statements help stakeholders and employees maintain focus during the strategic planning process and throughout the year.

HR plays an important role in the strategic planning process. HR professionals help create and decide on HR initiatives and are instrumental in communicating and disseminating the strategic plan to employees so that everyone within the organization can understand and support key initiatives. Additionally, through talent management and development, HR ensures that the organization is staffed with skilled individuals who move the strategic plan forward.

Developing Goals

When developing goals, leadership must define not only the goal but also the desired results. An organization's goals should be SMART:

- Specific: Goals must be clear and detailed enough to guide action plans.
- Measurable: Goals require metrics to determine their progress.
- Action-oriented: Goals should describe the actions needed to accomplish them.
- Realistic: Goals should be achievable.
- Time-based: Goals require a time frame for completion.

HR can play a key role in goal development by working with individuals, departments, and the organization to roll out SMART goals and train staff in achieving them.

Implementing the Strategic Plan

Once the strategic plan has been developed, organizational leaders, including HR, will consult with department heads, management, and other key employees to begin the implementation process. **Implementation** includes developing tactical goals and action plans, which can be specific to departments, work groups, or even certain individuals in the organization. The tactical goals and action plans should tie directly to the more broadly stated strategic plan and should be SMART.

After the goals and action plans are developed, leadership and management will address budgetary issues and resources needed to achieve the strategic plan. The organization may decide it needs additional personnel, new technology, or external assistance. Those involved in the budgeting process will make recommendations on the cash and resources needed, and leadership will determine whether these recommendations support the strategic plan.

Evaluating the Strategic Plan

Strategic planning does not end with the development of that plan. Rather, the process continues throughout the year or years. As the organization implements its plan, it should periodically evaluate whether it is on track to achieve its strategic goals. This includes evaluating the tactical goals and action plans. If the organization's leaders find that the organization is not on track, they may decide to revise the action plan or tactical goals or even reevaluate the strategic plan itself. Internal or external factors can sometimes cause an organization to change course. Organizations that can adapt accordingly to their environment are likely to succeed.

The Role of HR in Strategic Planning

HR leaders have an important role in the strategic planning process. HR develops its own goals and action plans that align with the overarching goals of the organization. The strategic HR plan—or human capital plan—addresses the same questions raised during the larger strategic planning process. As with any strategic plan, the strategic HR plan will differ from organization to organization; however, there are some commonalities, as described in Table 1.2.

Table 1.2. Components of a Human Capital Plan	
Component	**Explanation**
strategic direction	Strategic direction requires knowledge of the organization's strategic plans; budgetary constraints; internal and external forces affecting human capital; makeup of the current workforce; and customer and stakeholder expectations, challenges, and needs. HR must develop a vision of the future workforce in order to determine the ideal human capital necessary for the organization to achieve its strategic goals.
human capital goals	Human capital goals are related to the organization's talent (employees), performance management, and leadership. Goals may relate to the hiring, training, and allocation of employees to achieve certain objectives in the organization's general strategic plan.
strategies for accomplishing goals	These strategies specifically describe how goals will be achieved. Consideration should be given to the availability and capabilities of human capital.
implementation plan	The implementation plan describes the actions needed to accomplish goals and objectives. Implementation plans include the following components: ▪ a description of each task necessary to carry out the objectives ▪ stakeholders responsible for each task ▪ resources required (e.g., human, financial) ▪ time frames (e.g., milestones, deadlines)
communications plan	The communications plan describes how key stakeholders in the organization will stay informed about the progress of the strategic plan and the actions they need to take. HR must communicate regularly with all stakeholders to ensure their understanding of the plan and to solicit feedback. The communications plan is often a subset of the implementation plan.

Table 1.2. Components of a Human Capital Plan	
Component	**Explanation**
accountability system	The accountability system measures and tracks progress in executing the strategy or objective. People and teams identified in the implementation plan are held accountable. Specific targets are identified by describing the level of performance or rate of improvement needed for each part of the implementation plan. Establishing metrics provides essential direction to those involved in executing the objectives and shows progress of the plan's implementation.

First, human resources leadership establishes a human capital management plan. Then it develops a budget to implement the plan. Depending on finances, the human resources departmental budget may include the following costs:

- employee compensation (salaries, bonuses, and benefits)
- payroll taxes
- equipment and supplies
- training and development fees
- travel
- outsourced services (e.g., payroll, benefits administration, HRIS)

HR may also lead the development of budgetary items that are then allocated to other departments or verticals in the organization. These costs may include the following:

- recruitment fees
- training and development fees
- raises
- employee incentives or awards
- temporary staff

In some cases, it may be more cost-effective to outsource functions or repurpose HR positions to carry out new or different tasks. Furthermore, some processes can be streamlined so that HR personnel can focus on tasks that are more impactful to the organization.

Managing Organizational Change

As a result of the strategic planning process, an organization may decide that it needs to restructure itself in order to achieve its goals and remain competitive and viable in the marketplace. Organizational leadership may decide to explore or implement any of a number of structural changes.

In **restructuring** or **reengineering**, leadership may examine processes for redundancy within the entire organization or in certain departments or teams; it may also simplify operations to improve efficiency and reduce costs.

With an **expansion in force**, an organization grows teams by creating new positions and hiring additional personnel. This may lead to a culture clash between veteran employees and newcomers. It will also require resources to train the new employees and acclimate them to the new environment.

Conversely, a **reduction in force** decreases personnel expense by eliminating positions or departments. Also called **downsizing**, this may create anxiety for remaining employees, who must take on the extra workload while feeling uncertain about the security of their own jobs.

Mergers and acquisitions (M&As) are a combination of two or more entities. In a merger, two companies combine to leverage both of their assets while forming a new, stronger corporate identity. Acquisitions involve a larger company purchasing another company and integrating it into the existing culture and operations. With divestiture, a company's product line, service, or business unit is spun off or sold. Typically, the existing team involved in the divestiture remains intact.

In **outsourcing**, the organization uses external service providers to handle certain business functions, such as accounting, payroll, or IT. Finally, **offshoring** is when an organization moves certain jobs or functions to other countries where labor is cheaper. This has other implications, such as a loss of jobs elsewhere, cultural barriers, and time zone differences.

All employees are affected by organizational change in some way. In some cases, employee responsibilities may increase or change. Other employees may worry about losing their jobs and, unfortunately, some employees will lose their jobs. HR professionals help manage organizational change by establishing programs and communications to help employees understand changes, manage their emotions, and adapt to restructuring.

It is important for the organization to communicate regularly with employees about the changes, let them know how they are affected, and be truthful about the facts. If the organization is not truthful, or if employees perceive that information is being withheld, it risks losing longer-term employees with valuable historical knowledge. Decreased productivity could be another consequence.

Practice Questions

2. Strategic planning is centered around the organization's
   A) staffing plan.
   B) mission statement.
   C) needs analysis.
   D) competitor data.

3. To be effective, company goals must
   A) require the participation of line staff.
   B) be available in multiple languages.
   C) grow the company.
   D) be specific and measurable.

Navigating the Organization

Structures of Organizations

Every company is organized differently depending on industry, size, tax implications, and leadership; however, all businesses operating in the United States are formally organized into one of four basic structures:

- sole proprietorships
- partnerships
- corporations
- limited liability companies

A **sole proprietorship** is the most basic business structure. In a sole proprietorship, the business owner operates alone as the only responsible party for the business (including finances), and this person has the sole authority to make business decisions. Any profits made by the business belong to the owner, who is personally responsible for all debts and liabilities of the company. Many business owners of a sole proprietorship operate the company through an assumed name registered with the county or state in which they operate.

In a **partnership**, two or more people share ownership of the business. Depending on the structure of ownership as well as the intended duration of the partnership, partnerships can take various forms:

- general partnerships
- limited liability partnerships
- joint ventures

Many partnerships have formal agreements that outline how profits will be divided, how disputes will be resolved, how change in ownership may occur, and how the partnership may be dissolved.

Did You Know?

Both an LLC and a C-corp can file for an S-corp status through the IRS. The **S-corp** designation means that the entity will be taxed as a partnership and will therefore avoid double taxation, which happens when tax is paid on the incomes of both the business and the owner.

A **corporation** is a legal entity owned by shareholders in the form of stock or equity. Corporations are most commonly formed for large businesses. Unlike sole proprietorships and partnerships, the corporation itself (not the shareholders or owners) is liable for the actions and debts of the business. Shareholders are typically not involved in the daily operations of the business; instead, they elect a board of directors to represent their interests, and the company's senior leadership team makes decisions about the direction of the company.

Finally, a **limited liability company (LLC)** is a hybrid of a partnership and a corporation. LLCs provide the liability protections of a corporation while offering the simplified tax implications of a partnership. The "owners" of an LLC are called "members," and depending on the state, there can be one or more members.

Design and designation of a corporation or company depends on the desired tax implications. Typically, the LLC itself does not pay taxes; instead, the taxes pass through to the member's personal tax filing. **C-**

corporations, or **C-corps**, on the other hand, are taxed separately from the owner or shareholders. In other words, the organization itself is subject to corporate income taxation.

Operational Functions in an Organization

Regardless of size and formal structure, most organizations need certain core functions in order to operate. The general business functions below contribute to achieving the organization's objective:

- **Procurement, logistics, and distribution professionals** acquire resources (**inputs**) and deliver final products (**outputs**) to customers.
- **Product or service development professionals** design, revise, and improve products or services that are offered to the marketplace; their duties may include research, design, analysis, and engineering.
- **Operations professionals** and teams organize raw products and production processes to create a final product or service; they also determine methods for cost savings.
- **Marketing and sales professionals** target prospective clients, develop and maintain relationships with existing customers, and promote and advertise products and services through multiple channels.
- **Customer service representatives** support customers who buy products or services, resolve problems and complaints, and answer questions about products or services.

The following positions operate as support functions:

- **General management** oversees corporate governance, accounting, facilities, management, and administrative support.
- **Human resources professionals** oversee the recruitment, hiring, training, compensation, and termination of employees.
- **Information technology professionals** maintain, automate, and design the technical infrastructure of the organization, including equipment, hardware, and software.

Depending on the complexity and size of the organization, these functions may be handled by one person or multiple people. All of these functions are necessary components for conducting business.

Organizational Design and Development

Organizational design aligns people, processes, compensation, and metrics with the strategy of the organization to ensure that the organization embodies its core values as specified in its mission statement and can achieve the goals laid out in its vision statement. The design reflects the organization's need to respond to changes (internal and external); integrate new people, technologies, and processes; encourage collaboration; and offer flexibility.

A company can be organized in different ways, depending on its objectives. Leaders and managers must decide how to group people together so they can perform their work effectively. There are five common approaches to organizational design that help decision-makers group people (i.e., positions) together in the organization:

1. **Functional structure** groups positions into departments or units based on similar tasks, expertise, skills, and resources. Groups within a functional structure include accounting and finance, human resources, information technology, and marketing.

2. **Divisional structure** groups business units according to a type of output. For example, units may be aligned with specific geographic locales, products, or clients.
3. **Matrix structure** mixes functional and divisional structures. People work in teams that integrate disparate expertise. Employees working in a matrix structure belong to both a functional group and a divisional group (e.g., a project team or product team).
4. **Team structure** integrates separate functions into a group based on a particular goal or objective. Team structures foster collaboration, cooperation, problem-solving, and relationship-building among various functions.
5. **Network structure** involves external entities performing certain functions on a temporary or contractual basis. For example, work is assigned to a contractor for a period of time in order to achieve a certain goal.

Organizational structures evolve over time due to organizational growth, environmental change, and other circumstances. The strategic planning process identifies ways to maintain a sound structure that positions the organization to achieve its goals and objectives. The organization's structure should support what the organization hopes to achieve; otherwise, the organization will be at a disadvantage and may risk losing its competitiveness.

Centralized versus Decentralized Decision-Making

In addition to the physical structure of the organization, it is important to consider the structure of decision-making. Decisions are constantly being made: whom to hire, what products or services to offer, where to operate, what clients to target, and more. Decision-making in an organization can be either centralized or decentralized.

Centralized organizational structures depend on one individual (or group of executives) to make decisions and provide direction. Smaller organizations often use this structure because the owner is responsible for the company's business operations. As a benefit, centralized organizations often experience quick, efficient decision-making. Business owners typically set the company's mission, vision, goals, and objectives, which managers are expected to support and execute. However, centralized organizations can become bureaucratic as they grow, due to the hierarchy of management always leading to the owner. Accomplishing tasks may then take longer, resulting in slower operations and lower productivity.

Decentralized organizational structures, on the other hand, often have several individuals responsible for management decisions. Decentralized organizations depend on a team environment at different levels of the business in order to make decisions. (Individuals may have some autonomy to make business decisions but generally must align with the vision of the larger group.) Decentralized organizations typically employ individuals with a variety of knowledge and skills, ensuring that the company can handle various types of business situations; however, reaching consensus among decision-makers in decentralized organizations can be challenging. This can slow the organization's progress in achieving its objectives and harm productivity.

Organizational leadership should carefully consider work styles, personalities, goals, vision, and the overall environment when choosing the right structure for the organization. Small organizations typically adopt centralized decision-making structures because owners often remain at the forefront of business operations. Larger organizations often use a more decentralized structure because they have several divisions or departments. Additionally, business leaders may consider changing organizational structure depending on the growth of the business and overall strategy.

Distribution and Coordination of Labor

Regardless of their structure, all organizations are groups of people working together toward a common goal. To efficiently accomplish their goals, organizations typically divide work into manageable parts. They also coordinate the work so that all employees are working interdependently toward the same objectives.

Division of labor refers to the distribution of work into separate jobs that are performed by different people. Division of labor leads to job specialization as workers focus on one or a few tasks that are now essential to their positions. As companies grow over time, horizontal division of labor (many people doing similar jobs) is usually accompanied by a vertical division of labor (a hierarchy of managers and supervisors overseeing jobs performed). Job specialization also increases work efficiency.

Through a successful division of labor, workers can master smaller tasks quickly, and less time is wasted changing from one task to another. Training costs are also reduced because employees require fewer skills to accomplish the work. Finally, job specialization makes it easier to recruit and hire people best suited for the specific jobs. However, an organization's ability to divide work among employees depends on how well those people can collaborate and work with each other; otherwise, productivity suffers due to the misallocation of tasks or resources, or duplications of effort.

Coordination tends to become more challenging as jobs become more specialized; therefore, companies typically specialize jobs so that coordination is possible. Every organization coordinates work via informal communication, formal hierarchy, or standardization. Types of **informal communication** include the following:

- sharing information with other employees through face-to-face interaction
- email
- conference calls
- team meetings

Team meetings are a common method of informal communication. During team meetings, tactical matters are discussed and work is coordinated at a more specific level. Hierarchy gives authority to individuals at certain levels of the organization, who then direct work processes and allocate resources. This is also known as the **chain of command**. **Standardization** is the development of routine processes, measured outputs, and required training or competencies.

Span of Control

Span of control describes the extent of a manager's authority, which is evaluated by the number of employees reporting to that manager. A few employees reporting to each manager results in a narrow span of control and a lengthy hierarchical structure; this is known as a **tall organization**. On the other hand, many employees reporting to each manager results in a wide span of control, creating a **flat organization**. Because it is determined by so many factors, span of control is helpful in understanding organizational designs and behaviors.

One factor is organizational size: due to costs, large organizations tend to have a narrow span of control, while smaller organizations typically have a wider span of control. Required job skills must also be considered: Tasks involving fewer skills will require less supervision, resulting in a wider span of control. Complex tasks may need a narrower span of control, so supervisors can provide more individualized attention.

Another factor is organizational culture: flexible workplaces typically have a wider span of control because the organization provides a more autonomous environment in which employees need little supervision. Finally, manager workload is a key factor. Managers should be able to plan departmental activities, train staff, and manage performance while being accountable for their own responsibilities.

Spans of control can be purposefully widened by giving workers more autonomy and holding them accountable to manage themselves. Standardizing the work processes of junior employees in order to avoid costly mistakes will also widen the span of control. As the span of control widens in an organization, the number of relationships among managers also grows.

Practice Question

4. Decentralization works best in organizations where
   A) employees dislike management.
   B) unions are present.
   C) a quick response to problems is needed.
   D) the organization is too top-heavy.

Organizational Change and Growth

Like people, organizations have their own life cycles. They are "born" (established), they develop and mature, they decline, and sometimes they "die" (dissolve). Just like people, as organizations mature, they begin to understand the environment around them, develop knowledge and wisdom, and plan for the future. Organizations at any stage of the life cycle are impacted by both internal and external factors. In order to survive, an organization must adapt to changes, demands, and its internal and external environments.

According to scholar Richard L. Daft, an expert in organization behavior and design, as an organization progresses through its life cycle and grows in size, its functions and features evolve over time:

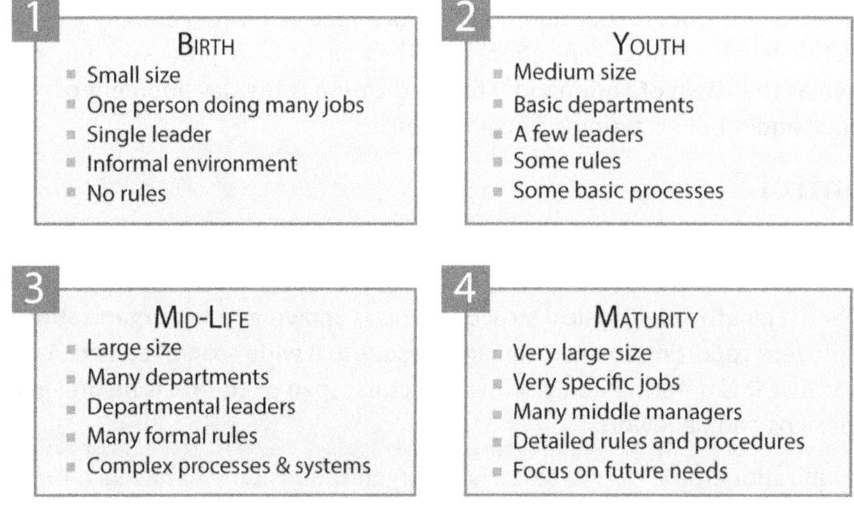

Figure 1.1. The Life Cycle of a Company

Growth Phases

In 1972, organizational development scholar Larry E. Greiner conceptualized five growth phases that an organization undergoes:

1. growth through creativity
2. growth through direction
3. growth through delegation
4. growth through coordination
5. growth through collaboration

According to Greiner, each growth phase is a period of organizational evolution of four to eight years followed by a period of organizational crisis. The phases and expected crises that result, according to his theory, are described in greater detail in Table 1.3.

Table 1.3. Growth Phases of an Organization

Growth Phase	Resulting Crisis	Organizational Needs	Action to be Taken
Growth through creativity	crisis of leadership	More formalized management practices are needed.	Leaders must adapt practices or hire managers to assume this authority.
Growth through direction	crisis of autonomy	Lower-level managers need more authority.	Leaders must delegate authority.
Growth through delegation	crisis of control	Employees need autonomy to do their jobs, while leaders need to feel in control.	Leaders must develop a system of checks and balances.
Growth through coordination	crisis of bureaucracy	Focus groups, planning processes, and staff cause delays in decision-making; innovation suffers.	Management must develop collaborative teams and break down silos.
Growth through collaboration	No formal crisis is indicated; however, employees may grow exhausted by teamwork and pressure.		

Effective leaders are aware of the growth phases of the organization and plan accordingly, typically through the strategic planning process. Understanding where the organization lies in the growth cycle also helps leaders respond appropriately to problems and crises and make decisions more efficiently. As organizations progress through the life cycle, it is important for leaders to manage change in order to ensure that management and staff are closely aligned with the strategic vision and objectives in order for them to be carried out effectively.

Not all organizations are able to survive the growth phase in its entirety. Some may collapse due to an inability to respond to changes and demands. Others may be acquired by another company and therefore cease to operate autonomously. If an organization does successfully progress through the growth phases, it will reach a point of maturity and eventually decline.

Maturity and Decline

An organization has reached maturity once it has resources to plan for the future, formalized policies and procedures, and a solid infrastructure in which it operates. In this stage of the organizational life cycle, it is typical for organizations to become bureaucratic, resulting in more difficulty making decisions or changing direction quickly. Bureaucratization harms the organization if its competition or industry evolves at a rapid pace (e.g., by developing new products and services).

On the other hand, an organization in the maturity phase also experiences stability. Functional departments and formalized procedures make it easier to hire and train staff. Additionally, mature organizations also have the financial resources and planning necessary to pay their employees competitively. The phase of maturity may last for several years or decades as long as the organization is able to respond to crises and changes in the environment.

Once an organization has reached a high level of inefficiency and bureaucracy, it will begin to decline. The organization's products or services may be outdated, and sales may decline due to a lack of innovation. Leadership may respond by reducing the workforce, closing facilities, or finding other cost-cutting measures that reduce redundancy. To revive the organization, leaders must innovate by developing new or refined products or services that meet the demands of the marketplace; otherwise, the organization may fail and cease to exist, or it may be acquired by a larger organization in a growth phase.

Practice Questions

5. What is a sign that an organization has reached maturity?
   A) It has formalized policies and procedures.
   B) It has a high level of inefficiency and bureaucracy.
   C) Leadership reduces the workforce.
   D) Bureaucratization harms innovation.
6. An organization has many detailed procedures and is resistant to change. Which phase of the organizational life cycle does this describe?
   A) birth
   B) growth
   C) maturity
   D) decline

Mergers and Acquisitions

When a company undergoes a merger or acquisition, the human resources department is a valuable partner in the process. In **mergers and acquisitions (M&As)**, an organization combines with or is absorbed by another organization. HR helps the organization conduct its due diligence when evaluating a potential merger, plan a strategy for integrating the other company's employees, and manage the change process. HR can conduct a risk assessment to identify possible conflicts before an M&A to address any problems. Given the complex nature of M&As, human resources professionals can provide particular expertise in several areas.

Evaluating Company Culture

Every company has its own unique culture, and when two companies combine (through a merger or acquisition), employees may experience culture shock. When a company is considering a merger or acquisition, its human resources department should evaluate the other company's culture and analyze how well that company would integrate with the other. HR processes and recognizing cultural differences should happen during the merger.

Organizational culture affects how employees work; what benefits they receive; the formality of the workplace; management methods; and shared work styles, attitudes, and values. HR uses the discovery process to determine this information; in this process, policies, procedures, communications, and other important documents are confidentially shared and evaluated. If there are significant differences between the two organizations, they should be thoroughly addressed prior to the merger or acquisition.

Identifying Compensation and Benefits Issues

During the due diligence process, the purchasing organization must also determine whether the deal makes financial sense. Part of the financial data includes compensation and benefits. HR should review the compensation structures and benefit plans that the other company offers. It should identify whether the compensation structures and pay levels are compatible with that of the purchasing organization. It should also determine whether there are any inconsistencies between the benefit plans, such as a difference in premium costs, coverage levels, or funding of retirement plans (e.g., company match on a 401(k) plan).

Managing Change

Change is not easy for most people. When a merger or acquisition occurs, employees may experience anxiety about their job security or the future in general. HR can help alleviate some of this anxiety by communicating regularly with employees, being responsive to their questions, and being open to feedback. HR should monitor employee morale and identify any challenges, fears, or rumors that arise due to the M&A. HR professionals can alleviate uncertainty, dispel rumors, and make the transition smoother.

Organizational Design and Development

When one company merges with or acquires another, some functions or jobs may be consolidated due to redundancy. **Workforce optimization**, the process of maximizing an organization's resources to achieve optimum performance, typically happens after a merger. In the event of a talent surplus, workforce optimization may include downsizing, which is a feature of some M&As. The process of downsizing may happen quickly or over a longer period of time. HR plays an active role in restructuring the organization, identifying ways to work more efficiently, and evaluating the impact of change. HR professionals are responsible for communicating changes to employees, revising job descriptions, handling difficult situations (e.g., layoffs or resistance to change), offering training as necessary, and motivating employees.

Practice Question

7. Which term describes the planned elimination of personnel in order to streamline operations?
   A) acquisition
   B) consolidation
   C) termination
   D) downsizing

Risk Management

Risk is defined as the probability that a specific outcome (or harm) will occur. In addition to dealing with the health and safety of employees, risk management also involves concerns the following:

- business interruption or enterprise management
- the prevention and handling of violence in the workplace
- security measures
- terrorism
- cybersecurity
- business continuity
- emergency planning

HR is involved in risk management on many levels:

- creating and disseminating a response plan
- investigating an incident
- purchasing insurance coverages
- offering support to an organization in the aftermath of an event

Risk management differs from workplace safety. **Workplace safety** focuses on reducing the risk of injury to the employee in the workplace, whereas **risk management** focuses on protecting the business and employees from external factors. A workplace security plan may include such issues as protecting intellectual property, developing crisis management plans, and taking steps to avoid theft and fraud. HR might work alone or directly with other parts of the organization, such as finance, technology, or operations to create teams to work on these threats and devise actions to mitigate future incidents.

Legal Compliance

Compliance means different things depending on the company or industry; however, all companies with employees must comply with federal and state employment laws. Many of these laws, such as the Fair Labor Standards Act and the Occupational Safety and Health Act (OSHA), are described throughout this guide. It is the responsibility of employers to understand all of the laws that apply to their business and in the location(s) in which they operate. Companies should develop sound, well-documented policies, and train employees to understand and follow them. There should also be procedures for managing employees who do not comply with a company policy (and may therefore be noncompliant with the law).

Companies must also understand and follow regulations and case law. **Regulations** are specific directives with the same force of law enacted by federal agencies in order to execute acts of Congress. The Family and Medical Leave Act is an example of a law passed by Congress that resulted in regulations and procedures developed by the Department of Labor, the regulatory agency that implements the law. The Internal Revenue Service (IRS) also creates regulations that can affect employee payroll and benefits.

Case law, on the other hand, refers to laws that are based on judicial decisions that arise out of court cases involving legal issues, such as regulations, established laws, or statutes.

The Federal Rulemaking Process

The **Administrative Procedure Act**, passed in 1946, outlines the method by which federal rules must be proposed, amended, and finalized. It is designed to govern the process that federal agencies must follow when developing and issuing new federal acts. The basic steps for promulgating a federal rule or regulation are described in Figure 1.2.

Figure 1.2. The Federal Rulemaking Process

The applicable law (which the regulation supports) specifies the process used to create accompanying regulations. Some regulations require only publication and an opportunity for comments to become final; others require publication and formal public hearings. Once a regulation becomes "final rule" and takes effect, it is published in the Federal Register, the Code of Federal Regulations (CFR), and on the website of the regulatory agency. Companies then must ensure regulatory compliance; their policies and procedures must be in accordance with regulations.

Practice Questions

8. Which term describes the level of probability that an organization may be exposed to a hazard or loss?
   A) risk
   B) adverse impact
   C) vulnerability
   D) loss analysis

9. Which of the following BEST describes risk management?
   A) reducing the risk of workplace injury to employees
   B) limiting financial losses a company may face year over year
   C) adhering to regulations to ensure regulatory compliance
   D) safeguarding employees and the organization from external factors

Organizational Culture

Organizational culture refers to the organization's internal identity and how it is perceived. It is the shared values and beliefs that set norms and govern actions. Organizational culture is not as rigid as a handbook or specific policies, but it may contribute to employee motivation.

Organizational culture also describes how people within the organization interact with one another in the workplace environment, and it is fostered by both leadership and employees. Culture is affected by the experiences, personalities, values, beliefs, and principles of leadership and employees. Everyone within the organization contributes to the organizational culture in some way, and every organization has its own unique culture. Culture is often a reason why employees decide to remain at—or leave—an organization; it can also affect an organization's success.

An organization's culture affects its overall identity, or the way that employees, clients, and the general public perceive it. For this reason, many organizations take great care to articulate and instill their values in everything they do. By developing a strong reputation, an organization attracts strong candidates for employment and reliable clients to purchase its products or services.

A shared organizational culture also helps to keep the workforce cohesive, especially when many employees come from different backgrounds, geographies, and cultures. Employees who feel supported by a sense of cultural unity and values are more likely to communicate effectively, work more collaboratively, and experience less conflict in the workplace.

Organizational culture is also a motivational tool. When employees feel connected to the organization and understand the significance of their role in it, they are more likely to feel invested in the organization's success. When they feel they have a stake in the success of the organization, they are more likely to work harder to accomplish the organization's goals. Having clear expectations and objectives set by management can help each employee understand his or her roles and responsibilities. This strategic management, combined with a system of recognition and feedback, helps keep employees aligned with the objectives of the business unit and organization. Employees will perform at their personal best to earn recognition and appreciation from management, and the organization will benefit from greater productivity and cooperation as a result.

Identifying Opportunities and Making Recommendations

An essential part of the Human Resources team's role is to understand and guide the organization's workplace culture. This requires not simply advocating for change but also understanding when *not* to advocate for change. A particular workplace's culture often emerges on its own as a natural "best fit" for the organization's business. For example, rigid hierarchies are effective in construction work because a firm chain of command improves safety. The PHR analyzes a culture's efficacy by surveying employee experiences and comparing them with business outcomes, such as financial or safety metrics. In particular, close attention to employee statements during exit interviews offers the PHR an opportunity to identify negative aspects of workplace culture. Prompt analysis and action allow the HR team to avoid propagating a toxic culture within the workplace.

Employer Branding

HR professionals need to be aware of two types of branding:

- **Company branding** is the organization's public story about products or services provided to customers.
- Meanwhile, **employer branding** is the story told to the organization's current and prospective employees.

In general, marketing handles the former while HR handles the latter; however, the PHR needs to ensure these stories are aligned. The prevalence of digital outreach in both hiring and marketing means both current and prospective employees consume branding messages. Consumers at times choose one company over another based on its reputation as an employer. Synergistic branding reduces recruitment costs and improves an organization's ability to meet its strategic goals.

Contributions to DEI Goals

The PHR contributes directly to an organization's diversity, equity, and inclusion (DEI) goals through demographic analyses of the workforce. Meaningful DEI improvement takes place not only by setting future goals but also by looking to past practices. Past demographics are important because they are the baseline from which DEI improvement is measured. The context provided by this historical data enables the PHR to accurately determine the efficacy of the organization's DEI programs. Once the efficacy (or inefficacy) of current programs has been determined, the PHR can provide relevant feedback to the leadership team members who have set the strategic DEI objectives.

Ethics

HR professionals play a key role in ensuring the integrity of organizations, and they are often the advocates, gatekeepers, and communicators of the ethical standards. HR professionals must therefore meet the highest standards of interpreting and overseeing corporate and legal policies. The organization and employees look to HR to be fair and to administer policies with principles.

HR is also involved in a company's ethics by supporting the establishment and institution of guidelines, policies, and procedures that govern behavior within a business. This may be through creating guiding principles or values that are communicated throughout the organization. By articulating how an organization desires to do business, employees, clients, and customers have a shared understanding of cultures and beliefs that guide their actions and decision-making.

Corporate Governance

Corporate governance refers to the set of systems, principles, and processes that guide everything a company does, including the relationships between its stakeholders (board of directors, management, and others).

Corporate governance is based on transparency, integrity, fairness, compliance, accountability, and responsibility. An active, independent board of directors provides corporate oversight and represents shareholders' interests. The board of directors typically includes **inside directors** (who work for the organization) and **outside directors** (who do not work for the organization). The board is elected by the **shareholders** (who are owners of the corporation). Management, including executives, are employees of the organization and oversee the daily operations of the organization.

Although a corporation is a legal entity, it cannot make a decision for itself. Instead, the board of directors and management make decisions for the organization. These stakeholders have a fiduciary responsibility to the organization, meaning their decisions should be in the best interests of stakeholders and the organization's survival. Of course, this does not always happen....

In response to corporate scandals in the early 2000s by Enron and WorldCom, among others, the Sarbanes–Oxley Act was passed in 2002 to ensure that stakeholders in public corporations appropriately maintain and uphold their fiduciary responsibilities.

The Sarbanes–Oxley Act of 2002

The **Sarbanes–Oxley Act** addresses unethical practices in public corporations and enforces penalties for violations. It includes the following provisions:

- The Public Company Accounting Oversight Board, a nonprofit corporation, was developed to require that all public accounting firms register with the board, which can audit the company's records for compliance.
- Standards were established to maintain the independent nature of auditors. Results of audits (including recommendations) are now provided directly to the audit committee of the organization's board of directors.
- Standards for corporate responsibility were established, and the organization's chief executive is held accountable for the accuracy of filings with the Securities and Exchange Commission.
- CEOs and CFOs are required to forfeit bonuses or gains through shares of stock for a one-year period when the organization files a restatement of financial reports with the SEC due to misconduct.
- Insider trading of stock is prohibited during pension fund blackout periods.
- CFOs must satisfy certain ethical requirements.
- Management officials who commit fraud or obstruct justice face criminal penalties.
- Whistleblowers who report misconduct they reasonably believe to violate SEC regulations or federal laws are protected.

Corporate Ethics

Ethical behavior begins at the highest levels of an organization. When the organization's directors, officers, and managers show their commitment to behaving ethically, employees are prone to follow their example. Many organizations, whether or not they are subject to compliance with Sarbanes-Oxley, demonstrate their commitment to corporate responsibility by developing organization-wide ethics statements, values statements, and codes of conduct:

- A code of ethics is an organization's ideals—what it wants to do when conducting business.
- A code of conduct is what an organization expects from employees; it also lays out how those who violate this code will be disciplined.

Within the code of conduct, the organization should indicate how conflicts of interest, insider information, and gifts should be handled. **Conflicts of interest** arise when an employee might personally benefit from the action of the organization. Employees are typically required to disclose potential conflicts of interest, and management will identify ways to avoid or mitigate the conflict.
Gifts from vendors or clients to an employee in the organization are a type of conflict of interest identified in such a policy. Insider information can lead to a conflict of interest when the employee has access to information that the general public does not have. Using insider information to make decisions on the purchase or sale of stock is prohibited by law and carries criminal and civil penalties.

Ethics Officers

Organizations committed to maintaining ethical standards often choose a key person to serve as an ethics officer. This may be a person at the executive level, the company's internal legal counsel, or the highest ranking human resources professional. Ethics officers advise all employees in the organization on acceptable and unacceptable conduct and their obligations to maintain an ethical workplace. They oversee the training of all employees on ethical matters and develop policies to maintain compliance with Sarbanes-Oxley (as applicable) and consistency with corporate values and ethics. Finally, ethics officers consult with other organizational leaders on ethical issues.

Within an organization, HR leaders are often asked to wear the hat of the ethics officer. This may be more likely in smaller organizations that do not have the resources or means to employ a designated individual for this role.

Practice Questions

10. Which statement about whistleblowers is MOST true?
    A) They cannot expect protection under the law.
    B) They enjoy protection under the Sarbanes–Oxley Act.
    C) They are protected under OSHA regulations.
    D) They are in violation of a company's code of ethics.

11. An HR team tracks the number of men and women who hold leadership positions in the organization as part of a DEI initiative. Using the graph below, which of the following DEI goals was accomplished at the end of Year 4?

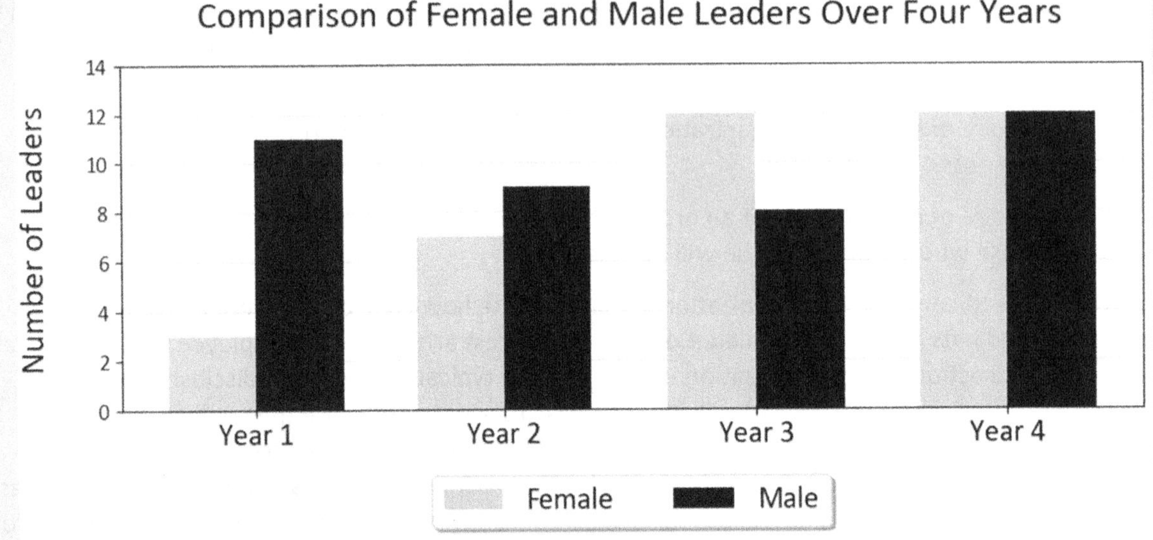

A) Equalize the gender balance in leadership positions.
B) Double the number of female leaders in Year 2.
C) Increase the number of leaders in the organization.
D) Reduce gender bias during internal promotions to leadership positions.

The Role of Stakeholders

Organizational Charts

Organizational charts (also called org charts) visually represent the relationships of authority and responsibility that the organization's stakeholders have toward one another. Typically, a single org chart is used to describe the relationships among all of the employees in the organization. Using a single chart ensures that the same types of organizational hierarchy are used from individual teams up to the executive team. The most common structures are as follows:

- **Functional Organization:** This classic top-down chart organizes stakeholders by what they do.
- **Flat Organization:** All stakeholders report to a single individual or team.
- **Matrix Organization:** Stakeholders report to multiple authorities within a two-dimensional "matrix" of projects and functions.
- **Team Organization:** Stakeholders are organized into teams with specific goals, and then reorganized as needed.

Shared Services

Using shared services in HR entails outsourcing specific roles or processes to external contractors. Some common examples include recruiting and payroll. The decision to utilize a shared services contractor is made based on the complexity of the service, the organization's internal ability to provide the service, and the contractor's reliability and credentials. Shared services are cost-effective for tasks that require technical proficiency or consume a lot of the PHR's time.

Centers of Excellence

Centers of excellence (COEs) are composed of an organization's subject matter experts who provide advisory or leadership roles on specific topics. These are often topics of critical importance to the organization's long-term health, such as hiring policies or regulatory compliance. COEs traditionally strengthen an organization through increased centralization of policy and decision-making processes; however, as more organizations have adopted agile project management strategies from the tech industry, the COE's role has shifted away from authoritative directives and toward adaptive guidance on the relevant topics. It is therefore important for the PHR to select a strategy that aligns with the organization's management strategy when leading a COE.

Practice Question

12. Which type of organizational chart is BEST characterized by multiple authorities providing oversight of each employee's activities?

A) functional
B) matrix
C) flat
D) divisional

Answer Key

1. C: An HR specialist has technical knowledge and skills in specific areas.

2. B: Strategic planning focuses on the organization as a whole and should therefore be centered around the organization's mission statement.

3. D: Goals should be SMART: Specific, Measurable, Action-oriented, Realistic, and Time-based.

4. C: Decentralization can aid in promoting a quick response to problems; with centralization, accomplishing tasks generally takes longer.

5. A: An organization has reached maturity once it has resources to plan for the future, formalized policies and procedures, and a solid infrastructure in which it operates.

6. D: An organization that is resistant to change and has many detailed procedures could be considered bureaucratized and in decline.

7. D: Downsizing is the planned elimination of personnel to streamline operations. Also known as a "reduction in force," downsizing may accompany mergers and acquisitions (M&As).

8. A: The definition of the term *risk* is the probability that a specific outcome (or harm) will occur.

9. D: Risk management focuses on protecting the business and employees from external factors.

10. C: Whistleblowers are protected under OSHA from pay reduction, discipline, and other forms of retaliation.

11. A: Option A is correct because the graph indicates that, in Year 4, about 50 percent of leaders are male and about 50 percent are female. Option B is incorrect because, while Year 3 saw double the number of female leaders compared to Year 2, the total number of female leaders went down from Year 3 to Year 4. Option C is incorrect because increasing the size of the leadership team is not a DEI objective. A DEI objective requires improving the representation of a specific demographic within the workplace. Option D is incorrect because this improvement in gender equality among leaders does not necessarily indicate that internal promotion practices have reduced bias. For example, this outcome could instead be due to improved external hiring practices, while internal promotions remain biased.

12. B: Option B is correct because a matrix organizational chart is structured around multiple axes of authority for the stakeholders. One axis is typically the manager for an employee's function in the organization; the other is the team leader for the employee's current project. Options A and C are incorrect because employees do not typically report to multiple authorities in flat or functional organizational structures. Option D is incorrect because divisional organization is descriptive of how large organizations are segmented but does not describe the structure by which multiple authorities provide oversight of each employee's activities.

Chapter 2 – Leadership, Relationships, and Communication

Leading and Communicating in the Workplace

Leadership takes many different forms, and different approaches are appropriate for different circumstances. There are several categories of leadership theories that have developed since the early twentieth century; these are discussed below.

Leadership Theories

Trait theories maintain that effective leaders share common traits, beliefs, and thought processes. Early trait theorists believed that leadership is an innate quality: either a person is naturally a leader, or they are not. Over time, theorists came to understand that people can develop leadership qualities.

Today, trait theories help managers identify qualities (e.g., integrity, charisma, empathy, assertiveness, and problem-solving skills) that help individuals lead others. However, there is no specific combination of traits that makes an ideal leader. Behavioral theories focus on how leaders act toward others.

In the 1930s, leading social psychologist Kurt Lewin discussed leadership behavior. According to Lewin, there are three styles of leadership:

- **Autocratic leaders** make decisions with little or no input from their subordinates. They dictate what needs to be done and how to do it. Autocratic leadership is useful when quick decisions are needed but input is not.
- **Democratic leaders** offer guidance to the team but allow team members to provide input before decisions are made. Democratic leadership is effective when team agreement matters; however, it can be challenging when individual perspectives and ideas clash.
- **Laissez-faire leaders** allow team members to make many decisions on their own. This approach works when the team is skilled, motivated, and does not need close supervision; however, oversight is still needed to make sure the team stays focused.

Effective managers use a combination of these three styles as appropriate. Leaders should be adaptable based on the needs of their teams and the organization.

Researchers agree there is no one correct type of leader, and that different leadership styles can be used effectively in different situations. **Contingency theories** address the best style for the circumstance. The **Hersey-Blanchard model** (discussed below), for example, links leadership style with the maturity of team members. Other contingency-based models include **Robert House's path-goal theory**, which says that leadership should depend on the needs of team members, the task at hand, and the environment in which they are working.

Power and influence theories consider the different ways in which leaders use their power and influence to accomplish tasks. Social psychologists John French and Bertram Raven identified five forms of power, known as **French and Raven's Five Forms of Power** and divided into positional power types or personal power types:

Positional Power Types

- legitimate
- reward
- coercive

Personal Power Types

- expert
- referent (charisma)

The model suggests that using personal, specifically expert power (becoming an expert at what you do), is more effective.

Transactional leadership is another leadership style. It assumes that people are motivated by rewards for accomplishments. This approach focuses on designing tasks and reward structures. In the transaction, the organization pays team members to complete a task or job. The leader penalizes those whose work does not meet an appropriate standard. This approach is used in most organizations to get things done, even though the approach does not focus on the human aspects of leadership, such as developing relationships.

Situational Leadership

When managing individuals and teams, leaders must incorporate **situational leadership**, which is the ability to adapt a leadership style to fit the needs of the individual, team, or organization. Situational leadership is based on the Hersey-Blanchard model. In their 1969 work *Management of Organizational Behavior*, Kenneth Blanchard and Paul Hersey recognize that all individuals are different, and, as a result, the leader's message must be tailored to the situation.

Situational leadership acknowledges four types of leadership styles:

- directing
- coaching
- supporting
- delegating

The goal of situational leadership is to move subordinates through the different leadership styles, enabling them to delegate on their own and complete tasks relatively independently. This model focuses on the employee rather than the leader. Each leadership style is measured by competency and the commitment of the employees.

Employees who need to be managed by **directing** are typically new to their roles or the organization. Since they are not yet knowledgeable about their roles, the manager focuses on giving clear direction and developing the skill levels of these employees. These individuals are usually highly committed and excited about their new tasks, so during this stage, the manager should also focus on positive feedback.

When the **coaching** style is used, it means that the employees have begun to develop their skill sets, though training and guidance are still needed. At this point, the manager might do more suggesting and less telling. The manager will emphasize motivating and building relationships in order to ensure the employee's commitment.

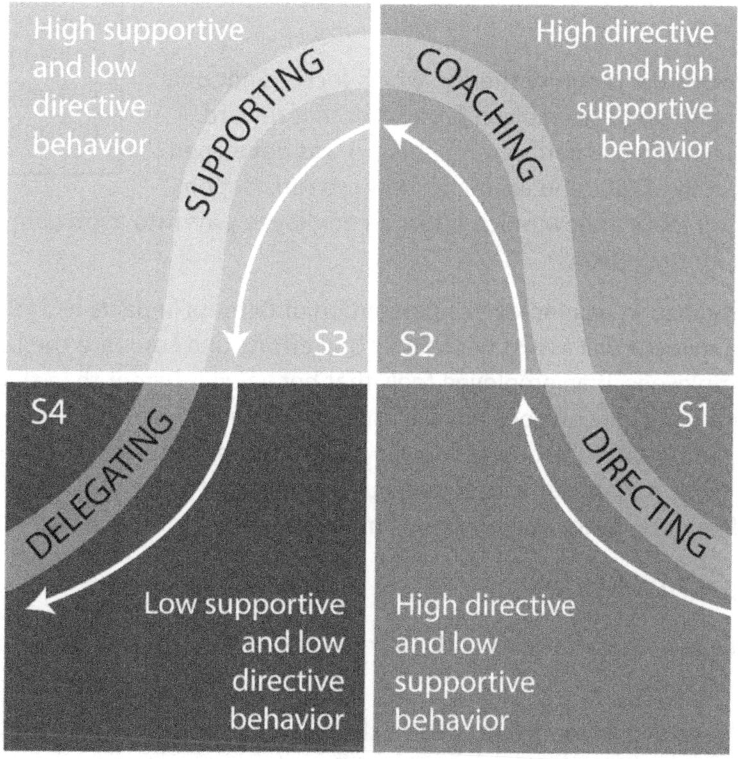

Figure 2.1. Situational Leadership

The **supporting** style is used with an employee who may be competent but, through performance issues or other factors, is not fully committed to the role or organization. At this point, the leader moves away from giving instruction or focusing on tasks and instead puts time and effort into engaging and motivating.

When leaders employ the **delegating** style, their subordinates feel empowered and secure in the knowledge that they have the competencies needed to perform their roles. The manager can now safely delegate tasks knowing they will be done effectively and in a timely manner.

People Management

In **people management**, managers must understand both the people they are leading as well as their own styles and behaviors. **Emotional intelligence** describes the ability of people to identify their own emotions and the emotions of others. Emotional intelligence allows leaders to adapt their style to a given situation.

Leaders may use rewards to manage people. These rewards can be positive, such as recognition or a bonus, or they can be negative, such as discipline or loss of pay. In 1964, Victor H. Vroom developed the idea of expectancy theory, which states that individuals are motivated by their perceived expected outcomes. In other words, if an individual thinks there will be a positive reward, he will be more likely to perform. The reverse of this can also be true: if an employee believes there will be no reward or punishment, his effort may be minimal or substandard.

A manager must strategically use rewards to encourage desired behaviors. Building relationships and dialogue with team members creates an understanding of their needs. The manager can use this information to design appropriate positive rewards and limit the use of punishment.

Helpful Hint:

Leadership cannot be executed the same way for all individuals or circumstances. A strong leader recognizes this and adjusts accordingly.

Another management tool is **equity theory**, which focuses not only on the reward but also on the perceived fairness of that reward. Equity theory (also known as Adams equity theory) was developed by John S. Adams in the 1960s and examines how job satisfaction relates to rewards. It looks at how much effort an employee puts into a job compared to the employee's perceived reward for that effort.

According to equity theory, an employee's perception of fairness impacts her job performance and satisfaction. The employee will assess her talents and efforts and compare them to the talents and efforts of other employees. If an employee feels that her value is higher than that of her coworkers, she will expect higher rewards. If she does not feel that her value is higher, she may change her level of effort or input to match what she now perceives is the appropriate reward. This perception may be accurate or inaccurate. A manager's responsibility is to create a sense of fairness for this individual, which may include a raise, other additional income if warranted, or coaching.

Other Leadership Styles

There are other leadership styles outside the frameworks previously mentioned, but they are still relevant in the workplace.

In **bureaucratic** leadership, leaders follow rules closely and expect the same of their team members. This style is effective when working in dangerous conditions (e.g., operating heavy machinery, working with hazardous substances), when working directly with money, or when performing routine tasks. This style is much less effective with teams that require flexibility, creativity, or innovation.

A **charismatic** leadership style seeks to inspire and motivate team members; however, leaders who rely on charisma often focus on themselves and their own ambitions rather than the organization as a whole. Charismatic leaders may seem infallible, which can damage the organization if significant, inappropriate decisions are made.

A **servant leader** leads by meeting the needs of the team. Servant leaders lead by example and with integrity; they often show great generosity. This approach can foster a positive culture and high morale. Servant leadership requires time and dedication and may not be compatible with more authoritarian, rigid types of leadership styles.

Transformational leaders expect individuals to meet their potential; they also take personal responsibility for their own actions. Transformational leaders are inspirational: they set clear goals and are able to resolve conflicts. This form of leadership encourages high productivity and engagement.

According to researcher Bernard Bass, transformational leaders gain the trust, respect, and admiration of others.

Clearly, leadership is not a one-size-fits-all concept; instead, leaders must adapt their approaches to fit specific situations. It is therefore important for leaders to develop a thorough understanding of various leadership frameworks and styles in order to adapt to changing situations.

Practice Questions

1. Which type of leadership theory examines the personal characteristics of a leader?
   A) trait theory
   B) situational theory
   C) behavioral theory
   D) contingency theory
2. What is a primary dimension of behavioral theories of leadership?
   A) common sense in the workplace
   B) consideration of employees
   C) self-confidence and assertiveness
   D) task-relevant knowledge

Relationship Management

Effective communication requires building relationships. This means knowing and acknowledging the members of a team and building connections with candidates, vendors, other departments, and even the executive team. The ability to build and manage relationships is a critical skill for effective leaders.

Interpersonal skills are as important to leadership as the ability to inspire people. Relationships should be strategically managed through clear communication, active listening, responsiveness, and showing interest in others. Relationship management builds loyalty, trust, and a culture of increased productivity, engagement, and tenure.

In the digital age, multiple avenues of communication are used to establish relationships. Knowing the audience and their preferred methods can go a long way toward enhancing communication. Going beyond the traditional meeting or phone call, leaders should consider how emails, texting, the internet, the intranet, and social media can build relationships.

Networking is one way to build relationships; it may occur within an organization, community, or profession. **Networking** establishes a mutually beneficial affiliation with other employees, clients, vendors, or organizations. It can be done in a casual setting (e.g., conference lunches where people share who they are and what they do). It can also take place in a more formal setting, such as through association meetings or management training programs. Finally, networking increasingly takes place online via social media and webinars.

Networking is more than just informing others about the organization's product or service. Through networking, employees gain additional knowledge, learn best practices, tap into problem-solving resources, and build successful teams.

Offering new hires mentoring opportunities can front-load their networking in an organization, opening up resources and collaboration to help them do their jobs effectively.

Relationship building happens when two or more people connect and associate. Relationship building at work is critical because it creates opportunities for coaching, collaboration, and idea sharing. When building a relationship, it is important to establish trust and to respect the psychological contract (explained below).

Did You Know?

The concept of the psychological contract was developed by organizational scholar Denise Rousseau in her 1989 article "Psychological and Implied Contracts in Organizations."

In order to build trust, both parties must be authentic, develop mutual respect, and create a meaningful connection. Trust is built over time as each party adheres to the unwritten set of rules that govern their interactions. These rules are called the **psychological contract** and refer to a set of expectations that are established between two parties (e.g., employers, managers, employees, or coworkers). Clear and effective communication can positively impact a psychological contract that is dynamic and changes over time. Breaking a psychological contract can lead to disengagement and turnover as the parties experience a loss of trust.

Teamwork happens when various people throughout a department, organization, or community come together to work on a single goal. This may involve creating, problem-solving, or advising. Often, teamwork results in a rewarding outcome since it brings together a diverse group of ideas, skills, and abilities.

Psychologist Bruce Tuckman created a model outlining the development sequence of a group. He concluded that there are four phases every group must undergo in order to become successful:

- forming
- storming
- norming
- performing

Team leaders should guide individuals through these stages so that they can complete them in a timely manner.

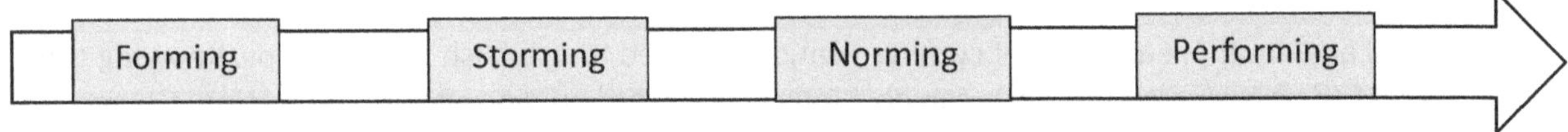

Figure 2.2. Development Sequence of a Group

Forming happens when a group first comes together: individuals are polite, and all of the rules are not fully understood. Forming is followed by **storming**, where participants start to push boundaries and conflict develops. This is normal, and groups should not only expect but also embrace this stage since it allows them to establish processes, roles, and rules. Likewise it allows the team to move into **norming**, during which they come together as a unit, resolve their differences, and create stronger relationships. In the final stage, **performing**, the team can work with the least amount of friction since processes have now been established.

Conflict Management and Resolution

Human resources must support the organization and individuals in conflict management and resolution. Ignoring conflicts can lead to distrust, lowered engagement and productivity, and higher turnover. Unfortunately, many people choose to avoid conflict because they are uncomfortable or they do not know how to solve the conflict on their own. A human resources professional can mediate and participate in conflict resolution. HR also trains employees and supervisors in order to reduce conflict.

It is important to understand that conflict is not only natural; it is to be expected. An organization must recognize this so that employees can resolve conflict in a safe and supportive manner. Conflict has many root causes. Understanding these causes and taking the time to determine them is a necessary part of resolving and reducing conflict. Conflict resolution involves exploring the underlying reasons for disagreement and lack of alignment among teams and individuals.

When resolving conflict, the involved employees should come together to discuss the issues. The following simple guidelines can be used to start this conversation:

- setting ground rules
- allowing each person an opportunity to share
- encouraging active listening and paraphrasing
- brainstorming mutually agreeable solutions

Sometimes outside resources are needed. For example, legal counsel is advisable when dealing with conflict that is severe or that could lead to liability issues (e.g., harassment or discrimination).

Organizational conflict describes the natural conflict or disagreement that develops between employees, departments, or functions. There are three basic sources of conflict:

- **Relationship conflict** involves interpersonal issues between individuals and affects how employees work together and the social issues surrounding interactions.
- **Task conflict** arises when parties disagree about the content or outcome of tasks, procedures, or goals. Task conflict focuses on "what" should be done.
- **Process conflict** involves disagreement over "how" the team should complete certain tasks.

Conflict can happen on a micro level between two people or on a macro level between two organizations. **Intraorganizational conflict** is between individuals, departments, or functions within the same company. **Interorganizational conflict** is between multiple companies or organizations. Conflicts between customers and vendors, or among competitors, are examples of interorganizational conflicts.

There are several styles of conflict resolution and negation. It is important to understand all of these styles since a particular situation may require one or more styles to resolve the issue:

- In **competing**, each side pursues their own interests, focusing on short-term gains. Competing is used when someone needs to act quickly or when there is no room to negotiate.
- In **accommodating**, one side wins and the other loses. Accommodating is used when maintaining relationships and goodwill is a priority.
- In **avoiding**, both sides lose. This style is often used by two individuals who want to avoid conflict. It can be a way of getting revenge or being passive-aggressive.
- In **compromising**, both parties win a little and lose a little. Often mistaken for collaboration, compromising is more about meeting in the middle than determining a mutually beneficial outcome.

- **Collaborating** creates a win-win outcome. This style focuses on meeting both parties' needs and arriving at mutually beneficial solutions.

Since human resources professionals are asked to be involved in conflict resolution, helping the parties move toward collaboration leads to positive outcomes that each side can agree on.

> **Did You Know?**
>
> Roger Fisher, William Ury, and Bruce Patton developed the concept of principled negotiation in their 1991 work *Getting to Yes: Negotiating Agreement Without Giving In.*

Negotiation

Many of the principles used in conflict resolution also apply to negotiation. The key difference is that conflict resolution focuses on an issue or problem that needs to be solved, whereas negotiation involves two parties sharing an objective. Human resources professionals use negotiation in many different areas, including employment offers, union contacts, benefit purchasing, and dispute resolution.

The **negotiation process** creates an agreement between two or more parties. These can be formal agreements or verbal agreements. It is important to know when these agreements are legally binding and approach such negotiations appropriately.

An important step in negotiation is **perspective-taking**—understanding the other person's point of view. A good negotiator helps the other party understand his point of view by speaking clearly about his needs, using data and information to support his position, or creating a story or narrative around his perspective. It is also important to take time to understand the other person. Doing this allows a negotiator to improve her position and know where her needs are in regard to the situation.

Principled bargaining, or principled negotiation, happens when both sides focus on objective outcomes, eliminating emotional disagreements or grandstanding. Principled bargaining includes the following actions:

- separating the emotions from the problem
- focusing on interests rather than positions
- looking for options that include mutual gains
- using objective criteria

Another negotiation tactic is auction. In an **auction**, buyers compete against one another for an item or outcome. The competitive nature of auction may drive the price higher if the outcome, such as a sale of a business, is in high demand. Auctions, however, may also lead to decisions based solely on monetary gain rather than on a win-win situation for everyone involved.

Interest-based bargaining, like principled bargaining, recognizes the importance of both parties and works toward a win-win outcome. Unlike auction, this type of bargaining keeps relationships intact, avoiding a win-at-all-costs mentality. This is in contrast to position-based bargaining in which there are winners and losers. **Position-based bargaining** is a competition that pits sides against each other; it can often breed resentment.

Since organizations use negotiation techniques for labor and employee relations, it is critical that both relationship management and teamwork are recognized as key influences. It is therefore important to choose the negotiation tactic that will best maintain employee trust and engagement, even after the negotiations are completed.

Practice Question

3. Which form of conflict resolution focuses on meeting the needs of both parties?
   A) accommodating
   B) avoiding
   C) compromising
   D) collaborating

Communication

Communication is an important aspect of trust, healthy relationships, conflict resolution, and negotiation. Understanding the basics of communication helps teams and departments collaborate effectively.

Aspects of Communication

Communication can be broken down into different components:

- the source (i.e., sender)
- the receiver

The **source** or **sender** is the individual or team that creates the original message. The source can communicate the message in different ways and use their communication skills to create the message. The message may be verbal, written, nonverbal, or electronic. The message itself is the content or idea that the sender is communicating.

The **receiver** is the person or audience who receives and interprets the message. It is important to note that the receiver's own experiences, skills, and abilities will impact how they receive and interpret the message. The sender should therefore create the message with the receiver in mind. When creating global messages, the human resources department must often assess the receivers' biases in order to ensure clarity and relevance within a communication.

Active listening happens when the receiver fully focuses on the message and does not allow external or internal distractions. During active listening, the receiver should give message feedback through nonverbal cues like nodding or smiling, or through paraphrasing or asking clarifying questions.

When giving feedback to an individual or a group, the manager must consider all elements of communication. In particular, managers should ask themselves, "Who is the receiver of the feedback and how will they receive the message I am trying to send?" Managers must be transparent with feedback even if it makes the sender uncomfortable. Employee must receive feedback and understand expectations so they can modify (or continue) behaviors.

One feedback tool is the **SBI model** developed by the Center for Creative Leadership. This model describes the situation (**S**), followed by the behavior (**B**), and finally the impact (**I**), or reaction, to the behavior. The SBI model shifts the focus from the individual to the actual behavior, creating a coaching opportunity.

Employee Communications

An organization uses employee communications to share knowledge with and get feedback from employees. The medium, manner, tone, and frequency of communications affect employee motivation and organizational success. People need regular and open access to information, the opportunity to ask questions, and the opportunity to provide feedback. They can then align themselves with the goals, strategies, and objectives of the organization, department, or team.

Employee communications can be organization-wide (macro level) or employee-specific (micro level). They can take many forms, including the following:

- announcement of a new product or service
- information about company-wide benefits and open enrollment
- disclosure of company quarterly earnings
- announcement of business changes
- formal and informal feedback
- invitation to company-wide events
- explanation of new processes

Using a combination of media to convey information is a good way to reach employees in different locations, those who have different schedules, and employees who have different learning styles. The following are just some examples of the types of media used:

- email messages
- bulletin boards
- company intranet
- company newsletters
- company-wide halls
- team or department meetings
- conference calls
- one-on-one conversations
- training sessions
- social media

The messages should be tailored to the type of communications media used as well as to the receiver (i.e., the whole company or a specific group of employees). Open lines of communication maintain transparency with employees and ensure that messages are conveyed to and understood by them. It is essential that information can flow upward from employees to leadership for free exchange between both sides.

A company and its employees can benefit from effective employee communications in many ways:

- Roles in the organization are clarified, and employees recognize how they contribute to the "bottom line," or mission.
- Employees better understand changes in the organization by asking questions and absorbing information to adapt to those changes. This reduces anxiety, which would lead to lower productivity or higher turnover.
- Customer service improves when employees fully appreciate the product or service and understand what is expected of them.
- Leadership can gain valuable input from staff about products and services, operations, or other issues, helping them to advance the organization's mission.
- Consistent and open communication establishes trust and encourages loyalty to the organization. Being up-front and honest can dispel rumors and encourage employees to ask questions.

Leadership should communicate information regularly to staff and solicit feedback. Furthermore, leadership must be responsive to feedback. Two-way communication will maintain a dialogue, reinforce trust, and generate new ideas. Companies undergoing change should establish a communications plan to ensure that messages are fully understood.

When creating a new product, process, policy, or program, focus groups can be a good source of ideas, input, and knowledge. A **focus group** is a small group of people whose response to a product or idea is considered representative of the larger population. A focus group's goal must be clearly defined before the group meets. Additionally, a trained facilitator must walk the team through predetermined exercises and questions that will allow the group to be productive. Conversations are facilitated through open-ended questions. There is often a separate recorder so that the facilitator is not distracted by taking notes.

Another type of group or team collaboration is a **staff meeting** or **team meeting**. These meetings should also have a recorder to ensure ideas are captured, action items are noted, and specific roles are assigned. When leading this type of meeting, creating and following an agenda can encourage productivity.

Communicating Policies and Procedures

As organizations grow, they must develop policies and procedures to promote consistency throughout the organization, convey important information to employees, and comply with federal and state laws. Clear, well-communicated human resource policies and procedures ensure that messages and administration throughout the organization are consistent. Documented policies can also protect the organization in case of lawsuits or complaints. Finally, HR policies and procedures help the organization formalize its approach to achieving compliance with federal law.

Policies should support managers in handling personnel issues. A supervisor who reads and understands the written policies of the organization can answer employee questions, respond to complaints, and handle minor disciplinary issues without always involving the human resources department. For example, if two employees in different departments are consistently late or are not meeting performance standards, having established policies in place will help managers treat those employees fairly. If an employee questions how the supervisor handles an employment issue, the supervisor can reference the HR policies, helping the supervisor maintain authority while remaining unbiased.

Policies and procedures help employees too. By providing handbooks to employees, organizations empower them with information and help them better understand their own responsibilities. Employees with questions about work hours, paychecks, dress code, paid time off, harassment, or other issues can find answers on their own. In addition, well-written policies provide employees with guidance on whom to contact with concerns about their employment or other issues. Because they may create an enforceable contract, handbooks should be reviewed carefully and updated regularly.

Finally, an employee handbook serves as an example of how the organization administers policies consistently and fairly. In the event of litigation or a complaint about an employment action, policies protect the organization. Human resource professionals should reference the policies when responding to questions and coach supervisors on the appropriate methods or procedures to document employee disciplinary problems. Policies and procedures should be reviewed periodically and updated to reflect changes in federal and state laws relating to employees as well as changes in the work environment or organizational structure.

Practice Questions

4. When using active listening, how should the listener behave?
   - A) interrupt the speaker to show an understanding of the speaker's message
   - B) actively acknowledge the speaker by taking notes and focusing on a notepad
   - C) nod, make eye contact, and paraphrase the speaker at the end of the talk
   - D) give verbal feedback as the speaker talks

5. What is the primary reason for which an employee handbook should be reviewed carefully and be continually updated?
   - A) so that it can be available to the public for review
   - B) so that it can create an enforceable contract
   - C) so that it can provide new employees with important information
   - D) to serve as the only method of communication between the employer and employees

Answer Key

1. A: Trait theory maintains that effective leaders share several common traits, beliefs, and thought processes.

2. B: Behavioral theories focus on how leaders act toward others.

3. D: Collaborating focuses on meeting the needs of both parties while looking for mutually beneficial solutions.

4. C: Active listening means being engaged with the speaker and demonstrating that engagement through message cues like body language (e.g., eye contact, nodding, facing the speaker) and paraphrasing the speaker's words at the appropriate time to show that the message is understood.

5. B: An employee handbook should be carefully reviewed and updated regularly because it may create enforceable contracts.

Chapter 3 – Talent Acquisition and Planning the Workforce

To plan a workforce and acquire the appropriate talent, HR professionals must balance numerous legal and ethical requirements while ensuring that the hiring needs to achieve the organization's goals can be met. Numerous federal laws have been established to help promote and support diversity and fair treatment in the workplace.

Equal Employment Opportunity

The doctrine of **Equal Employment Opportunity** prohibits discrimination against applicants and employees due to certain personal characteristics like race, color, sex, and other protected classifications. A **protected class** is defined as a group of individuals who have been granted specific legal protections. These protections are granted through legislation at the US Congressional level or through state legislatures. This doctrine ensures fair treatment for the following:

- finding work
- being paid
- getting promoted
- having opportunities for professional development

The Equal Employment Opportunity Commission

The **US Equal Employment Opportunity Commission (EEOC)** is an independent federal agency that enforces the numerous federal laws that prohibit employment discrimination. Several of these laws are discussed in Table 3.1.

Table 3.1. Federal Laws Prohibiting Employment Discrimination

Federal Law	Protections
Title VII of the Civil Rights Act of 1964	▪ It prohibits employment discrimination on the basis of race, color, religion, national origin, or sex. ▪ Employers must reasonably accommodate applicants' and employees' sincerely held religious practices, unless doing so would impose an undue hardship on the business. ▪ In 2020, the Supreme Court affirmed that gay and transgender people are

Table 3.1. Federal Laws Prohibiting Employment Discrimination	
Federal Law	**Protections**
	protected in the workplace under this law on the basis of sex.
Title VII of the Civil Rights Act of 1964 Pregnancy Discrimination Act (PDA)	▪ This amends Title VII to prohibit discrimination because of pregnancy, childbirth, or a medical condition related to pregnancy or childbirth.
Equal Pay Act of 1963	▪ The Act makes it illegal to pay men and women different wages if the employees are performing equal work in the same workplace.
Age Discrimination in Employment Act of 1967 (ADEA)	▪ The Act prohibits discrimination against applicants or employees based on age (forty or older).

According to the laws described in Table 3.1, federal law forbids discrimination in every aspect of employment, including hiring, compensation, discipline, and termination. It is also illegal to retaliate against anyone who reports discrimination, files a charge of discrimination, or participates in an employment discrimination investigation or lawsuit. Employers must post notices in the workplace that describe the federal laws prohibiting job discrimination based on race, color, religion, sex (including pregnancy), national origin, age (forty or older), disability, or genetic information.

Not all federal laws apply to all employers. As described in Table 3.2., employers with fewer than a certain number of employees may not be subject to nondiscrimination laws.

Table 3.2. Federal Discrimination Laws and Small Businesses	
Business Size	**Applicable Federal Laws**
Businesses with at least 1 employee	▪ Equal Pay Act of 1963
Businesses with 15 – 19 employees	▪ Equal Pay Act of 1963 ▪ Pregnancy Discrimination Act (PDA) of 1978 (an amendment to Title VII of the Civil Rights Act of 1964) ▪ Title I of the Americans with Disabilities Act of 1990 (ADA) ▪ Genetic Information Nondiscrimination Act of 2008 (GINA)
Business with 20 or more employees	▪ Equal Pay Act of 1963 ▪ Pregnancy Discrimination Act (PDA) of 1978 (an amendment to Title VII of the Civil Rights Act of 1964) ▪ Title I of the Americans with Disabilities Act of 1990 (ADA) Genetic Information Nondiscrimination Act of 2008 (GINA) ▪ Age Discrimination in Employment Act of 1967 (ADEA)

Additionally, some states and localities have enacted their own nondiscrimination laws that certain employers must follow. Employers should monitor employment laws in all states in which they operate and determine which laws apply.

Disparate Impact

The EEO laws also prohibit employers from using employment policies and practices that have a disproportionately negative impact on applicants or employees who are considered protected classes if the policies or practices are not based on reasonable factors. These adverse effects on protected classes are called either disparate treatment or disparate impact. Both disparate treatment and disparate impact refer to discrimination; however, they differ when it comes to intention:

- **Disparate treatment** is intentional bias against a protected class.
  - Examples include policies against hiring people who are pregnant or only promoting individuals of a certain race.
- **Disparate impact** is *unintentional* bias against a protected class.
  - Examples include requiring an individual to own a car even if it is not necessary for the job, or expecting employees to live in a certain area.

Precedent for disparate impact was established in the 1971 Supreme Court ruling in *Griggs v. Duke Power Co.* In *Griggs v. Duke Power Co.*, the Supreme Court ruled that the employer has the burden of showing that any selection process is job-related and that lack of intent does not make the practice lawful if it inadvertently causes discrimination based on a protected class.

Figure 3.1. Disparate Treatment

Figure 3.2. Disparate Impact

What Employers May Not Do

To comply with federal law and to provide equal opportunity to all employees and applicants, employers may NOT do certain things in their employment practices. Prohibited acts are based on race, color, religion, sex (including pregnancy, sexual orientation, or gender identity), national origin, age (forty or older), disability, or genetic information. The following acts are prohibited:

> **Helpful Hint:**
> Disparate treatment was established by the *McDonnell Douglas Corp. v. Green* case in 1973.

- advertising a job that shows a preference based on a protected class

- recruiting new employees in a way that results in discrimination based on a protected class
- discriminating against an applicant or refusing to give an application to a person of a certain protected class
- requiring preemployment or post-employment examinations that may be inherently discriminatory
- considering a person's characteristic (protected class) when making decisions about job referrals
- making decisions about job assignments or promotions based on an employee's protected class
- discriminating, based on protected class, as concerns the way in which employees are paid
- considering an employee's protected class when taking disciplinary actions
- refusing a reasonable accommodation to a disabled employee, unless doing so would cause an undue hardship to business operations
- refusing to accommodate an individual's sincerely held religious beliefs and attendance at religious services, unless doing so would cause a substantial burden to the business

Reasonable accommodations are changes or adjustments that do not create an undue hardship for an organization. These might include job restructuring, schedule changes, or flexibility in hours. Reasonable accommodations may also include tools or aids that help an employee complete a job. Personal items like medications, hearing aids, or wheelchairs are not reasonable accommodations.

Undue hardship describes when something requires a significant amount of expense and/or is significantly challenging to achieve. Undue hardship is determined on a case-by-case basis according to each company's situation. One key of reasonable accommodations is knowing the role's essential job functions and then determining which accommodations can be made so that the person can perform those job responsibilities.

Harassment

The same laws that prohibit discrimination also prohibit harassment based on protected class. Harassment and bullying can take the form of slurs, graffiti, offensive or derogatory comments, or other verbal or physical conduct. It is also illegal to harass anyone who has complained about discrimination, filed a charge of discrimination, or participated in an employment discrimination investigation or lawsuit.

Bullying is a type of harassment that creates an intimidating or offensive work environment. With enough frequency or severity, bullying can affect a reasonable person's work performance. Bullying behavior includes rudeness, sarcasm, or hostility if it is intended to interfere with the victim's ability to perform duties. **Illegal harassment** describes when this behavior is based on or targets an individual who is part of a protected class.

Sexual harassment is a specific type of harassment that includes unwelcome sexual advances, requests for sexual favors, and other sexual conduct. Any conduct of a sexual nature that makes an employee uncomfortable has the potential to be sexual harassment. The harasser can be the victim's supervisor, a supervisor in another area, a coworker, or someone who is not an employee, such as a client or customer.

Harassment outside of the workplace may also be illegal if there is a link with the workplace. For example, a supervisor who harasses an employee while driving that person to a meeting may be breaking the law. For these reasons, organizations typically develop strict policies against harassment with detailed procedures to report, investigate, and handle complaints.

Sexual harassment can take two main forms: quid pro quo or hostile work environment:

- **Quid pro quo**, (Latin for "this for that") occurs when certain employment outcomes are linked to sexual favors (e.g., job offers, promotions, raises, or other similar employment decisions).
- A **hostile work environment** is one in which intimidating or offensive working conditions impact an individual's ability to work or perform a job.

The law does not forbid mild misconduct like teasing, occasional comments, or some minor isolated incidents. But harassment becomes illegal if it is so pervasive or severe that it creates a hostile or offensive work environment, or if it results in an adverse employment decision (e.g., termination or demotion).

Several court cases have defined sexual harassment in the workplace. In 1986, the Supreme Court decided *Meritor Savings Bank v. Vinson*. This was the first case in which courts recognized a hostile work environment as discrimination under Title VII.

In *Meritor Savings Bank v. Vinson*, a bank teller named Mechelle Vinson was repeatedly sexually assaulted and humiliated by her supervisor. She was eventually fired, ostensibly for misusing sick time. Vinson said her supervisor coerced her into sexual relations and created a hostile work environment. In a unanimous decision, the Court found that a hostile work environment characterized by sexually inappropriate conditions is a form of discrimination based on sex under the Civil Rights Act of 1964.

In 1998, two landmark cases further defined sexual harassment. In *Burlington Industries, Inc., v. Ellerth*, Kimberly Ellerth accused her supervisor of sexual harassment, quit her job, and sued the company. She claimed her supervisor threatened her with retaliation if she did not engage in a sexual relationship with him. Even though Burlington Industries had a sexual harassment policy, Ellerth did not complain because she would have had to report the misconduct she endured to her harasser. The Court found that even though Ellerth had suffered no tangible adverse job consequences, Burlington Industries was still liable for the hostile work environment.

In *Faragher v. City of Boca Raton*, Florida lifeguard Beth Ann Faragher accused two male supervisors of inappropriate touching and making offensive remarks, which created a hostile work environment. Faragher did not immediately complain, but the Supreme Court still found the City of Boca Raton liable for the misconduct of the supervisors.

The outcomes of the Ellerth and Faragher cases demonstrate that, even if an employer is unaware that harassment is taking place, the organization is still liable when harassment is perpetrated by a supervisor. The company may have an affirmative defense *only* if it shows that it took reasonable care to promptly prevent or correct harassment and that the employee failed to report the incident through channels provided by the employer.

Retaliation describes taking an adverse action against an employee or applicant because that person has complained about harassment, raised concerns about violations, or engaged in other protected behavior. It is illegal to retaliate against an individual for raising a legitimate harassment complaint or concern. An organization should have policies and training concerning retaliation to ensure that those who do register a complaint are protected.

The 2016 Supreme Court case *Green v. Brennan* found that the filing period for an aggrieved employee to file a workplace discrimination complaint begins once the employee gives notice of resignation—not at the date of resignation.

Constructive Discharge/Forced Resignation

Another discriminatory practice under federal law is when an employer forces an employee to resign or makes the work environment so intolerable that a reasonable person cannot sustain employment. This is called constructive discharge. In **constructive discharge**, the work environment becomes unbearable to the point that an employee of a protected class feels there is no choice other than to quit his or her job. Such an environment often involves sexual harassment or discrimination.

Bona Fide Occupational Qualification

A **bona fide occupational qualification (BFOQ)** is a legitimate reason to exclude a person based on being a member of a protected class, which would otherwise be illegal to do. The courts define the legal use of BFOQ very narrowly, and it must directly relate to the ability to perform the job. An example is requiring an employee to stand for a certain period of time due to a piece of equipment that cannot be changed or modified.

Dress Code

Under the law, employers may establish dress codes. Dress codes might apply to all employees or to employees within certain job categories. There are some exceptions:

- Some dress codes might conflict with certain religious beliefs or practices.
- Dress codes may not be used to punish employees because of their national origin.

For example, an employer may not prohibit certain traditional or culturally significant attire while allowing casual attire. In addition, if the dress code conflicts with an employee's religious practices and the employee requests an accommodation, the employer must make an exception or modification to the dress code unless doing so would result in undue hardship. (The same rule applies to employees with disabilities who request a reasonable accommodation.)

Nepotism

Nepotism is a discriminatory practice in which one employee (typically a person in a leadership role) shows favor toward another employee due to their nonprofessional relationship—most often a personal friendship or a familial relationship. Nepotism is not prohibited by federal labor laws in the United States. While the Civil Rights Act and similar laws protect employees against discrimination on the basis of race, religion, gender, and other protected characteristics, these antidiscrimination laws do not prohibit favoring a person based on a personal relationship. This discriminatory practice is nonetheless unethical; furthermore, nepotism is illogical as nepotistic practices reduce the morale of other employees and deteriorate trust in the organization's leaders. These effects result in reduced productivity and innovation in the workplace. The PHR can prevent nepotistic practices in the organization through standardized hiring and promotion practices as well as transparent communication about how candidates are chosen. A robust grievance policy also reduces nepotism by assuring employees that they can safely express concerns about potential nepotism.

Equal Employment Opportunity Complaints

If employees or job applicants believe that they have experienced discrimination at work, they can file a charge of discrimination, or Equal Employment Opportunity (EEO) complaint.

Filing an EEO complaint does not automatically mean the company has committed any wrongdoing; rather, a **charge of discrimination** is a formal allegation that an employer has discriminated against the complainant. The Equal Employment Opportunity Commission (EEOC) must then investigate the situation and decide if there is reasonable cause to believe that discrimination has occurred. Furthermore, not every employee is protected by the EEOC. As addressed in Table 3.2., some employers are exempt from certain federal laws.

Complainants must file a charge of discrimination with the EEOC before filing a job discrimination lawsuit against an employer. The only law enforced by the EEOC that does not require a charge of discrimination is the Equal Pay Act. There are also time limits for filing a charge of discrimination. Employers must also adhere to EEO reporting requirements by keeping certain employment records; furthermore, private sector employers with more than 100 employees must make workforce data available to the EEOC via an EEO-1 Report. The EEOC collects this data whether or not a charge has been filed against the company. Workforce data is used in law enforcement, employer self-assessment, and federal research. Although a company's specific data remains confidential, aggregated data is available to the public.

Diversity, Equity, and Inclusion in Recruitment

Improving an organization's diversity, equity, and inclusion (DEI) metrics begins with recruitment. It's the PHR's responsibility to evaluate the recruitment process to ensure it both lacks bias against and is designed to facilitate the employment of persons who are members of a protected group. Eliminating bias against persons of a particular ethnicity, gender, gender identity, or other demographic is both an ethical and a legal responsibility. Best practices in DEI initiatives also require structuring the hiring process so that diverse candidates are encouraged to apply and diverse applicants are considered for the position. Without additional initiatives, reducing discriminatory bias has been proven insufficient to improve diversity within an organization; therefore, an organization's hiring process ought to also act as an outreach program for diverse persons. Implementing this type of outreach in the hiring process improves the variety of candidates who apply for positions.

The PHR's role in this aspect of a DEI initiative is to design and oversee the hiring process so that it fulfills the leadership team's strategic DEI objectives. It is important for the PHR to consider how the DEI hiring process is evaluated. Without a specific benchmark, a DEI initiative does not have a goal. Project management mindsets are useful when designing the hiring process because they are designed to establish goals, build a process for achieving the goals, and reflect on the efficacy of the goals and the process. There are two important questions PHRs must ask themselves during this process:

- Did we achieve our DEI goal?
- Does our goal truly reflect improved DEI?

Evaluating the goal as well as whether or not it was accomplished allows the HR team to reflect on whether the hiring process is creating meaningful change within the organization. Specific outreach practices (e.g., highlighting diverse employees in promotional materials) can then be adjusted to improve DEI outcomes during the next iteration of the hiring process.

Practice Questions

1. Which federal agency has the PRIMARY responsibility of enforcing employment nondiscrimination laws?
   - A) the Department of Labor
   - B) the Equal Employment Opportunity Commission
   - C) the Department of Homeland Security
   - D) the Office of the Attorney General
2. Which of the following laws deals directly with pay discrimination?
   - A) the Fair Labor Standards Act
   - B) affirmative action
   - C) the Patient Protection and Affordable Care Act (PPACA)
   - D) the Equal Pay Act
3. Which of the following workplace situations MOST likely exemplifies nepotism?
   - A) Bob was promoted to be the new manager because Ryan, Larry, and Ahmed believe he is tough and logical.
   - B) Jennifer is the founder's granddaughter; she received a better performance evaluation from her manager than anyone else on the team.
   - C) Laquisha's friend, David, was one of three managers evaluating her job application. After two rounds of interviews, Laquisha was selected.
   - D) Mr. Jones plays golf each weekend with his company's CEO, Mrs. Bannerjee. During an internal promotion, his resume was sent to the committee with the rest of the applicants.

Affirmative Action Planning

Affirmative action is the policy of providing opportunities specifically for, and favoring members of, a disadvantaged minority group that has historically experienced discrimination. Affirmative action may include outreach to minority candidates, special training programs, and other positive steps to ensure a diverse workforce. Employers who are subject to affirmative action typically develop formalized affirmative action plans (AAP) and policies. These plans are reviewed annually, and companies maintain documentation to ensure compliance with federal rules and regulations.

Developing Affirmative Action Plans

An **affirmative action plan (AAP)** or program is a tool employers develop and use to achieve their affirmative action goals. AAPs measure and evaluate the composition of the workforce, or the demographic makeup of the organization, and compare it to the relative composition of the available labor pools, or those in the same geographic region. An AAP also ensures equal employment opportunity by embedding this philosophy into the organization's employment practices, employment decisions, compensation programs, and performance management systems. Furthermore, AAPs include the practical steps an organization will take when people of certain classifications are underutilized.

AAPs typically outline a goal-setting process that is used to target and measure the effectiveness of affirmative action efforts to prevent and eliminate discrimination. Employers typically audit and report on their affirmative action plans on an annual basis, measuring their progress. Employers are prohibited, however, from establishing racial quotas or engaging in preferential treatment of certain groups (including women and minorities). AAPs must be signed by a company officer and be made available to internal employees and vendors.

Affirmative Action Requirements for Government Contractors and the OFCCP

In the United States, under **Executive Order 11248, Section 503 of the Rehabilitation Act of 1973**, and **Section 4212 of the Vietnam Era Veterans' Readjustment Assistance Act**, government contractors and subcontractors must provide affirmative action when recruiting, hiring, and employing qualified minorities, women, people with disabilities, and covered veterans. These policies require federal contractors and subcontractors to take affirmative action to ensure that all individuals have an equal opportunity for employment, without regard to race, color, religion, sex, national origin, disability, or status as a Vietnam-era or special disabled veteran.

The US Department of Labor's **Office of Federal Contract Compliance Programs (OFCCP)** enforces affirmative action laws, regulations, and executive orders with government contractors. To maintain a contract with the federal government, the OFCCP requires a contractor to practice affirmative action and nondiscrimination in employment. The OFCCP routinely investigates contractors' employment practices and complaints of discrimination. Failure to comply with nondiscrimination or affirmative action provisions of federal law is a violation of the contract. A contractor found to be in violation may have its contracts terminated or suspended, and the contractor may be deemed ineligible for future government contracts.

Under **Executive Order 11246**, nonconstruction contractors with fifty or more employees and government contracts of $50,000 or more are required to develop and implement a written affirmative action plan (AAP). The plan is kept on file and carried out by the contractor, and it is submitted to the OFCCP upon the agency's request.

Like other AAPs, government contractors' AAPs identify the utilization of women and minorities in the contractors' workforce. Underutilization occurs when fewer minorities or women occupy a particular job group than would reasonably be expected based on their availability. **Availability** is determined by the predominance of qualified women and minorities in the geographical location of the company or site.

Based on analyses of the availability of qualified individuals, contractors must establish goals to reduce or overcome underutilization. Employers are expected to consider the candidacy of qualified women and minorities and to provide them with employment opportunities and advancement; however, employment decisions are to be made on a nondiscriminatory basis. Finally, according to federal regulations, the OFCCP may not penalize contractors for not meeting goals.

For contractors in the construction industry, the OFCCP has established a distinct approach to affirmative action due to the seasonal and temporary nature of the construction workforce. For these businesses, the OFCCP, rather than the contractor, assigns goals and affirmative action that must be undertaken. In 1980, for example, the industry developed the goal of employing women for 6.9 percent of construction labor hours; this goal is still in effect today. The regulations also specify the good faith steps construction contractors must take in order to increase the hiring of minorities and women.

Practice Questions

4. Which statement about affirmative action plans (AAPs) is TRUE?
   A) All employers with over 100 employees are required to have an AAP.
   B) An AAP is required for employers who have been found to discriminate against employees.
   C) An AAP is required by the Fair Labor Standards Act.
   D) An AAP must be signed by a company officer and made available to internal employees and vendors.

5. What is the difference between affirmative action and equal employment opportunity?
   A) Equal Employment Opportunity is required by law in the United States.
   B) Affirmative action applies to small businesses and private organizations.
   C) Affirmative action is required of government contractors.
   D) Equal Employment Opportunity sets quotas for hiring in businesses throughout the US.

Recruitment and the Talent Acquisition Life Cycle

Talent acquisition or recruitment can be performed through internal recruiters, employment specialists, or HR generalists. As part of the overall recruitment process, these professionals advertise and post jobs, source resumes, screen candidates, conduct first-round interviews, and coordinate with the hiring manager (or team).

In many organizations, the success of recruiters is measured by the amount of time it takes to fill job openings (**requisitions**) and the number of positions that are successfully filled. Recruitment can also be performed by external agencies or headhunters.

Staff planning is a process by which an organization ensures it employs the right number of qualified people with the necessary skills to achieve organizational goals and objectives. Staffing plans require the cooperation of senior leadership, human resources, and management. The various components of a staff planning program include the following:

- job descriptions
- skills assessment of the current workforce (identifying gaps)
- turnover trends to predict how many people will leave an organization
- business trends examining both internal changes and external factors

Once all relevant information has been collected, the human resources department (or staffing department in larger organizations) can forecast its staffing and recruitment needs. Typically, HR or staffing professionals work directly with business unit leads to interpret staffing metrics and forecast staffing data for the fiscal year.

There are a few important metrics in staffing and recruitment:

- The **selection ratio** is the number of available job positions compared to the number of applicants.
- The **yield ratio** is the ratio of applicants at one stage of hiring versus the number that moves on to the next stage of hiring.

- The **acceptance rate** is the percentage of candidates who accept a formal job offer.
- **Recruitment costs** include items like testing, background checks, relocation, and signing bonuses.
- **The total cost of recruiting** is found by adding recruitment expenses for all of the people hired.
- The **cost per hire** is ultimately found by dividing total recruiting costs by the number of people hired.

During the planning process, HR and business unit leads will discuss the needs of the business unit, reevaluate jobs and processes, and identify a staffing model that supports the goals of the business unit. In some cases, a job may be redesigned, combined with another job, or divided into two or more jobs. The needs of the business as well as the available budget will determine how jobs are structured and how many employees a business unit will have during the year.

Recruitment Process

As jobs become available (through turnover or growth), organizations recruit candidates for these vacancies. The **labor market** is the pool of individuals an organization attracts as applicants or employees. The following is an overview of the typical steps in the recruitment process; these steps may vary depending on the organization:

1. Determine the recruitment process for the position: the number of candidates who will be identified, the estimated timeline for filling the position, the number of anticipated interviews, and the composition of the interviewing team.
2. Create or revise job descriptions to reflect the essential functions and requirements of the job.
3. Develop a job ad based on the job description; it should include information about the company, salary range, preferred requirements, and/or benefits.
4. Identify candidate sources and begin the search by posting job ads to job boards, social media, classified sections of newspapers, and at universities and colleges as well as other places where qualified candidates may be reached. Creating internal postings on a company intranet or bulletin board (for referrals) may be another useful method for sourcing talent. Advertisements should include instructions for applying (e.g., an email address to submit resumes or an online application system).
5. Prescreen resumes and identify applicants who meet the qualifications of the job. The **applicant pool** is the total number of individuals who have been evaluated for selection. Develop a short list of candidates for further consideration.
6. Conduct an initial phone screen of short-listed candidates and ask questions to understand their qualifications, gauge their interest, and evaluate their potential. Trim down the short list, and invite the most qualified candidates for an interview.
7. Interview candidates (with the interviewing team) and ask probing questions to further evaluate their qualifications and fit for the position. In some cases, a second or even third interview is conducted for the finalist(s).

8. Conduct preemployment tests, references, and background checks of finalist(s), if necessary, for the position or if required by the organization.
9. Make an offer of employment to the final candidate, including salary details, job role, responsibilities, benefits, start date, and other relevant information. In some cases, a verbal offer is made over the telephone and followed up with an **offer letter**, which is a written letter that lays out the salary details, start date, and so on. It is always a best practice to send a written offer with the terms of employment and have it signed by the candidate.
10. In some cases, the candidate may negotiate salary, benefits, perks, office location, and other factors. When an agreement has been made, it is also a best practice to update the written offer letter and have the candidate sign it.

Did You Know?

Employers must screen candidates thoroughly. **Negligent hiring** is a legal theory that makes employers liable for a harmful act if the employer knew about the employee's potential to cause harm.

Once the candidate has accepted the terms and is preparing to begin work, the organization should take steps to ensure that the new employee is properly transitioned and integrated into the organization.

Job Descriptions

Every position within an organization should have a corresponding job description that accurately and completely describes the activities of the job. The **job description** is a document that provides an overview of the position's major responsibilities and identifies the **knowledge, skills, and abilities (KSAs)** that are necessary to perform the job. A job description may also communicate the expected results of the position and explain how performance is evaluated; however, a job description does not need to include every detail of how the work is performed. A **disclaimer section** typically discusses changes in duties, the need to perform duties not listed, and the employment relationship.

Did You Know?

Employers generally must keep a record of on-the-job illnesses, accidents, and injuries for up to five years. They must also keep any medical records of such injuries or illnesses for thirty years.

To develop job descriptions for an organization, HR professionals use a combination of interviews, job shadowing, questionnaires, and sample job descriptions. The job description must accurately reflect the essential duties and requirements of the position. Table 3.3 describes the major components of a job description.

Table 3.3. Components of a Job Description		
Section	**Purpose**	**Examples**
General information	basic position and pay information, which may also be tracked in the HR Information System (HRIS)	• job title • position type (e.g., full time) • FLSA status pay grade department • direct supervisor • direct reports • job code
Position purpose	a summary of the position's essential functions and its role in relation to the department or organizational unit	• description of the role in relation to the department or organization • estimated duration of position
Essential job duties	a list of duties and responsibilities (An **essential function** occupies a significant amount of the position's time and requires specialized skills to perform.)	• functions of the job, arranged by importance and percentage of time spent • essential tasks related to the accomplishment of an essential function
Minimum requirements	the knowledge, skills, and abilities required to perform the essential functions of the job	• education • length of experience • soft skills • technical skills • specific experience

Job Specifications and Job Analysis

Job specifications list the KSAs needed to perform a role. Job specifications are often included within a job description, which typically focuses more on the particular tasks or duties of the role. The KSAs might include the following items:

- educational requirements
- personal abilities
- experiences
- physical requirements
- certifications

> **Did You Know?**
> **FLSA** status refers to the **Fair Labor Standards Act**. This differentiates exempt and nonexempt employees. Nonexempt employees must be paid overtime wages if they work over forty hours in a work week.

Understanding a job, creating a job description, and developing job specifications is a process. This process is called **job analysis**. There are many ways that HR practitioners can perform a job analysis:

- interviewing the incumbent of the position
- interviewing the manager of the position

- interviewing the colleagues who will work most closely with the position
- consulting clients/customers
- consulting other experts in the role
- thoroughly observing the tasks performed in the role
- thoroughly observing work samplings from the role

The type of job being analyzed defines which job analysis method is most appropriate:

- An observation or work sampling might reveal enough information about a manual job because the duties and tasks can be watched easily.
- Professional roles (e.g., accounting, legal) might require a questionnaire or diary to identify items that are not easily observed.

Different types of job analyses can be used to obtain different information about a role:

- A **task-based job analysis** focuses on specific steps a person must take to complete the required duties.
- A **competency-based job analysis** looks at the specific skills or capabilities that an individual must possess in order to perform the job effectively.

In addition to tasks and competencies, job analyses can also identify a division of responsibilities that can be used for labor planning and to determine department structures. The following steps are used to conduct a job analysis:

- planning and gathering data
- reviewing data and addressing inefficiencies
- communicating with people familiar with the role in question
- conducting the job analysis
- creating and writing the job descriptions and job specifications
- maintaining records

Physical requirements should be determined as part of the job analysis process and included in the job specifications. These physical requirements may be used as part of the recruitment process and to help identify any reasonable accommodations that might be made through the Americans with Disabilities Act (ADA). Note that the ADA requires that job descriptions list the essential functions of a job in order of importance.

The key to a thorough job analysis is to identify daily, weekly, and yearly tasks that must be performed in the role, along with the KSAs needed to do the job.

Employee Relations

Employee relations strengthen the employer-employee relationship by measuring job satisfaction, maintaining employee engagement, and resolving workplace conflicts or grievances. Employee relations also include coaching employees and managers to handle difficult situations, investigating sexual harassment and discrimination claims, placing employees on performance improvement plans, and terminating employees.

In a unionized work environment, labor relations functions may include negotiating collective bargaining agreements, facilitating the grievance process, and interpreting union contracts. The employee and labor relations functions of HR may be combined and handled by one specialist, or they might be entirely separate functions managed by two HR specialists with expertise in each area.

Employee relations and unions are discussed in greater detail in Chapter 7.

Compliance

Compliance describes adhering to local, state, and federal labor laws, and it is an essential HR function. Noncompliance can have serious consequences:

- litigation
- governmental complaints of unfair employment practices and unsafe working conditions
- fines from the government
- overall dissatisfaction among employees

HR staff must be aware of state and local employment laws as well as the following federal legislation:

- the Fair Labor Standards Act
- Title VII of the Civil Rights Act
- the National Labor Relations Act
- the Family and Medical Leave Act

Many more laws exist; to comply with these and maintain fairness in the organization, HR professionals help develop company policies and procedure manuals.

Compensation and Benefits

Like employee and labor relations, the compensation and benefits functions of HR are often handled by one HR specialist with dual expertise. HR functions include setting compensation and evaluating competitive pay practices. A compensation and benefits specialist may also negotiate group health coverage rates with insurers and coordinate with the retirement savings fund administrator. Payroll might be conducted by the compensation and benefits section of HR, but in many cases it is handled by the finance department or outsourced to an external provider.

Training and Development

Employers must provide employees with the training and tools necessary for their success. New employees should go through an orientation to help them transition to the new organization as part of the onboarding process and undergo adequate training for their positions. Many HR departments also coordinate leadership training and ongoing professional development activities. Depending on the organization's financial resources, programs such as tuition assistance programs for college or advanced degrees may be offered as part of training and development.

Workplace health and safety is also essential, especially in industries in which workers operate heavy machinery, are exposed to chemicals or harmful substances, or work in otherwise dangerous places or situations. Employee safety is mandated through the federal Occupational Safety and Health Act of 1970, and HR professionals must be able to recognize risks and promote best practices for preventing injuries. This is often achieved by facilitating or overseeing health and safety training and maintaining federally mandated logs for workplace injuries and fatalities that must be reported to the government. HR professionals also manage workers' compensation issues for on-the-job injuries.

Turnover

Depending on the internal and external environments, an organization may face a surplus or shortage of talent. In a **talent surplus**, the organization has more employees than it needs. During a talent surplus, employers must consider options like hiring freezes, limits on the number of hires, limits on the number of hours worked, a reduction in compensation, and the introduction of a voluntary separation program. All of these options are designed to control labor costs.

On the other hand, an organization faces a **talent shortage** when it cannot attract or retain enough workers to meet its needs. Short-term solutions to a talent shortage include outsourcing to a third party, using contingent workers, increasing employee hours through overtime, and initiating an employee referral program.

Turnover refers to the number of employees leaving an organization and the reasons for their departures. Turnovers can be involuntary or voluntary and are also known as separations.

Separation occurs when an employee leaves the organization. **Voluntary separation** may include resignation or retirement. **Involuntary separation** describes when an employee is terminated or fired.

HR can assist with separations in many ways. For instance, when dealing with a talent surplus, an organization may offer voluntary layoffs, during which staff are encouraged to voluntarily leave with downsizing assistance like payoffs, severance pay, or early retirement. **Outplacement services** provide support like interviewing workshops or career counseling for displaced workers.

HR professionals should also conduct exit interviews with employees who are separating. **Exit interviews** are conversations and/or surveys that departing employees have with HR and, as needed, other relevant personnel. They are useful for gathering feedback about the organization and HR processes and for communicating ideas for improvements that the company can make to increase employee engagement, retention, and satisfaction. Strong exit interviews usually use standardized questions that are sent to departing employees ahead of time. The goal of any exit interview is to solicit the most honest feedback possible and use it to help inform best practices for the company going forward.

When measuring turnover costs, HR professionals should study the costs of separation, replacement, and training in addition to **hidden costs** like employee morale, productivity impact, or customer satisfaction.

Outsourcing and Independent Contractors

Outsourcing simply means hiring outside contractors to do a job or certain tasks. Recruitment agencies find and screen candidates for organizations with small HR departments or that are short on time; however, these can be costly. An organization can achieve flexibility in staffing levels by using independent contractors during busy seasons or for specific projects. Additionally, using contractors allows the organization to work with individuals who are subject-matter experts in certain areas. A **professional employer organization (PEO)** supplies its own workforce to an employer, which can mean lower benefit costs for the employer but higher operational costs and limitations on HR management.

The term *1099 employee* is a common phrase used to describe an **independent contractor** who provides the organization with a service. This phrase is derived from a tax form required by the Internal Revenue Service (IRS). The distinction between employees and independent contractors impacts the employer's tax burden and legal relationships as defined in the Fair Labor Standards Act. In 2021, the Department of Labor added a new rule clarifying this distinction. The following are the most substantial factors:

- the worker's degree of control over the work
- the worker's opportunity for profit or loss

Employing remote workers makes this distinction doubly important. In general, anyone required to perform work during specified times or in specified ways is an employee. An example of an employee would be a person working from home during scheduled hours for a call center. In contrast, those who makes their own decisions about when, where, and how to work are considered independent contractors.

Practice Questions

6. Which type of information is NOT typically included in a job description?
   A) a list of responsibilities
   B) FLSA status
   C) required skills
   D) company history

7. According to the ADA, in what order should a job description list the essential functions of a job?
   A) in order of percentage of time spent on a task
   B) in order of importance
   C) in no order at all
   D) in alphabetical order

8. Which of the following recruitment methods is likely to result in greater loyalty?
   A) campus recruiting
   B) internet job board
   C) employee referrals
   D) newspaper ad

Immigration in the Workplace

Under the **Immigration Reform and Control Act of 1986 (IRCA)**, it is illegal for an employer to hire any person who is not legally authorized to work in the United States. Employers must verify the employment eligibility of all new employees. For organizations of certain sizes, the IRCA also prohibits discrimination based on national origin (as does Title VII) and/or citizenship status. The purpose of the law is to prevent employers from discriminating against job applicants based on their race, ethnicity, because they speak English with an accent, or other reasons related to national origin.

The **United States Citizenship and Immigration Services (USCIS)**, a component of the United States Department of Homeland Security, oversees and enforces immigration, including immigration that is related to employment.

It is against the law to hire an employee if the employer is aware that the employee is not legally authorized to work in the United States or if the employee is an "unauthorized alien." Under the law, an **unauthorized alien** is a federal term for a non-US citizen who either does not have status as a permanent resident in the US or who is not authorized for employment in the US. One way employers avoid noncompliance with the law is to hire US citizens. A US citizen is not considered an "alien" (and therefore is not an "unauthorized alien").

Table 3.4. Types of Temporary Work Visas

Visa Category	Description
H-1B	• person in a specialty occupation • requires a college degree or its equivalent
H-2A	• temporary agricultural worker • for temporary or seasonal agricultural work • limited to immigrants from designated countries
H-2B	• temporary nonagricultural worker • for temporary or seasonal nonagricultural work limited to immigrants from designated countries
L	• intracompany transferee • allowed to work at a particular entity or location of the current employer in a managerial or executive role, or in a position requiring specialized knowledge • requires one year of continuous employment by current employer within the past three years
O	• individual with extraordinary ability or achievement • for immigrant workers with extraordinary ability or achievement in business, science, arts, athletics, education, and other categories • must demonstrate national or international acclaim and continue to work in their fields of expertise • also includes people who provide essential services in support of a worker in this category

Another way of avoiding noncompliance is to hire "authorized aliens." **Authorized aliens** are noncitizens who are authorized to work in the US. Authorized aliens include permanent residents (individuals who have a "green card") or "aliens" who are authorized to work in certain conditions by way of a work visa. Table 3.4. contains an overview of common work visas that are available to immigrant workers. For more details and the most current conditions, check uscis.gov.

In general, a citizen of a foreign country who wishes to enter the United States must first obtain a visa (for a temporary stay or permanent residence). **Temporary worker visas** are specifically for people who want to enter the United States to work for a specific period of time (rather than permanently or indefinitely). Applications for all visas require the prospective employer to file a petition with USCIS. The petition must be approved in order for the visa to be issued. Hiring immigrants with approved visas is compliant with federal law; hiring immigrants without authorization from USCIS is illegal and can result in substantial penalties.

USCIS Form I-9

Form I-9 is a government-issued form that documents the evidence of a new employee's authorization to work in the United States. It also certifies the actions taken by the employer to verify the evidence. This form must be completed within the first three days of the employee's hire; however, if the employment is for less than three days, the form must be completed on the day of hire.

To validate an employee's ability to work, an employer's authorized representative must verify both the identity of the employee and the employee's status. Depending on the documentation, one or two documents may be required. Some documents (e.g., an unexpired US passport) prove both identity and authorization to work. Other documents (e.g., a driver's license) prove identity but do not prove authorization to work. Still other documents (e.g., Social Security card) prove authorization to work but do not prove identity. The instructions on the form indicate which documents are acceptable and which combination(s) of documents may be used to verify employment eligibility.

Documentation regarding I-9 verification must be kept for certain minimum periods of time as mandated by law—either for three years from the employee's date of hire or one year after the employee leaves, whichever occurs later.

E-Verify

E-Verify is an internet-based system managed by the federal government that allows employers to verify a person's employment eligibility electronically. E-Verify supplements Form I-9.

Participation in E-Verify is voluntary for employers unless the company is a certain type of federal contractor or otherwise required to participate. Employers may only use E-Verify after making hiring decisions. It is illegal to use E-Verify for screening applicants or for other purposes not connected to verifying employment eligibility.

The E-Verify system confirms an individual's eligibility to work in the United States. If the system reports a "tentative non-confirmation" (TNC) for a new hire, it means that the system found possible problems in verifying the person's eligibility to work in the US. In that situation, the employee may contest the TNC, during which time the employer may not take adverse actions against the employee. If it is determined that the employee is in fact not eligible to work in the US, the employer may no longer continue to employ the individual.

Practice Questions

9. Who is responsible for verifying that an employee is eligible to work in the United States?
   A) the USCIS
   B) the Department of Labor
   C) the employer
   D) the employee

10. For the purposes of the I-9 form, which document confirms an employee's identity and verifies that individual's eligibility to work in the US?
   A) an unexpired US passport
   B) a driver's license
   C) a birth certificate
   D) a foreign passport

Succession Planning

The Succession Planning Process

To remain viable and competitive, organizations must retain key talent to lead, manage, and execute their missions and visions. As employees resign, retire, or otherwise turn over, it is important for the organization to anticipate these separations and plan to keep key positions filled with the most qualified people.

Succession planning is an organization's systematic approach to building a pool of future leaders to ensure leadership continuity. It develops potential leadership successors, identifies the best candidates for positions to meet future needs, and allocates resources to develop internal talent and create meaningful career paths.

Succession planning recognizes that some jobs are critical to the organization and therefore must be filled by the most qualified persons. Good succession planning is critical to mission success and sustains an effective process for recognizing, developing, and retaining top leadership talent; it can be achieved through the following steps:

1. **Align strategic planning with workforce planning:** Identify the long-term vision and direction of the organization, and analyze future needs to develop and offer products and services. Use data to understand the current composition of the workforce and to make projections for future workforce needs.
2. **Analyze gaps in future workforce needs:** Identify needs for competencies or skills, and determine talent needed for future demands. Develop a business plan based on long-term talent needs, not specific positions.
3. **Identify talent pools within the current workforce and categorize talent based on career level, path, and potential:** Assess the competencies and skills of employees by using formal appraisals and 360-degree feedback. Analyze external sources of future leadership as well.
4. **Develop strategies for succession, including recruitment, relocation, and retention programs:** Identify learning and development strategies. These can include job assignments, training programs, job shadowing, coaching and mentoring, and feedback mechanisms.
5. **Implement succession-planning strategies:** Maintain the commitment and involvement of senior leadership. Communicate activities with employees regularly and actively.
6. **Monitor and evaluate succession-planning efforts:** Solicit and consider feedback from leadership as well as potential future leaders. Analyze employee satisfaction through surveys and informal feedback. Assess the responsiveness of the organization to change and adjust to future needs.

Benefits of Succession Planning

Successful succession planning initiatives are based on the long-term needs of the business; they are an investment in the future. Senior leadership is invested in the process and helps to prepare emerging leaders. Future leaders are also accountable for their own development. The pipeline of future leadership is based on anticipated needs. Careful analysis of the organization's workforce and needs guides the process, while the process itself creates meaningful career paths for employees, which can be a motivational tool. Finally, succession planning addresses workforce challenges, such as recruitment and retention.

Practice Question

11. Why is succession planning important?
    A) because it ensures that key roles in the company will not be vacant
    B) because it provides feedback for all employees
    C) because it requires managers to go through training
    D) because it controls the company's operating budget

Answer Key

1. B: The Equal Employment Opportunity Commission (EEOC) is an independent agency that enforces federal laws prohibiting employment discrimination.

2. D: The Equal Pay Act of 1963 makes it illegal to pay different wages to men and women if they perform equal work in the same workplace.

3. B: Option B is correct because it is likely that Jennifer received favorable treatment due to her family relationship with the founder. This is nepotism even if Jennifer does not have a personal relationship with her immediate manager. Option A is incorrect because this situation demonstrates gender bias: an all-male leadership team chose a male candidate due to stereotypically "masculine" traits, such as being tough and logical. Option C is incorrect because the presence of additional managers and multiple interview rounds suggests that Laquisha's personal relationship with David did not influence her receiving the position. Option D is incorrect because the inclusion of Mr. Jones's resume with the rest of the applicants indicates that he is being treated equally with the other employees.

4. D: AAPs must be signed by a company officer and made available to employees and vendors.

5. C: Equal Employment Opportunity is a doctrine that prohibits discrimination in employment. Several laws exist to enforce EEO that apply to companies throughout the US. Affirmative action is not required of all businesses, but under Executive Order 11248, Section 503 of the Rehabilitation Act of 1973, and Section 4212 of the Vietnam Era Veterans' Readjustment Assistance Act, government contractors and subcontractors must provide affirmative action.

6. D: Company history is not typically included in a job description.

7. B: According to the ADA, a job description should list the essential functions of a job in order of importance.

8. C: Employee referrals are most likely to result in greater loyalty.

9. C: The employer is responsible for verifying an employee's eligibility to work in the United States.

10. A: An unexpired US passport verifies both an employee's identity and eligibility to work in the United States.

11. A: Succession planning recognizes that some jobs are critical to the organization and therefore must be filled by the most qualified persons.

Chapter 4 – Development, Learning, and Training

Employee Integration: Onboarding and Training

Once an organization's hiring needs are met, the HR professional must ensure that new employees are integrated into the organization and its culture. This is accomplished through onboarding, orientation, and training programs.

Onboarding

Once new employees are hired, they typically go through new hire training, or onboarding. **Onboarding** is the process of helping new hires integrate into their new work environments, learn their jobs, and transition into their roles. Onboarding is a critical component of the overall recruitment process for the employer and the employee; it typically includes the following activities:

- a tour of the office or facility
- an overview of the organization
  - an explanation of the company's history
  - information about the company's products or services
  - an explanation of the company's mission, strategy, and vision
- completion of required HR and payroll forms, as well as benefits enrollment (if applicable)
- training on the rules, culture, and procedures of the organization
- on-the-job training and job shadowing
- mandated training on safety, sexual harassment, nondiscrimination, whistleblowers, and other topics as required by law

In many cases, onboarding typically lasts only a few days or weeks, but a robust onboarding process can span one to two years. Lengthier onboarding processes monitor the employee's progress, provide mechanisms for ongoing feedback, and help the employee understand how she fits into the organization as a whole. Many organizations integrate lengthy onboarding processes into their overall performance management programs.

Depending on the structure, size, and resources of the organization, onboarding programs may be simple or complex; however, they should, at a minimum, address the following:

- logistics
- training
- safety

New employees should have ample time to train on the job and shadow others, if possible, in order to gain a total understanding of the company's products or services. With a holistic understanding of the organization and its operations, as well as a foundational knowledge of their own jobs, new employees are better positioned for long-term success.

Training and Learning

Encouraging ongoing training and learning among employees is a key function of HR. HR professionals need an understanding of learning styles and theories in order to support their efforts in planning, developing, and implementing training programs.

A **learning organization** is one where employee development, learning, and training are part of the culture. Employees of learning organizations are offered learning opportunities and are encouraged to continue learning throughout their careers.

Career management, or **career development**, is the process of encouraging and enabling employees to understand, plan, and develop their career skills and interests. Career management does not just encourage employee growth; it ensures succession planning within the organization. An organization can foster career development in various ways:

- career counseling
- mentoring programs
- career development plans
- established training programs (internal or external) that are made available to employees

Employee training programs are important for educating staff, preparing them to perform a job, and helping them acquire valuable skills that are relevant to the job. In other words, **training** helps employees acquire the tools, strategies, and techniques necessary to be successful at their jobs.

Through training and development programs, the organization can establish desired cultures and move toward long-term goals. HR plays a critical role in developing culture, and strategic initiatives that support cultural development should be incorporated into the training planning. Staff education should reinforce organizational values and ensure that those values are understood and practiced.

Furthermore, it is key to include diversity and equity training in personnel development to promote an understanding of the benefits of a diverse workplace. Education programs can reinforce and instruct employees on awareness, organizational commitment, sensitivity, and the value of diversity throughout the organization.

Organizations benefit from the perspectives and contributions of employees of various backgrounds. It is therefore essential to ensure that employees of every race, ethnicity, gender identity, sexual orientation, religion or lack of religion, ability or disability, and age are respected and treated fairly in the workplace. Beyond the legal implications, a diverse workplace strengthens the organization, its product or service, and its workforce. Employees from different backgrounds can bring their perspectives to improve both internal and external processes.

Training Methods

Training methods fall into two main categories: cognitive and behavioral.

Cognitive training methods are based on theoretical training that focuses on processes, guidelines, methods, and rules. Information is provided either in verbal or written form and results in increased knowledge or a change of mindset. The following are examples of cognitive-based training:

- live demonstrations and tutorials
- lectures to provide information
- group discussions for process-based problem-solving
- computer- or web-based training (eLearning)

Behavioral training methods are interactive and intended to spark creative thinking. They focus on employee behaviors and problem-solving rather than processes. Examples of behavioral training include the following:

- role-playing with open-ended problem-solving
- behavior modeling to compare scenarios
- case studies with open discussion about outcomes
- group brainstorming to solve sample problems

Cognitive training can also be useful for providing consistency; however, it does not encourage creative thinking. Behavioral methods challenge trainees to develop their own solutions, but they do not offer uniformity. When determining which training method to use, the organization should account for the advantages and disadvantages of each method and the desired outcome of the training. In addition, although these two methods of training are the most commonly used, other effective training methods also exist:

- one-on-one coaching and mentoring
- soft skills training
- formal and informal feedback

Adult Learning: Styles and Conditions for Learning

Adult learning styles describe the methods by which adults best absorb new concepts. Some people understand a message by seeing it. Others most effectively absorb a message by hearing it. Still others learn by acting out a process or through other means.

To effectively communicate with staff, organizational leadership and human resources must be cognizant of adult learning styles:

- **visual (spatial):** learning through pictures, drawings, and images
- **aural (auditory-musical):** learning through sound or music

- **verbal (linguistic):** learning through words (verbal and writing)
- **physical (kinesthetic):** learning through touch or movement
- **logical (mathematical):** learning through logic or reasoning

While it is not always practical to tailor a message or concept to every learning style, organizations should strive to use a combination of methods and media that are appropriate for the particular message and the available resources.

Adult learners have several distinct traits that HR and the organization should consider while developing learning and development programs:

- Adult learners are **independent and self-directed:** in training programs, employees should be actively engaged in the learning process.
- Adult learners are **results-oriented and practical:** these learners should receive information that they can apply immediately.
- Adult learners may be **resistant to change and will require justification for new behaviors.**
- Adult learners may **be more skilled at integrating new knowledge with previous experience**, despite the possibility that they learn more slowly than younger learners.

There are also domains of learning. Psychologist Benjamin Bloom described three of these:

- The **cognitive domain** includes collecting, synthesizing, and applying knowledge.
- The **affective domain** involves emotions and attitudes, including the ability to be aware of emotions and respond to them.
- The **psychomotor domain** relates to motor skills, including the ability to perform complex skills and create new movement patterns.

Program design and implementation plans should address all three learning domains. For example, an employee who is learning about a new online filing system may need to be taught about the positive impacts of the new system (cognitive domain), how to manage negative emotions related to changing systems (affective domain), and how to correctly use the new system (psychomotor domain).

Helpful Hint:

Developing employees is a team effort: managers coach and counsel employees, and HR provides the tools for management to help employees grow.

Motivation

A training program should assess the learners' sources of motivation in order to better educate, encourage, and advocate for them:

- **Intrinsic motivation** is the desire to achieve a goal, seek challenges, or complete a task. This type of motivation is driven by enjoyment and personal satisfaction. For instance, an employee who completes a training exercise because it is enjoyable or who learns a skill she has desired to know is intrinsically motivated.
- **Extrinsic motivation** is the desire to accomplish a goal; it is driven by external factors like praise, financial rewards or other benefits, or punishment. An employee who completes a training exercise to avoid a disciplinary action or to earn a bonus is extrinsically motivated.

Did You Know?

The knowledge, skills, and abilities (KSAs) align with the three learning domains: knowledge is cognitive learning, skills are psychomotor learning, and abilities are affective learning.

An individual's readiness to learn can be shaped by many factors, including openness to new information, emotional response (e.g., denial, anxiety), and support systems. In the workplace, HR or management must review an individual's readiness to learn because it will impact that person's ability to learn as well as the success of the development program. Employees who are struggling with readiness to learn may need proactive steps to help them become open to training or development. This may include creating time for training outside of the person's normal routine, instilling motivation, or providing remedial training.

Program Design and Implementation

A critical part of any training and development program is the design. Without fully understanding the needs of an organization or individual, an educational program may have little impact and fail to deliver the return on investment that was desired. HR must understand the strategic needs of an organization and carefully analyze the performance gaps. By completing this step, the programs can be designed to reinforce strategic initiatives and build the necessary skills required of the workforce moving forward.

When designing a training program, the previously discussed principles of adult learning, learning styles, and training methods must be incorporated. One tool that can be used for program design and implementation is the **ADDIE model:**

- Analysis
- Design
- Development
- Implementation
- Evaluation

During the **analysis phase**, the designer will consider the desired new behaviors, delivery options, the individuals who will participate, the participants' abilities and skills, and the timeline of the project. An **individual development plan (IDP)** can be one source to identify the needs of individuals. An IDP is a commitment between an employee and supervisor that identifies the employee's growth opportunities and development needs.

The designer might also use a training needs assessment to identify the training requirements and skill levels throughout the organization during the analysis phase of the ADDIE model. By looking at the gap between the needs and the actual abilities, the designer can identify the causes and reasons for these gaps. By taking this step, the instruction can focus on the right personnel, prioritize the training needs, engage the staff by showing the gap and ROI of the training, and identify tools and methods to be used within the training itself. A training needs assessment can focus on the organization as a whole, specific roles within the organization, and/or individual personnel.

After the designer completes the assessment phase, he will move on to the **design phase**, where specific content, methods, and goals are identified. Training can be delivered in a variety of ways:

- in person within a traditional lecture or classroom style
- through digital or technological resources (also known as eLearning)
- through on-the-job training, coaching, and mentoring
- through job rotation or shadowing
- via outside programming or classes

Each of these methods has advantages and disadvantages that should be assessed for the specific training needs. For instance, eLearning is flexible, cost-effective, and can often be accessed at any time and delivered over a large region or to a group of employees. However, eLearning often limits the ability of participants to interact with an instructor or to allow more modified content. Additionally, employees who lack time-management skills might struggle with self-paced courses.

When designing training, it is important to remember the **70-20-10 model of learning**:

- 70 percent of learning happens through doing.
- 20 percent of learning happens by coaching or mentoring from others.
- 10 percent of learning happens through formal learning.

By using this type of model and the principles of adult learning, a program that incorporates multiple methods can be designed.

After the ADDIE design phase, the designer moves into the **development phase**, where the actual content and course materials are created. The selection of these items should only happen after assessment and design are completed. If using an outside resource or platform, the same holds true: selection should happen only after the first two phases are completed and the needs are fully understood.

The ADDIE implementation phase is when the instructor preps and delivers the actual course material. At this point, the training should be set up for success; however, it is important to always include the last ADDIE phase—evaluation—so that any training can be improved upon and issues can be identified. During the **evaluation phase**, time should be spent developing specific questions that will allow the organization to determine the effectiveness of the education in reaching the established goals. This may include not only looking at the participants' reactions to the training but also at the learning, changes in work, and overall results of the training.

One model that can be used for the ADDIE evaluation phase is Kirkpatrick's Four Levels of Training Evaluation, which facilitates the effective evaluation of training programs. Historically, most organizations only focus on reaction, or level one of Kirkpatrick's model; however, reaction only measures how participants felt *during* the training. **Kirkpatrick's Four Levels of Training Evaluation** look deeper at not only the participants' reactions but also at how well they learned and whether this training will impact their future performances. The four levels of this model are reaction, learning, behavior, and results:

1. **Reaction:** This level measures satisfaction with training, learner engagement, and whether the learners thought that the training was valuable. Questions might include: "Was the training worth your time?" "Did you like the location?" "Did you enjoy the activities?" "How will you use what you learned?"
2. **Learning:** This level describes the degree to which participants' skills or knowledge increased due to training. The degree of learning can be measured through evaluation that may include a before-and-after test to determine change.
3. **Behavior:** This training evaluation level measures the degree to which participants' behavior increased due to training and how participants are applying their new knowledge. This evaluation takes place weeks or months after the training and examines whether the trainees have used the new skills, if there has been a change in the behaviors of the trainees, and/or if the trainees have shared this new information with others within their respective teams.
4. **Results:** This level examines the results achieved due to training. Results looks at quantitative measurements, such as improved productivity and the quality of work. By looking at these results, a return on investment (ROI), for the training can be computed.

A **learning management system (LMS)** is an application that supports an organization's training and development activities. It facilitates online training, tracks and reports on employee progress, and maintains learning aids. An LMS intersects easily with eLearning, which may be self-directed. Corporate training departments use LMS applications to deliver online training, maintain electronic records, and automate employee registration in training programs. An LMS system is often part of an overarching human resource information system.

Practice Questions

1. What is employee training?
   A) the development of skills that apply to an employee's job
   B) teaching employees about the requirements of the workplace
   C) one-on-one tutoring
   D) an intervention with employees who need special attention

2. Which of the following is an example of behavioral-based training?
   A) self-directed online learning
   B) live demonstrations
   C) case studies with open discussion
   D) tutorials

Ongoing Learning and Development Programs

In addition to playing a key role in developing and implementing training programs for new hires, HR professionals spearhead career growth learning opportunities for existing employees. HR professionals develop the tools, processes, and structures for managers and employees to use to facilitate the growth and development of personnel.

Professional Development Programs and Their Benefits

Professional development refers to the acquisition of skills and knowledge, both for personal development and career advancement. It can take the form of formalized training programs, external training opportunities, and financial assistance with work-related degree programs. Some examples of common professional development programs that companies offer to employees include the following:

- training seminars and workshops (internal)
- external seminars and workshops
- tuition assistance for advanced (work-related) degrees
- reimbursement for certification exams and recertification fees
- mentoring
- career coaching

Professional development programs are key to a competitive total rewards package and are mutually beneficial to the employee and the employer. Employees acquire new skills and knowledge to improve their work, advance them in the organization, and increase their competitiveness in the marketplace. (Note that, in some cases, professional development activities are required to maintain mandatory professional certifications.) Employers benefit by having a smarter, more efficient workforce that can attain higher goals. Employers may also benefit through reduced costs, thanks to improved innovation and operational efficiency that can result from professional development opportunities.

Diverse and Inclusive Workplace Development

Most successful organizations understand that diversity within the workforce leads to higher creativity and profitability. Still, a more diverse workforce can mean differences in perceptions and expectations based on experiences, norms, and attitudes.

The human resources team is the heart of cultural and diversity integration. HR provides opportunity for open dialogue and training in inclusion and equity. An inclusive work environment not only promotes a diverse membership but also ensures welcoming behaviors and social norms. An inclusive environment encourages access, choice, opportunity, and policies that incorporate and support all employees.

Equity promotes fairness by providing support and resources to individuals to allow them to reach their full potential. It also focuses on the removal of barriers that prohibit specific classes of people from succeeding. This may be as simple as allowing a flexible schedule to accommodate parents with childcare needs. It may also include translating documents so employees can read communications in their first languages. It is important that all employees are able to assimilate into the organization's culture, but assimilation also requires that the culture be open and welcoming.

Training in sensitivity and unconscious biases can have a positive impact on inclusion. An **unconscious bias** is an unintentional stereotype or perception a person has. Unconscious biases can adversely affect the workplace if not addressed. It is therefore important that individuals recognize any actions they take or words they use that might alienate other people. Addressing unconscious biases may be done in a group setting or one-on-one.

When creating an inclusive environment, it is important to involve the workforce, solicit feedback, and embrace disagreement. HR professionals should create opportunities for relationship building and dialogue, which may be done in social settings or formal meetings.

Learning to Operate in a Global Environment

Companies with locations around the world must balance their culture with the cultures of different countries and regions. Communication in multiple languages and time zones can be a challenge; it is therefore critical to create communication programs and strategies to account for a diverse and changing workforce.

To facilitate communication in a global environment, organizations can take additional steps, such as providing language and cultural classes. Language and cultural classes not only give employees additional skill sets, they also help people eliminate unconscious biases and raise awareness about diversity.

Helpful Hint:

Cultural awareness and training—beyond language classes—should be incorporated into the fabric of a company. All employees should be exposed to this type of training on a regular basis.

Several human resource information systems (HRISs), learning management systems (LMSs), payroll, and communication platforms operate on a global level. Choosing the right one allows the organization to roll out global programs where employees around the world have access to the same type of educational information.

Expatriates—employees living outside their home countries—require preparation and training before their assignments begin. Regular check-ins on performance and progress should take place over the course of the assignments. When expatriates return to their home countries, clear career paths should be determined.

Cultural Intelligence

Although most organizations operate within the global economy, those that do not must still acknowledge multiple cultures and diversity within the workplace. **Cultural intelligence (CQ)** is an outsider's ability to understand the unfamiliar aspects of a different culture and even blend in. There are a number of models that help employers understand cultural diversity on both global and organizational levels.

According to anthropologist Edward T. Hall, cultures are characterized by high and low contexts. In a **high-context culture**, numerous rules are understood but not defined. A high-context culture can be confusing for someone who is unfamiliar with the many unwritten rules that are understood. Norms may not be clearly articulated, people may rely more on body language, and emotions may not be expressed openly.

On the other hand, a **low-context culture** has clear rules that are more easily communicated to newcomers, which eliminates confusion early on. People from a low-context culture may be more outspoken and expressive, and emphasize spoken communication over body language.

Social psychologist Geert Hofstede developed a cultural dimensions theory that organizations use to help employees understand cultures and perform globally. Hofstede's model is based on six cultural dimensions, as described in Figure 4.2.

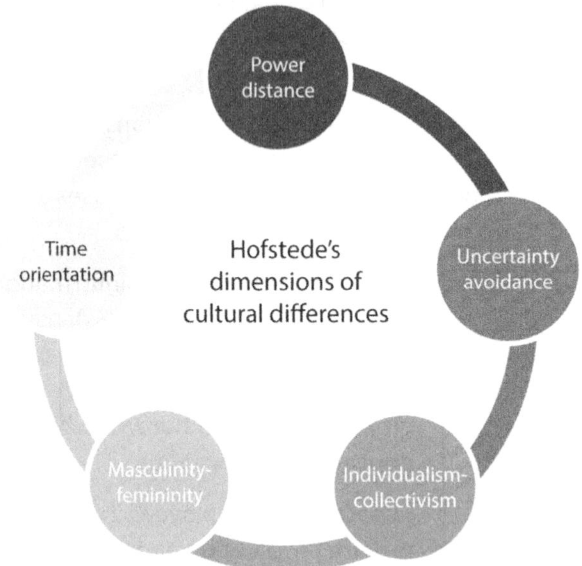

Figure 4.2. Hofstede's Cultural Dimensions Theory

1. The **power distance index** refers to the extent that inequality in power is accepted.
2. **Individualism versus collectivism** describes the degree to which individuals are reliant on or obligated to others.
3. **Uncertainty avoidance** describes the extent to which uncertainty and risk are accepted.
4. **Masculinity versus femininity** describes attitudes toward gender equality. (A "masculine culture" features distinct gender roles, whereas a "feminine culture" has fluid gender roles.)
5. **Short-term versus long-term orientation** describes how a culture views future rewards versus present gratification.
6. **Indulgence versus restraint** is the degree to which a culture controls or regulates gratification.

A similar cultural model is **Trompenaars model of national cultural differences**. Dutch author Fons Trompenaars developed the following seven cultural dimensions:

1. **Universalism versus particularism:** Universalism focuses on consistent rules for all, whereas particularism focuses on relationships and embraces decisions based on nepotism.
2. **Individualism versus communitarianism:** In individualism, the outcomes of one's life are based on one's actions; in communitarianism, people succeed or fail as a group.
3. **Specific versus diffuse:** In a specific culture, work and home are kept separate; in a diffuse culture, these two parts of life are interconnected.
4. **Neutral versus affective:** In a neutral culture people conceal their emotions; in an affective culture people are emotionally demonstrative, even in the workplace.

5. **Achievement versus ascription:** In an achievement culture, individuals gain status through knowledge and skills; in an ascription culture, individuals have status based on predetermined positions or connections.
6. **Sequential time versus synchronous time:** In a sequential culture time is literal, and punctuality is very important; in a synchronous culture, time is flexible and punctuality is less important.
7. **Internal direction versus external direction:** In a culture based on internal direction, individuals believe they can control their environments, whereas people in a culture based on external direction believe they work with the environments they are given.

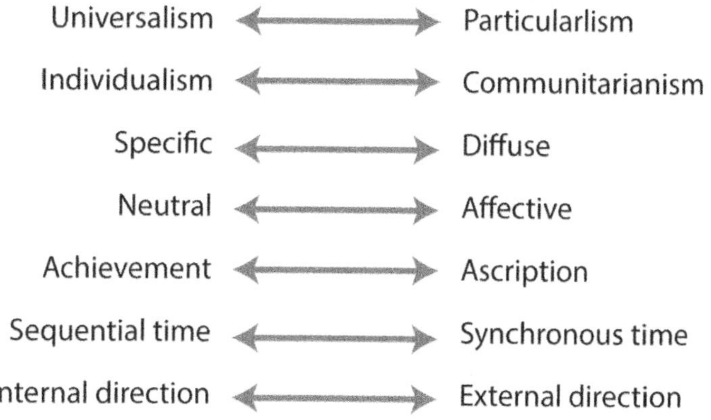

Figure 4.3. Trompenaars Cultural Dimensions

Management professor Edgar Schein developed another model of organizational culture. Schein's model contends that an organization's values shape its practices and behaviors. In other words. Schein believes that culture is not created quickly but rather over time as different practices are put into place.

Schein's model has three levels of organizational culture: artifacts, values, and basic assumptions.

1. An organization's **cultural artifacts** are the visible parts of the culture that can be seen by outsiders. Cultural artifacts may include actual physical items such as trophies, office designs, or pictures. Artifacts may also be invisible items like language, stories, and traditions.
2. The organization's **values** are shared understandings of how business will be conducted.
3. **Basic assumptions** are shared ideas among individuals, such as how space is used, what is moral, or what is ethical.

Practice Question

3. How can HR professionals promote culture intelligence in the workplace?
   A) by using cultural theory learning models
   B) by encouraging managers to assign projects to teams composed of various cultures
   C) by implementing mandatory weekly cultural exchange sessions
   D) by encouraging employees to connect with each other socially outside of work

Performance Management Strategies

In addition to spearheading training and professional development in the workplace, HR professionals must also support and drive efforts to evaluate how employees are performing. This type of information is not only helpful in identifying gaps that could be bridged through various training and development programs; it can also affect the employees' motivation, compensation, and other components of their professional lives.

Feedback is one of the most important duties of managers and is critical to an employee's success. HR practitioners have a key role in collaborating with management to ensure that feedback is timely, consistent, and impactful. Feedback can be formal (e.g., performance reviews, write-ups) or informal (e.g., conversations, meetings).

Feedback and appraisals can also affect an employee's compensation. Performance management involves measuring an individual's performance, coaching and developing employees, and recognizing and rewarding performance.

Informal Feedback

Informal feedback is instant, in-the-moment advice that occurs outside the formal performance review (which typically occurs once a year). Examples of informal feedback include the following:

- praising an employee for accomplishing a goal
- correcting a mistake
- providing constructive criticism

Feedback should be specific, immediate, and use data or examples. Providing feedback can help effective employees sustain their success and coach poor or average employees in taking immediate steps to improve.

Managers can—and should—provide feedback to employees in the following situations, which are categorized as either positive reinforcement or constructive criticism:

Positive Reinforcement:

- when an employee demonstrates improvement in a development area
- when an employee goes "above and beyond," or exceeds, her job responsibilities
- when an employee "pitches in," helping colleagues in a way that is beyond the scope of his individual duties
- when an employee reaches an important goal or milestone
- when an employee sets a good example for others

Constructive Criticism:

- when an employee is not performing the job correctly and is making mistakes
- when an employee is being disruptive to the team or not following rules

- when an employee is not meeting the expectations of the job
- when an employee needs to develop a particular skill

Employees usually perform better when they receive timely and specific feedback from their managers. Sometimes employees are not aware that their performances are problematic, or they may not be aware that they are exceeding expectations. Feedback provides employees with specific information they need about the manager's expectations. **Constructive feedback** allows employees to correct their behaviors, and **praise** lets employees know that they should stay on the same path. When an employee's behavior changes, it is important for the manager to follow up and give new feedback as necessary.

Helpful Hint:
Ranking is a method used to compare the relative performance of employees. A forced distribution method of rating employees ranks them in order of productivity.

Performance Appraisals

In addition to informal feedback, formal feedback is an important way to support the success of the organization's workforce. The most common type of formal feedback is the **performance appraisal**, or **performance evaluation**, which is a documented assessment of the employee's performance in a specific period of time (typically a year) that contributes to the employee's overall development.

Performance appraisals complement the organization's strategic plan, which determines individual job tasks and requirements. The appraisal is based on results achieved by the employee during the course of his duties. It measures skills and accomplishments with reasonable accuracy and uniformity, often using a predetermined rating scale, rubric, and criteria. The evaluation should be conducted using specific data, examples, and feedback from colleagues or customers. Done thoroughly, the appraisal identifies areas where performance can be improved and helps the employee grow professionally. Performance appraisals should recognize the employees' achievements, evaluate their progress, and identify ways to improve or expand their skills.

Periodic reviews enable managers to stay aware of their employees' abilities, set clear paths for moving forward, and help their teams work more effectively. If the manager has been providing ongoing and specific feedback during the year, the performance appraisal should not present many surprises to the employee. In these cases, the appraisal is a tool for documenting the employee's progress. Typically, the appraisal is signed by both the manager and employee to confirm receipt of the document and confirm that the performance conversation took place.

Appraisals are also tools for managing organizational risk. Sometimes these documents are requested during litigation or hearings with governmental agencies (e.g., for unemployment or discrimination claims). Organizations that have thorough, timely, and relevant performance appraisals documented in the employee's file can respond to complaints more effectively. If an organization does not document performance appraisals, or if it carries out appraisals inconsistently, it places itself at risk. A licensed employment attorney can help employers understand their particular risk and respond to complaints if they arise.

One type of appraisal that has gained popularity is the 360-degree review. With the **360-degree performance review**, multiple sources are asked to contribute to an employee's evaluation. These could include coworkers, subordinates, customers, the supervisor, and the employee herself. The 360-degree review is a way to obtain a full picture of the employee's impact on the company.

Needs assessments can help managers identify the development needs of individuals. These assessments types include the following:

- assessment centers
- psychological testing
- performance appraisals

Assessment centers offer a collection of tests or exercises that determine an individual's skills and abilities concerning identified activities and tasks. Exercises such as role playing and behavioral interviews are often part of assessment centers.

Understanding and Providing Data

In evaluating the organization's employee efficacy, the PHR's role is to assess and communicate information about the workforce to the leadership team. This data allows leadership to then assess whether or not the organization is meeting its strategic objectives in developing and utilizing human resources effectively. Throughout this process, it is important to strive to gather a holistic picture of the workforce. HR teams that focus only on a single type of employee information—such as average time to complete a task—overlook other types of workforce data. This leads to blind spots that hinder the organization's ability to use data to identify new opportunities to reduce costs, improve efficiency, and foster innovation. The HR team has three key sources of data:

- employee performance evaluations
- hiring interviews and exit interviews
- demographic information

Each data source gives insight into a different aspect of the larger picture. For example, the questions typically asked by candidates during hiring interviews provide information about the typical concerns of prospective employees. These can then be contrasted with the causes of turnover revealed in exit interviews. Comparing the two interviews, over time, can reveal trends in perceived and actual sources of employee discontent. These interview processes in particular are important sources of information regarding the efficacy of an organization's DEI initiatives. Often, those persons intended to receive support by the leadership team's DEI goals do not perceive themselves to be receiving meaningful assistance in furthering their careers. Such complaints are likely to emerge in exit interviews where former employees feel freer to speak their minds.

A data-first approach to HR benefits the organization by allowing leadership to set goals based on specific objectives rather than vague promises. This improves transparency and makes it possible to rationally assess the organization's performance. For example, "improve African American representation in leadership" is a less meaningful goal than "in three years, at least 30 percent of leaders should be members of the African American community" because the former is less specific and less quantifiable than the latter.

Demographic information about the organization's workforce provides key context for the traditional performance evaluations as models of employee productivity. Poor performance outcomes in a particular demographic often indicate a need for increased managerial focus on providing appropriate support to certain groups or individuals. Additional coaching or mentoring programs help traditionally marginalized populations feel valued by the organization. Over time, this additionally furthers DEI initiatives by improving the skills of such persons. Fostering skills training and leadership mentoring empowers persons who historically have experienced discrimination to achieve expertise and leadership roles through their own abilities.

An important tool in utilizing these data sources is reframing low performance outcomes as growth opportunities. While not every performance deficit is an opportunity—at times, an employee is not a good fit for the position—it is important for the PHR to analyze the data for its causes rather than simply provide the data directly to the leadership team.

Analysis requires comparing multiple data sources to one another to search out sources of inequity and structural problems in the workplace. For example, data showing that 95 percent of women in the organization never receive a promotion provides important context to a statistic that 20 percent of employees receive a promotion to management during their career. This comparison of performance and demography highlights discrimination in the organization's internal promotion process. When analyzing performance metrics, consistently poor performance among a particular demographic often indicates a flaw in the organization's managerial practices rather than in the employees themselves. Employees who experience (or believe they are experiencing) discrimination are less motivated and less productive. This is the organization's fault—not the fault of the employee. By providing data to management that frames the data contextually, the PHR improves the leadership team's ability to direct goal setting effectively.

Data-first HR practices also enable the PHR to assess the financial costs and benefits of the leadership team's strategic goals. Doing this provides valuable information when assessing the viability of merit-based compensation, mitigating turnover and employee attrition, and retaining a consistent knowledge base within the organization. For example, if improved compensation is not improving productivity, that likely indicates something has gone wrong elsewhere in the organization, such as in the workplace culture. Analyzing data allows the PHR to put a dollar value on effective and ineffective management practices, which improves the leadership team's decision-making process by clarifying how meeting employee needs will support business outcomes.

Communicating the results of this analysis requires the PHR to understand how the organization's leadership team best comprehends information. Communication is most effective when the message is crafted for a specific audience. A single presentation about how the organization is performing will not be maximally effective with both the front-line employees and the senior leadership. When presenting to leadership, it is important to focus on the conclusions that align most closely with the leadership team's stated objectives. Keeping information on topic and highlighting how it impacts strategic goals strengthens communication. Use the leadership team's own preferred method of presenting information to employees to determine the best way to communicate with them. For example, if a leader frequently utilizes charts as a visual aid, the employees will likely appreciate a chart explaining the HR team's findings about the organization's use of human capital.

Practice Questions

4. What is a performance evaluation also called?
   A) a performance appraisal
   B) a write-up
   C) progressive discipline
   D) informal feedback

5. Who typically provides feedback on an employee's performance during a 360-degree performance review?

A) peers
B) subordinates
C) current supervisor
D) all of the above

6. Which of the following is NOT a key source of data for analyzing employee outcomes?

A) annual skill evaluations
B) exit interviews
C) hiring interviews
D) leadership's strategic objectives

Answer Key

1. A: Employee training refers to helping employees develop skills that apply to their jobs or career paths.

2. C: A case study with open discussion would spark creative thinking and is an example of behavioral-based training.

3. A: Cultural theory models, such as Hofstede's Cultural Dimensions Theory, can be used by organizations to help employees understand cultures and perform globally.

4. A: A performance evaluation is a formal, documented assessment of an employee's performance in a given time period (usually a year). It is also called a performance appraisal.

5. D: In a 360-degree performance review, multiple sources are asked to contribute to an employee's evaluation; the employee may also contribute.

6. D: Option D is correct because the leadership team's strategic objectives are not a source of data; instead, the PHR uses data to assess whether or not those objectives have been achieved. Options A, B, and C are incorrect because each of these three answers lists an important source of employee outcomes data. Remember that both hiring and exit interviews are useful for acquiring data because they provide contextual insight into an employee's performance metrics.

Chapter 5 – Total Rewards: Compensation, Benefits, and Nonmonetary Rewards

Managing Total Rewards Programs

Total rewards describe all of the tools an employer uses to attract, motivate, and retain employees. Total rewards include anything an employee perceives to be valuable as a result of working at the organization. There are five components of total rewards:

1. compensation
2. benefits
3. work/life programs
4. recognition programs
5. professional development

Depending on available resources, employers offer these various programs or components as part of a total compensation package to employees. A competitive and appropriate compensation package is key to retaining and motivating employees, who in turn will deliver performance and results for the organization.

Salary and Benefit Surveys

To remain competitive, the organization should monitor its competitors' packages and overall total rewards packages for the industry. **Salary and benefit surveys** are reliable sources of data for an organization to consider when determining compensation and benefit programs.

The total rewards program encompasses the whole life cycle of an employee. The **employee life cycle** has five stages:

1. attracting and recruiting
2. onboarding
3. developing
4. retaining
5. separating and offboarding

At every stage of the employee life cycle, the organization must consider each aspect of the total rewards program, including wages, benefits, recognition, and development, and consider how the total rewards program impacts the performance of the company and its employees. Additionally, as employees move through the life cycle stages, their needs may change as they are impacted by varying situations, abilities, and experiences. It is therefore important that a total rewards program is dynamic enough to meet the needs of the five stages of the employee life cycle.

Compensation

Employee **compensation**, sometimes referred to as **remuneration**, is the money employees receive in exchange for the work they perform or the time they work. Compensation can include a wage, salary, commissions, or bonuses. Cash compensation can be categorized as fixed pay, variable pay, or premium pay. According to the **Equal Pay Act of 1963**, there are four basic compensable factors:

- effort
- skill
- responsibility
- working conditions

Other compensable factors include the skills, years of experience, licenses, value to the organization, and any other factors that determine the worth of the job. When determining employee compensation, all forms of remuneration should be considered: wages and salary, bonuses and variable pay, and other types of remuneration.

Pay Classifications

Employees can be paid either on a salaried or hourly basis. Salaried employees are paid a predetermined amount based on the expectations and outputs of the job. This is an annual amount paid in regular intervals throughout the year according to the pay schedule.

Hourly employees are paid for time worked. They are paid an amount based on the number of hours worked in a pay period. There are no minimum required hours that an employee must work, though benefit plans typically define part-time and full-time workers based on the number of hours worked.

According to the Fair Labor Standards Act (FLSA), an employee can be considered exempt or nonexempt:

- **Exempt employees** are exempted from the FLSA, so that act does not apply to them.
  - ▷ The FLSA has strict guidelines on what types of positions are exempted.
- **Nonexempt positions** have specific requirements, including paying overtime wages when an employee works more than forty hours in a workweek.

(See Chapter 3, "Talent Acquisition and Planning the Workforce," and Chapter 7, "Employee and Labor Relations," for more details on the FLSA.)

All hourly employees are nonexempt due to the nature of the classification, but salaried employees can be either exempt or nonexempt. Nonexempt salaried employees are paid fixed sums based on their annual salaries, but they may also receive overtime when they exceed forty hours during the workweek.

The amount of overtime pay that employees receive depends on how many hours they worked in a pay week—not a pay period. If a pay period goes over multiple weeks, the employer cannot use an average of hours to pay overtime; overtime must be calculated each week.

Additionally, some employers or union contracts pay overtime for over eight hours worked in a day. The FLSA, however, requires only that overtime be paid when more than forty hours have been worked in a week.

Types of Compensation

Fixed pay, also called **base pay**, is nondiscretionary compensation. This means that it does not fluctuate based on performance or results. Nondiscretionary compensation is linked to the organization's pay philosophy and structure as well as market conditions; examples include salary pay and hourly wages.

Variable pay is compensation that changes directly with performance or results achieved. It is a payment based on performance over a specified period of time and can be linked to either or both the employee's and employer's performance. Examples include commissions, bonuses, short-term incentives, stock options, performance-sharing incentives, and profit sharing. **Pay-for-performance** is when employees are rewarded for achieving goals. **Piece-rate pay** rewards individuals on the number of units they produce.

Premium pay is compensation that is tied to nontraditional work schedules, shifts, and skills; premium pay is provided *in addition to* fixed pay. Some examples of premium pay are shift differential pay, weekend/holiday pay, on-call pay, and skill-based pay (see "Pay Increases" below).

Deferred compensation means that some of an employee's compensation is paid out long after the employee earns the money. Examples may be a pension plan or stock options.

Direct compensation typically refers to monetary payouts that have been discussed previously in regard to monies paid for work or time performed. On the other hand, **indirect compensation** refers to nonmonetary items paid for by the company for the employee. **Fringe benefits** is another term used for indirect compensation; it includes items like tuition reimbursements, gym memberships, mobile phones, and company cars.

Fringe benefits are taxable unless the law specifically excludes the benefit. Excluded fringe benefits include the following:

- health and other similar insurances
- educational assistance up to a specific dollar amount
- qualified deferred retirement plans
- de minimis, or low-cost, gifts (e.g., coffee cups)

Common, taxable benefits include the following:

- mileage reimbursement
- moving expenses
- awards and prizes (e.g., gift cards)

Remuneration Data Analysis

When determining compensation levels and structures, organizations need to consider data from many different sources. Furthermore, organizations should compare this data with internal data to determine individual pay.

> **Did You Know?**
>
> Many organizations will "mark up" the benefit so that the amount, once taxed, hits the targeted level of the benefit. This way, the company—not the employee—assumes the cost of taxation.

Comparable worth describes the idea that employees who perform roles or work with relatively the same value should be paid a similar wage. Historically, comparable worth has described pay equity between men and women ("equal pay for equal work"). Comparable worth can be established by using a formal pay structure and compensation philosophy.

When analyzing pay, it is important to consider both the internal and external market data. Analysis of current employee wages can determine internal alignment. **Internal alignment** compares the compensation level of one job with that of another within the same organization. On the other hand, **external competitiveness** assesses the pay level of an internal job in relation to the market value of that job more broadly. Finally, **internal consistency** uses job analysis, wage data, and job descriptions to analyze the relative value and pay of a role as they relate to other roles in the organization.

When determining pay and creating pay structures, it is important to consider both internal alignment and external competitiveness. For instance, the market may indicate that a specific job is worth more than other jobs within the department, but a company may choose to pay this specific job below the market average in order to maintain the same level of pay within that department. By the same token, a job in high demand that is difficult to recruit may be paid more than others within a specific department based on market wages. Any decision to create internal inequities must be based on data so that the decision can be supported.

Pay Structures

A company's **pay structure** refers to its method of administering pay. There are two common types of pay structures:

- The **internal equity method** pays based on the job's placement in the organizational hierarchy.
- In **market pricing**, each job's pay is tied to the prevailing market rate:
    - Employees who are paid below the established pay range of a job are considered green-circled. Employees who are paid above the market rate are considered red-circled.

Red-circled employees typically have their pay held or receive smaller increases until the market or target pay level meets their salaries. Employees can be overpaid for a number of reasons, including a demotion whereby wages are held at a previous level or when an employee's skills do not keep up with the changing demands of a job.

A green-circled employee typically receives larger increases to help the individual catch up to the market or target. Due to costs, it is often difficult for an organization to move an employee to a targeted level within one year. Rather, when an employee is green-circled, a plan is put into place to move that employee up over the course of a few years.

A pay structure helps clarify the value the organization places on each role; it also shows why employees are compensated differently. Furthermore, a pay structure helps human resource professionals equitably administer the organization's overall pay philosophy. The pay structure also helps HR professionals administer incentive compensation, especially for people with higher levels of responsibility and accountability.

The first step in establishing a pay structure is to create a **compensation philosophy**, which is a statement that articulates how the company wants to pay and reward employees. The compensation philosophy defines how the organization compensates employees relative to the market. A pay structure should align the compensation and benefit strategies with the mission, vision, and values of the company.

An organization may have a **lag method** in which it pays below average due to limited funds or a new business model. The company may want to **meet the market**, which means paying average market rates. On the other hand, the company might want to **exceed the market** by paying above-average wages in order to attract and retain employees. Exceeding the market can be an important strategy for a high-tech company that needs to attract employees who are in high demand.

Factors to consider when creating a compensation philosophy include the size of the organization, its financial performance, turnover levels within the organization, and candidate availability. A compensation philosophy should also account for the total compensation of an employee (e.g., wages, variable compensation, and benefits).

After establishing a pay structure or philosophy, the organization must perform a job analysis to determine the content of a job and the knowledge, skills, and attributes (KSAs) necessary to perform it. (See Chapter 3, "Talent Acquisition and Planning the Workforce," for details on performing a job analysis.)

Organizations use the information obtained through the job analysis process to establish job descriptions. An accurate and up-to-date job description must be available during the compensation process so that the job and its required KSAs are properly represented when examining internal and external markets.

With the job analysis and the job description in place, the pay grades and pay bands can be established. These tools establish compensation of a role relative to other roles in the organization. The organization uses factors like level of responsibility, span of control, and required education to rank the roles within the company. It is important to look at the role itself rather than the individuals performing the job.

Pay grades describe a system of establishing a range of compensation through a fixed framework. Minimum, middle, and maximum pay levels are determined. There may be anywhere from five to fifteen pay grades depending on the size and complexity of an organization. There is no set standard or number of grades; instead, each organization must determine the number based on its own needs. Each job is then assigned a pay grade based on the established factors. This sets up a transparent pay progression for employees as they enter new roles and develop their skills and abilities.

Pay bands are similar to pay grades but include a broader segment of the roles. In general, there are fewer bands in a structure than grades. Pay bands can be used to determine pay for certain levels within an organization (e.g., entry level, mid-managers, and executives).

To establish pay structures and determine the appropriate pay levels for jobs, HR professionals typically conduct a **structured compensation analysis**. Steps of the compensation analysis are described in Table 5.1.

Table 5.1. Compensation Analysis
1. Determine the Payroll Budget.
• Research merit increases and salary adjustments in the company and in the industry. • Determine how many jobs need to be priced. • Project upcoming payroll budgets to account for these adjustments.
2. Benchmark Each Job's Value.
• Use salary surveys to match the compensation of the internal job to an external job with similar duties; compare with other jobs in the same industry or geographical location. • Determine the benchmarked value based on the organization's compensation philosophy. For example, if the organization decides to pay "at market," the fiftieth percentile should be reviewed.
3. Create Salary Ranges and Pay Grades.
• Use the internal equity method to create a series of grades or bands, with wider ranges at the top of the structure and narrower ranges at the bottom. Each grade should be tied to a different level of responsibility within the company. • Pay grades should have a spread by which employees can progress in their jobs. There should be a minimum and maximum amount for each pay grade. Typically, the midpoint of a given grade should be 15 percent higher than that of the lower grade. • Slot jobs into pay grades based on their market value and/or relative value in the organization.

Pay Increases

An organization will rely on the pay structure to manage pay increases. Pay increases may occur on several different schedules:

- annually
- by calendar year
- at the time of promotion
- randomly

At the time of a wage review, financial performance, market data, and internal grades or bands should be considered.

Organizations award increases based on performance or merit. A **merit adjustment** rewards employees for high performance. Similarly, an organization might offer compensation to employees who exceed their duties in the form of **incentive pay**. **Skill-based pay** rewards employees for mastering new skills and is typically given to those who perform physical or production work.

Many organizations award annual increases based on inflation or a **cost-of-living adjustment (COLA)** increase. A **seniority adjustment** refers to a pay adjustment based on an employee's length of service or seniority at the organization. Each organization must consider culture and performance in order to determine the types of increases that should be awarded.

Creating strong compensation models is dependent on good data. Internal data can be collected through a payroll or human resources information system (HRIS). When looking at internal data, all factors should be considered. These include overtime pay, variable compensation, and other forms of remuneration.

External data can be more challenging to collect depending on the demographics of a company's location(s) and the relevant types of jobs. When determining the validity of wage data, sources and statistics must be considered. This can be done by asking the following types of questions:

- "How was the data obtained?"
- "Is there enough data for a specific role to make the data statistically valid?"
- "How does the stated role align with the job that is being evaluated?"

The **Bureau of Labor Statistics (BLS)** publishes wage data on the national, state, and regional levels. This data is provided directly by employers. An organization can use other statistical and business surveys when conducting a wage survey, depending on the company's specialty. When looking at the data, it is important to look at the average, or mean, as well as the median—the middle of the highest points being reported and the middle of the lowest points being reported. After establishing a compensation philosophy, the organization can then use the data to establish pay structures and compensation levels.

The PESTLE analysis is useful for studying external markets because it incorporates political, social, economic, and technological factors. (See Chapter 8, "Information Management in Human Resources," for more information on the PESTLE analysis.)

Executive Compensation

To attract and retain the most qualified executive team, organizations sometimes offer a unique package of executive benefits and compensation for presidents, C-level executives, vice presidents, and senior directors. Executive compensation differs from packages offered to lower-level employees. **Executive compensation** packages often include the following:

- a base salary
- bonuses or performance incentives
- a signing bonus (e.g., cash bonus for joining the organization)
- stock options (the opportunity to buy stock in the company)
- income protection in the event of a company sale or liquidation
- a predetermined severance package for termination without cause
- executive-only benefits (e.g., additional insurance coverage)
- company perquisites, or "perks" (e.g., club memberships, company car, or the use of a company plane)

As with any other compensation, executive compensation is negotiated between the potential executive and the employer; however, the structure or terms may be substantially different from the "regular" package offered to

Helpful Hint:

Skill-based pay should not be confused with **pay-for-knowledge**, which is a compensation system based on an employee's KSAs; it is not an increase or a bonus.

other employees. It may be specifically customized for the executive; in other words, each executive has a unique compensation structure.

Typically, executive salary and benefits are documented in an employment contract or agreement. This document outlines the terms of employment, including the full spectrum of compensation, benefits, perks, performance incentives, and severance agreements. In contrast with compensation agreements provided to lower-level employees, executive compensation agreements are more detailed and contain a variety of benefits and perks not offered to other levels of employees.

Helpful Hint:

It is best to get wage data from a reputable source such as the Bureau of Labor Statistics (BLS), an association that runs surveys, or a paid service. Employee feedback can be useful, but employees themselves may provide biased information, intentionally or not.

Sales Compensation

Typically, an employee in a sales role has a full or partial compensation program that is tied to a sales commission program. In other words, salespeople are compensated based on the sales they make by either "receiving a commission" or "getting paid by commission." Each organization must consider its goals to determine the appropriate sales commission program. Commissions may be based on overall revenue, sales above budget, profit margin, or number of units sold. Additionally, a sales commission may be a percentage of an individual's overall compensation, or it may be the only monies or compensation paid to an employee.

Global Compensation

When offering compensation and benefits to international employees, HR professionals need to be knowledgeable of the country or region's culture and regulations.

A **centralized compensation structure** can provide simplified financial planning, increased transparency in compensation practices, consistency in the enforcement of compensation practices, and reduced administrative expenses.

However, global companies must be able to manage variations in compensation structures due to economic factors, local expectations that dictate the types of compensation and benefits that are expected, and holiday schedules that impact employee compensation and the organization's operations. To ensure compliance with international customs, laws, and regulations, companies must address many issues concerning the compensation of their global workforces.

One important issue is maintaining pay equity. Base pay and traditional compensation structures vary from country to country. In France, for example, base pay can include vacation pay and overtime payments. Regional differences must be factored in to the overall compensation program, and they must be accounted for when analyzing internal pay equity.

Accounting for cost of living is also a major matter of global compensation. The value of a US dollar in a given country affects the pay levels of employees in that country. For example, due to the difference in cost of living, a position paying sixty thousand US dollars annually in the United States may pay a local employee in another country eleven thousand US dollars for the same work.

Managing cultural differences is essential for effective global compensation. Appropriate communication with employees (especially with respect to their compensation and benefits) must be handled in accordance with the country's customs. In some cases, the organization may decide to outsource its administrative payroll and HR functions for international employees in order to better manage the costs of operating abroad.

Another part of global compensation is the remuneration for expatriates living outside their home countries. A global organization needs to develop a pay structure for its expatriate personnel. This may include a base salary plus housing, transportation, visits to the home country, cost-of-living allowances, assignment incentives, premiums, and allowances. Though the standardization of expatriate compensation is desired, it is often difficult to achieve based on the actual assignment, its duration and location, the home country location, the cost of living in each country, and other components.

When considering expatriate base salary levels, there are a number of different approaches:

- In the **home country approach**, the home country's salary levels are used.
- In the **host country approach**, the host country's salary levels are used.
- Finally, in the **headquarters-based approach**, the salaries at the location of the headquarters are used.

Another consideration is "where" expatriate employees are paid: will they be paid in the currency of their home countries or the assignment countries?

Due to the assignment, some expatriates are awarded a hardship allowance or hazard pay to incentivize living in difficult contexts. If the employee's family moves with the employee, for example, there can be educational assistance for the children to attend specific schools or spousal support for finding a job in the new country.

Extreme differences in compensation and benefits between expatriate and local staff may negatively affect morale within the organization. It is therefore important to consider not only the expatriate staff but also the local staff to ensure internal alignment within the organization.

Other factors to consider are insurance coverage while abroad, taxes, and employment laws and regulations. Finally, an employer must also be thinking ahead to repatriation and the impact of the assignment compensation when expatriate employees return to their home countries.

Practice Questions

1. Health insurance benefits are a component of which of the following?
   A) total rewards
   B) organizational development
   C) work-life balance
   D) pay for performance

2. In determining compensation structure, what does the term *meet the market* mean?
   A) The compensation structure pays by salary and not by the hour.
   B) The compensation structure uses market analyses to determine compensation.
   C) The compensation structure pays at average market rates.
   D) The compensation structure leads its competitors in compensation.

3. Which of the following is NOT a category of exempt status under the FLSA?
   A) outside sales
   B) management
   C) hourly assistants
   D) executives

4. Which of the following is generally true about executive compensation?
   A) Executives receive a wider variety of compensation than other employees.
   B) Executives receive cheaper health insurance than other employees.
   C) Executives are guaranteed pay even if they do not work.
   D) Executives do not receive a base salary.

Payroll

Payroll departments manage employee compensation, including tax withholdings and deductions. Payroll administrators manage the following processes to ensure the proper and timely compensation of employees:

- calculating time cards
- calculating salaries, wages, reimbursements, commissions, bonuses, overtime, and retroactive pay
- tracking and paying company-paid holidays, vacation time, and sick time
- handling paycheck deductions for taxes, wage garnishment, insurance, and retirement savings
- coordinating with the accounting and finance departments to report all payments and deductions accurately

While human resources and payroll are considered two distinct functions, they often work together and may be combined in smaller organizations. For example, when HR initiates the hiring of an employee, payroll introduces the employee's information to the payroll system, collects and processes the employee's tax withholdings and deductions, and adds the employee onto the roster for paycheck processing.

Smaller organizations may outsource their payroll and/or human resources duties to **third-party administrators (TPAs)**. A TPA can help the organization administer payroll, benefits, and HR records for less cost than hiring full-time staff. Other organizations, especially growing ones, may employ an internal staff member (e.g., an office manager) to act as a liaison between employees and TPAs to ensure that administration is handled accurately and quickly. Even larger companies may outsource all or part of their payroll or HR functions if doing so is in the best interests of the organization's budget, operations, and long-term goals.

Organizations often include both human resources and payroll management in the strategic planning process to ensure that those processes are closely aligned with the strategic goals of the organization. For example, human resources leadership can develop the appropriate strategies to attract, hire, and retain the best employees for the company. Meanwhile, payroll leaders can develop strategies to streamline processes, ensure high accuracy in recordkeeping, and provide excellent service to employees. Both functions collaborate to conduct or assist in internal audits to ensure the accuracy of employee records and employment practices, such as paying employees.

A paycheck or pay stub typically summarizes the amount of pay, deductions, taxes, and year-to-date compensation information; however, many employees find it difficult to fully understand their overall compensation when benefits and other fringes are included. One communication device that helps show employees the values of their total compensation packages is a compensation statement. A **compensation statement** includes information about pay as well as details about direct and indirect compensation and benefits, including both the employer's and the employee's contributions. For clarity, these figures are communicated as an annualized number.

When administering, running, or managing payroll, it is important to understand basic accounting principles. These ensure that the payroll, when integrated into the financial statements, is balanced and accurate. Payroll will impact several financial reports:

- The **balance sheet** is a financial summary of a company's assets and liabilities.
- The **profit and loss statement (P&L)** summarizes the organization's revenue, costs, and expenses; it also shows overall profitability and performance.

The payroll function might also work directly with the accounting department in regard to accounts payable (the money that is owed *by* the company) and accounts receivable (money owed *to* the organization). This might be especially true when working with an outsourced payroll organization and managing the flow of monies to the employees from the employer's bank accounts.

The payroll professional will also need to understand the basic accounting principles upon which the organization's accounting standards and processes are built. These may include the **accrual principle**, in which the financial statements reflect the costs when they occur rather than when they are paid. In this type of system, even if a pay run falls into the next month, the cost of that payroll will be recorded in the month in which the hours were worked. Other principles would record the cost of the payroll only when it is actually paid. Knowing how the organization operates is key to effectively managing and recording payroll.

Helpful Hint:

The P&L is sometimes known as the **income statement**.

Severance Pay

Severance pay is payment awarded to employees upon their termination. Its purpose is to help the terminated individual bridge the gap between jobs while looking for their next position. Though there is no one formula to compute the severance pay amount, it is usually based on length of service. Typically, the amount of severance is equal to one or two weeks of pay for every year of service.

Severance pay can be paid in one lump sum or it can be paid over several weeks. Additionally, a severance package might include an extension of benefits or the company paying the COBRA premium for the terminated employee.

Strategically, severance pay should be tied to a severance agreement, which is a contract made between the terminated employee and the organization that releases claims toward the employer for a specific amount of money or benefits.

Did You Know?

Severance plans must comply with the Employee Retirement Income Security Act (ERISA), which regulates employers who offer pension or welfare benefit plans to their employees.

Severance pay can affect a worker's unemployment because it is considered income by many state plans. Typically, unemployment is impacted the week or weeks during which severance pay is allocated.

Executive severance agreements or packages are designed for the top executives of an organization. These protect executives who are at-will employees and who are terminated without good cause. These agreements are typically agreed upon at the time of hire and provide monetary protection for executives who are asked to leave the organization. Reasons for termination without good cause may include downsizing, plant closings, mergers, acquisitions, or the avoidance of lawsuits.

Executive severance agreements are more generous than typical severance agreements and can include pay from six months to a year or more. They also may include bonuses and benefits.

Benefits

Employee benefits are important to the livelihood of employees and their families. Benefits support employees with their health, financial, and personal needs and make a total compensation package competitive and rich. The benefits package offered by the employer may be the deciding factor that convinces a talented individual to work at the organization. There are two categories of employee benefits: mandated benefits and optional benefits.

Mandated benefits are those that must be provided by law, such as workers' compensation and unemployment insurance. Table 5.2. provides an overview of benefits that are mandated by federal law. (Certain health-related benefits are covered in more depth later in this chapter.) Note that additional benefits may be required for workers in certain states according to the regulations in those states.

Helpful Hint:

Employers with more than fifty employees are subject to the PPACA, which means that health care becomes a mandated benefit.

Table 5.2. Mandated Benefits

Mandated Benefit	**Purpose**
Social Security taxes	• Social Security funds retirement income. • Employers must pay Social Security taxes at the same rate paid by their employees.
Unemployment insurance (UI)	• Workers who become unemployed through no fault of their own and meet other requirements under state law receive UI. • States administer their own UI programs under federal guidelines.

Table 5.2. Mandated Benefits	
Mandated Benefit	**Purpose**
Workers' compensation insurance	• Employees who become injured or ill due to their jobs receive workers' compensation benefits to cover payment for lost wages and medical bills. • Employers must carry workers' compensation insurance coverage through an insurance carrier, on a self-insured basis, or through the state's program.
Disability insurance	• Certain states require businesses to provide insurance for wage loss due to employees' non-work-related sickness or injury. • These benefits provide partial income replacement during the period of disability.
Family and medical leave	• The Family and Medical Leave Act (FMLA) provides up to twelve weeks of unpaid leave to eligible employees for the following instances: ○ the birth and care of the employee's child, or the placement for adoption or foster care of a child ○ care of an immediate family member (spouse, child, parent) who has a serious health condition ○ care of the employee's own serious health condition • The employee maintains group health benefits during the leave.

Table 5.2. Mandated Benefits

Mandated Benefit	Purpose
Military family leave	• The FMLA was amended in 2008 to provide protections specifically for military families. • Eligible employees receive up to twenty-six weeks of leave to care for injured family members and up to twelve weeks to tend to matters related to deployment. • These leaves are also unpaid, but the employee maintains group health benefits.
Patient Protection and Affordable Care Act (PPACA)	• PPACA requires employers with more than fifty employees to provide affordable health insurance that provides minimum value to their full-time employees (and their dependents).

Optional benefits are benefits that the employer chooses to offer as a way to compensate employees (or to comply with a collective bargaining agreement in a unionized environment). Examples of optional benefits include health insurance coverage (in some cases) and retirement plans.

In addition to major health, welfare, and retirement benefits, companies may also offer the following types of **voluntary benefits** to employees:

- critical illness coverage
- long-term care coverage
- wellness programs
- automotive insurance
- home insurance
- other coverage at a group discount
- pet benefits
- student debt forgiveness programs
- new parent programs

> **Helpful Hint:**
>
> According to the IRS, **minimum value** on an employer-sponsored health plan is met when the plan "covers at least 60 percent of the total allowed cost of benefits that are expected to be incurred under the plan."[1]

These programs might be purchased by the individual employee through a payroll deduction program or bought by the organization itself.

Offering a complete package of benefits to suit the various needs of employees helps attract well-qualified talent to the organization and serves as a retention tool.

Health and Welfare Benefits

Health and welfare benefits are the most common discretionary benefits offered by employers. These benefits are typically offered in the form of group health plans established or maintained by the employer (or union). They provide medical care coverage for participants (and often their dependents) either directly or through insurance, reimbursement, or other means.

Employers may offer the following health and welfare benefits to their employees as part of their total compensation packages:

- medical plan
- dental plan
- vision plan
- prescription drug plan
- flexible spending account (FSA)
- health reimbursement account (HRA)
- health savings account (HSA)
- life insurance
- accidental death and dismemberment insurance
- short- and long-term disability insurance

Most welfare plans can be provided by an employer to its employees on a pretax basis (i.e., the cost of the plan is not taxable to the employee). As an exception, some welfare plans will result in additional gross income to a highly compensated employee or a key employee unless the plan meets the nondiscrimination requirements determined by the Internal Revenue Code. A few benefits and plans are discussed in more detail below.

A **cafeteria plan** allows employees to reduce their compensation in order to pay their share of employer-provided benefits coverage on a pretax basis. In a cafeteria plan, employees can choose from two or more cash or qualified benefit plans (hence the name "cafeteria"). Pretax benefits like health insurance, group-term life insurance, flexible spending accounts, and certain voluntary supplemental benefits (e.g., dental or vision coverage) could all be available through the plan. A cafeteria plan must not discriminate in favor of either highly compensated employees or key employees.

In a **flexible spending account (FSA)**, an employee sets aside a portion of earnings to pay for certain expenses as established in the cafeteria plan. Usually, employees use an FSA for medical expenses, but FSAs can also be used for dependent care or other expenses. FSA contributions are made on a pretax basis. The FSA is a "use it or lose it" program whereby the unused dollars are not available to the employee after the plan year. Rather, these dollars either go back to the employer to offset the administration costs or are distributed to all the participants of the plan depending on the plan design.

A **health reimbursement account (HRA)** is an employer-funded account that can be used to cover qualified medical expenses of the employee and their dependents. This account may be used to pay for the participant's out-of-pocket, qualified medical expenses until insurance covers the expense or the funds are depleted.

> **Helpful Hint:**
>
> A cafeteria plan is sometimes called a **Code Section 125 plan** or a **flexible benefits plan**.

A **health savings account (HSA)** is a pretax medical savings account available to participants in a high-deductible health plan (HDHP). The funds contributed to the HSA are not subject to federal income tax upon deposit. Funds are used to pay for the participant's out-of-pocket, qualified medical expenses (and those of their dependents). This account can roll over year after year, allowing the employee to build a balance for future medical needs.

Employers (as plan administrators and/or fiduciaries) and the health plans they offer must comply with several health- and welfare-related federal laws:

- The **Employee Retirement Income Security Act (ERISA)** covers most private-sector health plans. ERISA provides protections for participants and beneficiaries covered under employee benefit plans. Plan administrators and fiduciaries are required to meet certain standards of conduct that are outlined in the law.
- The **Consolidated Omnibus Budget Reconciliation Act (COBRA)** grants employees the right to keep the group health insurance (and pay the premium) that they would otherwise lose after they separate from the employer or reduce their work hours. Most people can retain their insurance coverage for up to eighteen months (and longer, in some situations).
- The **Health Insurance Portability and Accountability Act of 1996 (HIPAA)** provides opportunities for people to retain (or obtain) health insurance during qualifying events. It also protects the confidentiality and security of health care information and provides mechanisms to control administrative costs.
- As discussed in Table 5.2., the Patient Protection and Affordable Care Act (PPACA) requires certain employers to offer affordable health insurance that provides minimum value to their full-time employees and their dependents. Employers must also communicate about health care marketplaces to employees and offer a standardized summary of coverage to employees (among other requirements). Insurers must cover preexisting conditions and all applicants.
- The **Pregnancy Discrimination Act (PDA)** requires certain health plans to provide the same level of coverage for pregnancy as for other conditions.
- The **Mental Health Parity and Addiction Equity Act (MHPAEA)**[1] requires that when a health plan covers mental health services, the annual or lifetime dollar limits, copays, and treatment limitations must be at least the same as the limits for other medical benefits.

---

[1] "The Mental Health Parity and Addiction Equity Act (MHPAEA)," Centers for Medicare and Medicaid Services, accessed March 14, 2024, https://www.cms.gov/marketplace/private-health-insurance/mental-health-parity-addiction-equity

- The **Americans with Disabilities Act (ADA)**, among other protections, requires that disabled and nondisabled individuals be provided the same benefits, premiums, deductibles, and limits under a given health plan.
- As discussed in Table 5.2., the **Family and Medical Leave Act (FMLA)**, among other protections, requires employers to maintain health coverage for qualified employees for the duration of the FMLA leave.
- The **Uniformed Services Employment and Reemployment Rights Act (USERRA)** allows employees to continue group health coverage while absent from work due to military service.

Time-Off Benefits

Employers may offer their employees several types of time-off benefits. These benefits include both paid time off and unpaid time off.

Paid time off is when the employee receives continuation of pay while away from work due to agreed-upon reasons. Paid time off can mean paid vacation time, sick days, personal time, or holidays. Some organizations offer nontraditional paid time off, such as paying for volunteer days and exercise or wellness time. **Sabbaticals** are paid extended leaves for job development or rejuvenation. More companies are also beginning to offer paternity leave or nongendered parental leave.

An employer may also offer a leave program, which may be an unpaid or paid leave from work. A **leave** is time off from work due to a specific reason. The most common leaves include those for sickness, the birth of a child, bereavement or a funeral, and jury duty.

Leaves may coincide with other paid benefits, like disability or workers' compensation programs. Or, the employer may choose to pay the employee a certain amount during the leave. Other times, the leave is taken unpaid with an agreement about returning to work within a specific period of time.

Employers with more than fifty employees are subject to the FMLA. The FMLA covers leaves for the birth or adoption of a child, a serious health condition of the employee or immediate family, or military family leave for the care of a wounded service member. The FMLA offers job protection to employees for up to twelve weeks (or longer in the case of military family leave). Under the FMLA, employees on leave are guaranteed to keep their jobs when they return, but they are not guaranteed compensation for the time during which they are on leave. In other words, FMLA leaves may be unpaid. To qualify for FMLA leave, the employee must have been employed at the company for at least twelve months and have worked a minimum of 1,250 hours in those past twelve months.

Many employers have moved away from the traditional siloed time-off programs such as vacation, personal time, and sick days to a more consolidated paid time off (PTO) benefit. In a **PTO program**, the employees are awarded a higher number of hours to use when away from work with the expectation that this time will be used for most absences. The employees' vacation, sick days, jury duty, bereavement, and personal days are typically all rolled into PTO. Rather than pulling from multiple accruals or programs, the time is managed by just one plan.

Income Replacement Programs

There are a number of income replacement programs—both legally mandatory and voluntary—that organizations offer employees to ensure financial support if the employee is unable to work.

Mandatory income replacement benefits include workers' compensation, which is paid when a worker is injured or becomes ill as a result of the employment, and unemployment insurance (UI). In most states, workers' compensation insurance is purchased by the employer. Some states have state-run plans to which the employer contributes in order to avoid having to purchase an insurance policy.

Employers pay both federal and state unemployment taxes. Individuals can collect unemployment when they are ready and willing to work but are unable to due to a termination of employment for reasons beyond their control (e.g., layoffs, job elimination). Generally, employed workers will not qualify for unemployment benefits if they leave their jobs voluntarily, if they are unable to work, or if they are fired for cause.

Voluntary income replacement benefits are benefits which employees are not required to have but may choose to add as payroll deductions in order to provide stability should their main sources of income be eliminated. Voluntary income replacement programs include leaves-of-absence benefits, such as short-term disability insurance (in some states) and income continuation insurance.

Retirement Benefits

In addition to health and welfare plans, many organizations also offer retirement plans to their employees. A **retirement plan** is a savings plan that supports employees once they retire. Retirement plan income replaces employment income. These plans may be set up by employers, unions, or other institutions. Retirement plans fall under three categories: defined benefit plans, defined contribution plans, and profit-sharing plans:

- **Defined benefit plans** are company-provided pension plans through which an employee's pension payments are calculated (defined) according to the employee's length of service with the company and earnings prior to retirement.
- **Defined contribution plans** are retirement savings plans in which the employer or employee (or both) contributes on a regular basis (typically pretax, assuming certain conditions are met). There is no guaranteed benefit. Employees have limited access to their accounts until retirement, though there may be a loan provision in the plan or the option to take hardship withdrawals. Any withdrawal before the age of fifty-nine and a half is usually penalized.
  - Examples of defined contribution plans include individual retirement accounts, such as IRA, 401(k), and 403(b) programs.
  - These are governed by the IRS and are subject to specific tax regulations.
  - The ability of employees to transfer money from one retirement account to another ("roll over") if they change jobs depends on the organization's vesting schedule.
- **Profit-sharing plans** are typically offered in conjunction with defined contribution plans. They allow the company to allocate profit to the employees' retirement accounts using a predetermined formula and vesting schedule.

Retirement plans may have a vesting schedule. When employees **vest**, it means they have rights or ownership to the monies within the plan. When 100 percent vested, employees have 100 percent ownership of that money. There are two types of vesting schedules: cliff and graded:

- A **graded schedule** means an employee earns a specific percentage ownership to the company contributions until 100 percent vesting is met, which can take up to six years within a defined contribution plan.
- A **cliff vesting schedule** is one in which the employee is 100 percent vested upon reaching a specific milestone. This may be immediately upon hire or after reaching a designated anniversary year.

Fiduciary Responsibility

Under the Employee Retirement Income Security Act (ERISA), the owner, CEO, CFO, or even the human resources representative may have fiduciary responsibility. The individual with **fiduciary responsibility** is held accountable for decisions that are made concerning the company's retirement plans.

A **fiduciary** can be anyone who has authority or control over the administration of an ERISA employee benefit plan, such as a 401(k) program. The "prudent man rule," or "prudent person rule," insists that the fiduciaries invest another person's assets as they would their own: with caution and care. An individual who does not meet the "prudent man standard of care" may face civil penalties or even lawsuits on the basis that decisions concerning the plan were not made with the employees' best interests in mind.

Practice Questions

5. Which of the following is typically considered a taxable benefit?
   A) vacation pay
   B) health insurance
   C) flexible spending account
   D) 401(k) matching contribution

6. How long does COBRA allow an employee who has been terminated to continue coverage under the employer's health insurance policy?
   A) twelve months
   B) eighteen months
   C) thirty-six months
   D) indefinitely

7. The prudent person rule is associated with which law?
   A) FLSA
   B) ERISA
   C) FMLA
   D) OSHA

8. An employee comes to HR upset because his pay stub shows large deductions for taxes, Social Security, Medicare, and health insurance. He feels that he is not getting his full compensation. What is the BEST way for HR to clarify the employee's annual compensation, including deductions and employer and employee contributions?
   A) several months' worth of pay stubs
   B) the employee's W2
   C) a compensation statement
   D) instructing the employee to speak with his supervisor

9. What is the MAIN reason employers offer a comprehensive benefits package?
   A) to reduce operating costs
   B) to do what other companies are doing
   C) to help attract and retain employees
   D) to save money on taxes

Work-Life Balance Programs

In addition to overseeing financial compensation, it is the PHR's job to determine and implement employee benefits that support a healthy work-life balance. This concept is important in the modern environment because of changing employee values and the increased flexibility enabled by recent technologies. As a member of the HR team, the PHR must advocate for policies that support work-life balance, implement nonmonetary benefits for employment with the organization, and evaluate the ongoing efficacy of these programs.

Human resources personnel are not generally tasked with policy creation; instead, it is the PHR's role to advise the leadership team on the efficacy of policies. This includes retaining policies that support work-life balance as well as changing policies that are detrimental to employee well-being. Policies are an effective way to establish boundaries throughout the organization because they are sources of authority. For example, a communication policy dictating that managers may not email their team members after hours is more forceful than leadership orally encouraging managers to use healthy boundaries.

Establishing firm boundaries between work and personal life reduces employee stress and improves engagement during working hours. In addition to encouraging employees to maintain healthy boundaries, policies that support work-life balance also send explicit messages to employees that they are valued by the organization. Typically, employees recognize that rules enforcing boundaries are designed to support their well-being rather than restrict their work behavior.

While advising leadership on policy creation, it is also important for the PHR to advocate for leaders to set an example for the organization's employees. Leaders who asks managers to follow the email policy in the example above but do not follow the same boundary with their managers are setting a negative precedent. Such behavior leads to work-life balance policies remaining "on the books" as one of the organization's values but not being pursued in day-to-day work. This double standard harms employee morale by implying that they are not truly valued by the organization.

While the role of HR professionals is somewhat passive in policy creation, their task is more active when creating and implementing employee benefit programs for the sake of work-life balance. This project may entail programs that occur at the workplace or benefits provided outside of the work environment. On-site benefit programs tend to remain fairly traditional:

- employer-provided meals and beverages
- exercise equipment or an on-site gym
- on-site child care
- recreational spaces for socializing with coworkers
- designated quiet spaces for privacy and stress management

In contrast, employee benefits that can be taken advantage of outside the workplace continue to evolve and change. This aspect of human resources is a result of the increased digitization of the modern workplace following the COVID-19 pandemic.

Demand for flexible schedules and remote positions is increasing. In the current work environment, providing off-site benefits gives organizations a key edge in attracting and retaining high-quality employees. Immediate options for the PHR include expanding remote options for employee roles and implementing flextime to offer employees greater freedom as to when they complete their tasks. Once the organization has begun the transition to a more flexible working environment, the PHR can begin implementing an employee assistance program.

Employee assistance programs (EAPs) support an organization's employees by providing services to the employee at little or no cost to them. EAPs commonly focus on the employee's mental health by providing counseling and emotional support to mitigate stress, reducing burnout, and helping to maintain a positive work-life balance. For example, free counseling to an employee struggling with grief can help the employee compartmentalize the grief in her personal life and avoid overworking as a way to avoid that grief. No two EAPs are identical because an organization's needs change over time. An organization with an aging workforce may benefit from an EAP with robust retirement or estate planning services. In contrast, a younger workforce is unlikely to make full use of those services. By determining the services most desired by the organization's employees, the PHR optimizes the EAP's cost-effectiveness. A cost-effective EAP is less likely to be targeted by budget cuts in times of need, thus retaining positive employee morale.

When supporting a flexible or off-site workforce, the PHR must keep in mind the importance of good work-life boundaries. Remote positions and off-site perks risk eroding these boundaries because employees do not physically compartmentalize work and home as different locations. Boundaries around working hours and communication can support all types of organizational structures and workplace cultures.

Another employee benefit that can be implemented in both on-site and flexible workplaces is an employee recognition program. Traditionally, this practice has looked similar to the stereotypical "employee of the month" award distributed by upper management; however, in the modern workplace, employee recognition is best implemented as a collaborative process in which both leaders and employees participate. A democratic recognition process increases the value of the praise to the employee because it comes from both their peers and their supervisors. This reduces the perception that a leader is playing favorites and increases employees' self-esteem through the sense that they have earned the respect of their coworkers.

Once these practices are in place, the PHR must monitor their effectiveness on an ongoing basis. The workforce's needs change over time; using performance metrics, anonymous surveys, and transparent conversations will allow the HR team to assess which benefits best support the mental health and work-life balances of employees.

Practice Questions

10. What is the purpose of an EAP?
    - A) to provide free, confidential counseling on work-life and personal matters
    - B) to assist employees with finding a job when they are laid off
    - C) to help employers find the best candidates for a position
    - D) to provide legal counsel to employees who want to sue the company

11. A workforce is struggling with employee retention due to long working hours at the end of each project cycle. Which of the following recommendations should the PHR make to the leadership team?

A) Implement a maximum limit on the number of overtime hours an employee may work.

B) Create a policy that dictates when a manager is allowed to communicate about work with employees after business hours.

C) Provide recreational amenities in the workplace in order to foster a stronger sense of camaraderie among the employees.

D) Utilize performance metrics to optimize the effectiveness of overtime hours so that the organization spends less on overtime pay.

Answer Key

1. A: The term *total rewards* refers to compensation, benefits, work-life programs, recognition programs, and professional development.

2. C: The term *meet the market* means that the company pays at average market rates.

3. C: Due to the nature of the classification, all hourly workers are considered nonexempt under the Fair Labor Standards Act (FLSA).

4. A: Executives generally receive not only higher compensation than other employees but also more variety in compensation (e.g., stock options, signing bonuses, income protection, executive-only bonuses, predetermined severance packages, and perks).

5. A: Compensation is taxable even if it is for paid time off.

6. B: In most cases, Consolidated Omnibus Budget Reconciliation Act (COBRA) coverage allows a terminated employee to continue coverage under the employer's health insurance policy for up to eighteen months.

7. B: In HR, the prudent person rule is mainly associated with the Employee Retirement Income Security Act (ERISA). A fiduciary should invest according to the prudent person rule and manage employees' retirement assets with care.

8. C: In this situation, the best solution would be to offer the upset employee a compensation statement since he might not have a full understanding of the costs of certain taxes and benefits. This overview of the employee's annual compensation, including employer and employee contributions, and a clear explanation of mandated benefits and required deductions (e.g., taxes), can help him better understand his net pay and the actual costs of taxes and certain benefits (e.g., health insurance). He will also be able to see the amounts that his employer contributes to these benefits.

9. C: A comprehensive benefits package attracts and retains the most talented employees.

10. A: Employee assistance programs (EAPs) provide employees with counseling on work-life and personal matters. Along with work-life balance programs, they can help reduce burnout.

11. B: The crunch at the end of a project cycle can be tricky to eliminate entirely. Establishing healthy work-life boundaries reduces burnout by giving employees adequate distance to reduce stress; therefore, option B is correct. Option A is incorrect because an arbitrary maximum limit on overtime hours does not actually address the stress caused by working overtime hours. Option C is incorrect because these amenities will not build stronger relationships within the team if the team does not have the spare time to utilize them. Option D is incorrect because this answer focuses on whether or not overtime is cost-effective; it does not address how overtime increases burnout and makes retention worse.

Chapter 6 – Employee Engagement

Employee engagement goes beyond the strategies, such as performance appraisals and exit interviews discussed in Chapter 3 ("Talent Acquisition and Planning the Workforce") and Chapter 4 ("Development, Learning and Training"), which are designed to glean feedback from employees and gauge the functional effectiveness of their roles.

Organizational programs and data-first HR practices that aim to increase and improve employee engagement are also critical components that allow organizations to maximize employee performance.

Using Data to Support Employee Engagement

Metric and Conversation Tools

Data-first HR practices require the PHR to understand how to acquire the data needed for analysis. **Anecdotal information**, such as a positive or negative story told by a colleague about the workplace, may act as a valuable "red flag" indicating a topic to address; however, data drawn from across the entire workforce is needed in order for the PHR to discern the causes of any anecdotal "red flags."

To do this, the PHR must engage with employees using both metric tools and conversation tools. **Metric tools** include processing performance evaluations (performed by leadership personnel, not the PHR) and utilizing anonymous employee surveys. Anonymity is important because it improves the likelihood that staff will answer questions honestly and with reduced fear of reprisal. Well-designed surveys ought to have the following components:

- be focused on a single topic of concern, such as employee satisfaction
- be intentionally timed so that surveys are neither too frequent nor too scarce
- be intended to produce actionable information that fosters positive change

For example, an employee survey that reuses old questions about employee satisfaction with management is unlikely to provide relevant data about a DEI initiative's success in the workplace. An unsuccessful DEI initiative, for instance, might increase employee dissatisfaction, but if the data collected does not provide a way to discern actionable information about how to improve the DEI initiative, the survey will not be useful.

Conversation tools use discussions between the HR team (or occasionally leadership team members) and employees. These discussions become tools when they occur on a consistent basis and with an intentional agenda. Chatting in the hallway produces anecdotal information; a weekly group discussion about hiring practices produces data. Mutually arranged focus groups of employees and HR team members are most effective for determining the workforce's opinion on possible courses of action. This is, of course, only possible if the discussion environment fosters transparent and honest communication.

Attitudes, behaviors, and opinions that would be inappropriate in the workplace may be permissible within such a group so long as they do not carry over into completing day-to-day tasks.

Focus Groups and Employee Resource Groups

Engaging employees through a **focus group** requires more time than using metrics-based tools but pays dividends in improved employee engagement and retention. Such a group improves the employees' feeling of ownership in the organization and the feeling that they are valued by the employer. Furthermore, a focus group often provides the specific feedback needed to create an action plan that will address sources of discontent.

An increasingly prevalent method of identifying and implementing employee desires is the employee resource group. An **employee resource group (ERG)** is an employee-led type of focus group that emphasizes the needs of employees who self-identify based on specific characteristic (e.g., race or gender). An ERG is analogous to a labor union in some important respects:

> **Helpful Hint:**
>
> Metrics identify employee emotions; conversations articulate employee desires.

- Both are led by employees.
- Both are intended to point out challenges in the workplace.
- Both function best when employees and leadership work together in a spirit of mutual support.

In contrast to a union, an ERG advocates for policy changes without direct negotiation with the employer. The ERG provides support to employees who share its characteristic in order to increase inclusion and visibility of potential biases in the workplace.

ERGs that are supported and welcomed by leadership and the HR team have been shown to consistently improve employee engagement and satisfaction. This improves overall productivity, often without a substantial increase in the organization's costs. It is easy, however, for an ERG to fail due to a lack of synergy between the employee-led group and the organization's own DEI initiatives. If an ERG and the organization's DEI initiatives both advocate for a marginalized group in different ways—such as the ERG focusing on internal hiring while DEI initiatives focus on external hiring—employees tend to feel dissatisfied with both programs. Teamwork from HR and leadership that supports the ERG is necessary to maximize employee engagement.

Practice Question

1. Which of the following survey questions is BEST designed to assess employee satisfaction with an organization's internal promotion process?

   A) How many managers have you worked with who are members of a marginalized group?
   B) How often have you applied for a position with increased responsibility?
   C) On a scale of 1 to 10, how accurate do you feel your performance evaluations are?
   D) On a scale of 1 to 10, how important do you feel seniority is as a factor in promotions?

Organizational Programs

Recognition Programs

Recognition programs can have a significant impact on business performance and employee morale. Some organizations have formal recognition programs with monetary rewards; others offer informal or low-cost recognition programs. Regardless of budget, successful recognition programs share the following characteristics:

- They reward results or behaviors, such as meeting sales targets, saving the company significant money, completing an important project, or otherwise affecting the business in a notably positive way.
- They give feedback that is immediate and frequent and provide positive reinforcement for positive behaviors; furthermore, they can be used as motivational tools.
- They offer opportunities for peer-to-peer recognition, which creates a positive team dynamic, camaraderie, and strong working relationships.
- Recognition is public and embedded into the company's values. When employees are recognized publicly by leadership, they feel appreciated and essential to the company's success.

A culture of recognition is an important tool to retain good employees and motivate new ones. Moreover, when employees celebrate their successes together, synergy in the workplace improves.

Finally, recognition programs help meet basic psychological needs. Psychologist Abraham Maslow theorized that human beings have a series of needs (Maslow's hierarchy of needs). These range from the most basic needs (physical) to the most complex needs (self-actualization). Maslow's hierarchy of needs is depicted in Figure 6.1., which shows the levels of needs each human being must satisfy in order to reach psychological fulfillment.

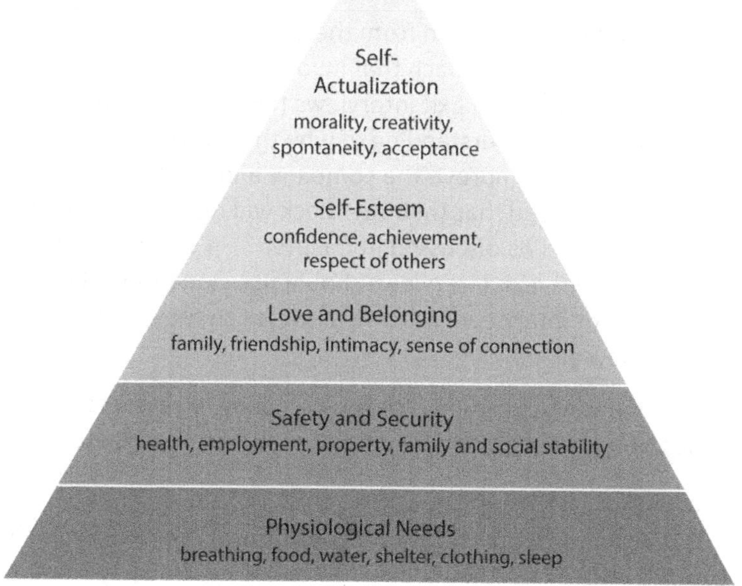

Figure 6.1. Maslow's Hierarchy of Needs

According to Maslow's theory, two of the most important psychological needs of humans are the need for appreciation and the need to belong. Having psychological needs met is an important element of an employee's decision to remain at an organization. Organizations can meet these psychological needs through recognition programs.

Alumni Programs

As recruitment methods continue to shift, the creation of **alumni programs**, also known as **corporate alumni programs**, has emerged as a strategic way for companies to expand their talent pool. Along with increasing the company's network of possible new employees, alumni programs can support a company's sales and development objectives, provide a boost to the company's branding, and help meaningfully support other company initiatives. Creating an alumni program also offers companies an opportunity to proactively confront the dwindling rates of employee retention, which currently stands at roughly 4 years[2].

Supporting employees who have separated from the company forms the foundation of a successful alumni program. The emphasis of a successful alumni program is to build and maintain a lifelong network of past employees, but the rationale behind this is somewhat twofold:

- Past employees who still feel engaged with and appreciated by the company will feel inspired to refer new talent, become brand ambassadors, advocate for the company, and perhaps even return to the company at some point.
- Successfully fostering a lifelong relationship with past employees also allows companies to retain some of the investments they made to train and compensate the employees while they were still with the company.

For many companies, creating a robust alumni program starts during the onboarding process, since many employers already anticipate that their new hires will be unlikely to stick with the company for the long haul. At this stage, the HR professional should have discussions with new hires about their goals and opportunities for advancement that may interest them. These discussions can help shape an alumni program by identifying what employees are seeking and how an alumni program can help support these goals—and maintain engagement with employees—when they almost inevitably decide to move on.

When employees do announce their separation from the company, HR professionals should encourage the company to take a gratitude-based approach that involves recognizing and thanking the employees for their contributions during their tenures. Exit interviews (discussed in greater detail in Chapter 3) should be leveraged to gain a clearer understanding of why the employee has decided to leave and any changes the employee may suggest to improve the company and its relationship with employees. Departing employees should be assured that their feedback will remain confidential and be used solely for company improvement purposes. As discussed in Chapter 3, in order to help elicit the most honest feedback from departing employees, exit interviews should use standardized questions that are sent to the employees ahead of time. Exit interviews will also allow HR to reevaluate, fine-tune, and improve future exit processes for employees.

The exit interview also serves as an opportunity for the company to reassess the goals of the departing employee and determine the type of support the employee would appreciate in a corporate alumni

[2] "Employee Tenure in 2022," Bureau of Labor Statistics, US Department of Labor, accessed March 15, 2024, https://www.bls.gov/news.release/pdf/tenure.pdf

program, such as networking or community volunteer opportunities. Finally, departing employees should be encouraged to officially sign up for the alumni program and given information about how they can meaningfully participate in it.

The following steps should be used to help build a successful alumni program:

- Create a dedicated team who will spearhead the recruitment of alumni and team management.
    - This often requires collaboration from numerous departments, notably HR, marketing, and IT.
    - Identify and use company resources, such as CRM databases and HR records, to help recruit alumni and identify program goals.
    - Determine budgetary considerations.
- Create a mission statement for the alumni program.
    - Use company resources and collaboration to identify objectives and goals of the program.
    - Goals and objectives can include increasing the talent pool, bolstering networking opportunities, increasing brand visibility, and offering various forms of assistance to alumni.
- Determine the type of technology needed for alumni engagement.
    - Prioritize the use of automated technology that can be integrated into the company's system.
    - Use in-house talent to create an alumni program platform or plan to launch the program through a third-party host, which often enables companies to launch programs much more quickly than if they design the platform in-house.
- Strategize the program's launch, and launch the program.
    - Send out teasers to help build anticipation and excitement about the program.
    - Share messaging across numerous channels (e.g., dedicated alumni portals and social media).
    - Integrate virtual events into the launch to promote engagement.
    - Identify executives from the company who can participate in the launch.
- Continue building the program.
    - Plan networking and similar event types.
    - Create channels for feedback and communication from group members.
    - Share information that will help the company achieve the objectives of the alumni program (e.g., information about job opportunities to encourage alumni referrals).

Finally, HR professionals should look for ways to promote alumni communities that are socially responsible. Corporate social responsibility, which is discussed in the next section, has been identified as a motivating factor for employees when choosing where to work. As such, alumni programs should have components built into them that encourage members to work together to improve their shared communities.

Practice Question

2. Which of the following should NOT be an objective of a corporate alumni program?
   A) to expand the company's talent pool
   B) to offer a platform for former employees to discuss their grievances
   C) to support former employees in achieving their goals
   D) to provide another mechanism through which the company can promote social responsibility

Corporate Social Responsibility

HR plays a crucial role in corporate social responsibility. **Corporate social responsibility (CSR)** is how and to what level an organization focuses funds and capital toward improving one or more segments of society that are in need or are underrepresented by positively impacting their standard(s) of living.

Organizations that incorporate some level of social responsibility are generating long-term value for their shareholders: studies have shown that these types of programs can increase both revenue and customer commitment. Social responsibility is integrated into the business strategy through numerous philanthropic endeavors:

- monetary or in-kind contributions
- employee volunteerism
- community activities

Businesses can use social responsibility efforts to not only support specific causes but also to engage employees and create goodwill for the organization.

Some larger organizations have roles or departments that are specifically designed to carry out annual giving and participation throughout the year. This may include deciding—according to the strategic plan—who or which organizations will receive funds and which types of fundraising and similar events should be attended.

Fundraising events and galas provide opportunities for an organization to expand its profile and create a positive impression across a vast network. Corporate donors often have the chance to receive high-level introductions, make speeches, and enjoy visibility through promotional items (i.e., "swag") that are made available to guests. Additionally, corporate donations might come with tickets or seats to events that can be used in the entertainment of customers or employees, which creates a win-win situation for both the giving and receiving organizations.

Community Inclusion

As discussed above, one way in which an organization can create community inclusion is through philanthropic efforts. **Philanthropy** includes the donation of monies or the time and talents of employees.

Many organizations practice charitable giving. **Charitable giving** may be as simple as the company itself donating funds to one or more specific nonprofit organizations. It may also be conducted through providing mechanisms for the employees to donate. Payroll deductions or matching contributions are some of the ways in which businesses can encourage and support personnel who donate their own funds.

One way in which an organization may enact corporate social responsibility is through a volunteer program or policy. In these programs, employees are encouraged to volunteer their time to nonprofit organizations, especially through incentives like paid time off for volunteer time or bonuses tied to volunteering. HR can work with organizational leaders to create a volunteerism policy and promote it throughout the organization. Typically, these policies include information concerning which organization(s) the employee can support or which types of services the employee can provide in order to receive their corporate-sponsored volunteer benefits.

Additionally, companies might even organize volunteer events or days of service where groups of individuals have the opportunity to work together on a project. This not only supports the selected organization but also creates a team-building opportunity for the company.

Companies can also encourage their employees to join and participate in boards of directors for certain nonprofit organizations. This type of volunteer opportunity will allow the chosen organization to be supported and help employees grow in the process since, as board members, they will be exposed to the organization's strategic decision-making and financial planning. Employee participation on boards also spreads goodwill for the organization since the name recognition for the company for which the board member works will also be expanded.

Corporate Citizenship

All of these philanthropic efforts support a business's corporate citizenship. **Corporate citizenship** refers to an organization's responsibility to create a higher standard of living or improve the quality of life of its neighboring communities or other areas throughout the globe.

Corporate responsibility goes beyond charitable giving and extends to the moral and ethical treatment of an organization's suppliers, employees, distributors, and customers. In other words, in addition to simply donating money, an organization should integrate its designated causes and annual agendas into its overall strategy.

Practice Question

3. Which of the following is an example of corporate social responsibility?
   A) An employee donates to a political campaign and lists her place of work on the form.
   B) The company sponsors a group of employees who are volunteering at a beach cleanup.
   C) A company pays taxes owed to the state and federal governments.
   D) An employee volunteers at his church in his spare time on the weekend.

Answer Key

1. D: Option D is correct because this question asks employees whether or not they consider a reasonably important metric (seniority) to be actually used in the promotion process. Considering the fact that seniority is often a valid basis for fair internal promotions, this survey question is effective. Option A is incorrect because this question would provide data about a DEI initiative's effectiveness but does not describe how those persons got hired. Option B is incorrect because the frequency of application does not provide data about how the employee feels about getting passed over for promotion. For example, the employee may feel that each person who received the promotion did in fact deserve it. Option C is incorrect because the accuracy of performance evaluations provides data on how effective the organization's managers are, not whether or not their promotion process is fair.

2. B: Using a corporate alumni program as a platform through which former employees can air their grievances about the company should never be the objective of the program, nor should it be allowed. The purpose of alumni programs is to inspire past employees to continue to give back to the company in some capacity, be it through new hire referrals, as brand ambassadors, or as supporters of the company's initiatives. An alumni program should help both the members and the sponsoring company achieve their respective goals.

3. B: A group of employees participating in a volunteer cleanup event is a great example of corporate social responsibility through volunteerism and is a good way to build teamwork and camaraderie.

Chapter 7 – Employee and Labor Relations

Employee and Labor Relations

Employee and labor relations are concerned with maintaining positive employer-employee relationships to ensure high productivity and morale; however, the two terms differ in meaning:

- **Employee relations** refers to the relationship between management and employees.
- **Labor relations** is the term used to discuss relationships in a unionized environment.

Employee Relations

HR professionals perform employee relations when they work with an organization to create and maintain a positive culture, which could include advising managers on handling poor performance or employee misconduct. Employee relations should also focus on the proactive activities that ensure strong relationships between the employees and the organization. Proactive activities to meet these goals include the following:

- creating a strategic plan to implement cultural goals
- ensuring good communication throughout the organization
- designing workplace activities to build relationships
- conducting surveys to understand current employee issues or morale

The HR professional should also understand federal labor laws (discussed in Chapter 3), the history of organized labor in the United States, and protections for workers. HR professionals also play a role in resolving disputes and grievances, and disciplining and terminating employees. Ensuring these activities are done in a fairly, legally, and consistently can support a positive culture.

Practice Question

1. Which of the following would most likely NOT be described as part of employee relations?
   A) creating a policy that prohibits managers from communicating with subordinates after hours
   B) organizing a company-led drive for school supplies for local children in need
   C) gathering payroll data for management ahead of planned union negotiations
   D) setting benchmarks for achieving DEI goals

Labor Relations

The term ***labor relations*** refers to the interaction between employers and bargaining unit employees in a unionized environment; however, in some cases, it also applies to nonunion workers. Labor relations, like employee relations, also examine how employees are affected by economic factors like globalization and recession, and strive to minimize their negative impacts on the workforce.

When labor relations are strong at an organization, management works effectively with employee representatives (typically labor unions) to solve problems among the employees and the organization. For example, if the cost of materials rises substantially and threatens mass layoffs, the labor relations process could find ways to cut costs elsewhere; adapt to the changes; and innovate new, sustainable products or business strategies, thereby protecting jobs.

In the United States, labor is closely regulated by federal and state law. Under the **National Labor Relations Act (NLRA)**, unfair labor practices are defined as acts that violate the NLRA; they apply to both labor and management. Some of these acts include the following:

- discrimination
- coercion
- intimidation

Management cannot form company unions or use coercive tactics to discourage union organization. Unions negotiate many aspects of the workplace through contracts with management. For instance, a worker's length of service with an employer is called **seniority**. In union contracts, seniority often determines layoffs from work and recalls back to work.

On a global level, the International Labour Organization (ILO), the only tripartite UN agency, brings together governments, employers, and workers from 187 member states. The purpose of this organization is to set standards, develop policies, and devise programs to promote fair and equitable work for people around the world. The mission statement of the ILO is "to promote rights at work, encourage decent employment opportunities, enhance social protection and strengthen dialogue on work-related issues" (www.ilo.org).

Organized Labor in the Workplace

An organized workplace can take a number of different formats, types, and structures:

- **Organized labor**, or a **labor union**, is a single entity that represents member employees collectively; it can be organized vertically or horizontally.
    - **Horizontal unions**, also known as **trade unions**, are composed of workers across the same industry rather than within a single business or organization. Examples of horizontal unions include the International Brotherhood of Electrical Workers (IBEW) or the United Brotherhood of Carpenters.
    - **Vertical unions**, also known as **industrial unions**, allow workers in various positions practicing different crafts to join. Membership is determined by industry or geographic location. Examples of these types of unions are the International Brotherhood of Teamsters or the United Automobile, Aerospace and Agricultural Implement Workers of America (UAW).

On a global level, worker representation can take on different forms. Many countries legislate **work councils**, which may or may not be within a unionized setting, that create local representation within an organization. **Trade union federations**, where local trade unions are affiliated with a national organization, are another type of worker representation.

Labor unions use tools to negotiate with management; their greatest strength is in their bargaining power:

- A **bargaining unit** is a group of employees who bargain collectively (i.e., through a union) with their employer.
- **Collective bargaining** is a negotiation process between the union and the employer about wages and other conditions of employment.
    - Generally, if a company wants to change the terms of a collective bargaining agreement while it is in effect, it must give sixty days' notice.
    - If the union and management cannot resolve a dispute, it may go to **arbitration**, which is the referral of disputes to an impartial third party (an arbitrator rather than a court of law). The arbitrator's decision is typically final and binding.

If bargaining fails, unions take other actions:

- **Picketing** is the public protest of an employer by workers who discourage non-striking peers and customers to enter the business. Picketing typically takes place during a strike, when the bargaining unit refuses to work until a collective bargaining agreement is reached.
- Unionized workers may also engage in **boycotts**, which describe when groups refuse to buy certain goods or services in order to put pressure on a supplier.

Management may respond to organizing workers in the form of a **lockout**, whereby they close a facility to coerce workers to meet a demand.

Union Security Clauses

Some workplaces are unionized, some are not, and some are partially unionized. These statuses are determined by a union security clause.

A **union security clause** is a clause in the collective bargaining agreement that provides for a union shop, maintenance of membership, or an agency shop. Common types of union security clauses include the following:

- In an **open-shop** workplace, people are employed without respect to union membership.
- In a **union shop**, the employer is allowed to hire individuals who are not currently members of the union, with the provision that those individuals are required to join the union after a specified amount of time.
- In an **agency shop**, employees are not required to join the union, but they are still obligated to pay dues or fees to the union.

- A **closed shop** refers to the practice of hiring only individuals who are current union members. Closed-shop workplaces were made illegal under the Taft-Hartley Act in 1947.

Union contracts may include a union security clause stating that, as a condition of employment, workers must be members in good standing of the union. This may include payment of union dues and fees.

Some states have **right-to-work laws**, which prohibit or limit union agreements that require the employees' membership or payment of union dues or fees as a condition of employment. Despite their name, these laws do not provide a general guarantee of employment.

Collective bargaining agreements typically include a provision for union stewards to represent the members at a local level. A **union steward** is usually a volunteer position; the steward may be elected by the members. There may be one or more stewards depending on the contract and size of the organization. Stewards may receive some preferential treatment in the event of a layoff and may be paid by the employer for reasonable union activities.

Did You Know?
Collective bargaining among federal workers was legalized by Executive Order 10988, which allows federal employees to collectively bargain with management. It was signed by President John F. Kennedy in 1962.

Labor Relations in Federal Law

Labor relations are regulated by the US government, which provides guidance on the treatment of employees. The **National Labor Relations Act (NLRA)** of 1935, also called the **Wagner Act** or **Wagner-Connery Labor Relations Act**, is enforced by the National Labor Relations Board (NLRB). This act grants most private sector workers several labor rights, including the right to strike, to bargain as a union, and to protest the conditions of their employment. It does not apply to management, government employees, independent contractors, and certain other employees.

Helpful Hint:
TIPS stands for "Threats, Interrogation, Promises, and Surveillance." The National Labor Relations Board (NLRB) prohibits all of these behaviors by management during a union organization campaign.

Employees covered by the NLRA are granted certain rights to join together to improve their wages and working conditions, with or without a union. This means that, although a union may not be present in an organization, employees at that organization still have the right to discuss the conditions of their employment and to take action as a group.

Under the NLRA, employees have the right to form a union if one does not already exist. If they no longer support an existing union, they have the right to decertify (i.e., no longer recognize) it. In exchange for membership dues, the union represents employees on matters related to their pay, benefits, and workplace conditions. The union will assist employees when they file complaints or grievances, or when an employer is not abiding by a collective bargaining agreement. It is illegal for employers to retaliate against employees who form a union or who engage in a protected activity covered under the NLRA.

The NLRA also protects employees who are not represented by a union but are engaged in concerted activity. **Concerted activity** occurs when two or more employees take action to protect themselves in the workplace or improve their work situation. For example, concerted activity may involve a group of employees asking a manager to raise their wages. It may also apply to two or more employees speaking to each other about work-related issues, such as safety concerns. Concerted activity may also apply to one employee if that employee is acting on behalf of a group of employees by raising complaints or trying to coordinate a group action.

The effects of the NLRA were changed substantially when the **Labor Management Relations Act (LMRA)** was passed in 1947. Also known as the **Taft-Hartley Act**, the LMRA outlawed closed shops, jurisdictional strikes, and secondary boycotts. Taft-Hartley also established mechanisms to decertify unions. It permitted anti-union legislation at the state level (e.g., right-to-work laws). Finally, Taft-Hartley prohibited unions and employers from contributing funds from their treasuries to candidates for federal office. According to the LMRA, management is not afforded union protection, and the unions seeking the services of the NLRB must file documents with the US Department of Labor.

While the NLRA and Taft-Hartley are the most well-known laws involving labor relations, a large amount of legislation can be accurately described as labor relations. The following types of laws were all passed because of influence from organized labor:

- minimum-wage laws
- fair-practice rules
- wage theft laws
- legislation mandating danger pay

Weingarten rights refer to the rights of union employees to have union representation during an interview if they are being investigated. This term stems from the 1975 court case *NLRB v. J. Weingarten, Inc.* (1975).

J. Weingarten, Inc., operated a chain of convenience stores. Weingarten had denied an employee her request to have her steward or other union representative accompany her during a disciplinary investigation. The court held that this was in violation of the NLRA and that a union employee has a right to have a union steward present during investigatory interviews.

Union organizing is also subject to important legislation. In the 1992 case *Lechmere, Inc. v. NLRB*, union organizers used a shopping plaza parking lot in front of a Connecticut retail store to contact store employees. The parking lot was partially owned by the store owner, and the union organizers were not employees. The store owner barred the organizers from the parking lot, and they were forced to use other, public areas to work. The union organizers alleged that the owner violated the NLRA by prohibiting them from the parking lot. Initially the NLRB ruled in favor of the union; however, on appeal, the Supreme Court reversed the decision, concluding that an employer does not have to allow distribution of union literature by nonemployees on the employer's property. The exception is if the location of the business and employees' residences puts them beyond reasonable reach (e.g., a very rural area).

Helpful Hint:

The exam will test on federal law, not state or local laws.

Practice Questions

2. When was the National Labor Relations Act enacted?
   A) 1910
   B) 1929
   C) 1935
   D) 1950

3. What is the GREATEST strength of a labor union?
   A) collective bargaining
   B) union dues
   C) right-to-work laws
   D) strikes and lockouts

4. How much notice must a company give the bargaining unit if it wants to change the terms of a collective bargaining agreement while it is in effect?
   A) 30 days
   B) 60 days
   C) 90 days
   D) 120 days

5. Which union security clause requires workers to join a union?
   A) closed shop
   B) union shop
   C) open shop
   D) agency shop

6. State right-to-work laws limit or prohibit which of the following?
   A) the formation of unions
   B) termination of employment
   C) unfair labor practices
   D) union shops

Federal Labor Law

The US Department of Labor (DOL) is a federal agency that administers and enforces more than 180 federal laws. These mandates—and the regulations that implement them—apply to numerous employment contexts, including specific industries and sizes of companies. Employers must understand and comply with certain laws. Some of the following laws are also discussed in Chapter 5 ("Total Rewards").

Individual states (and sometimes localities) create and enforce their own laws related to the employment of workers. Employers should be aware of the employment laws in all states in which they conduct business and employment. The state's department of labor can be contacted for state-specific information about employment laws. In order to remain compliant and avoid penalties, employment practices and policies should be consistent with all laws that affect the organization.

Wages and Hours

The **Fair Labor Standards Act (FLSA)** mandates standards for the payment of regular wages, overtime, and the employment of minors. The FLSA affects most private and public employers. Employers are required to pay covered employees (i.e., nonexempt employees) *at least* the federal minimum wage and overtime pay of one-and-one-half times the regular rate of pay ("time and a half"). Children under age sixteen can only work certain hours, and children under age eighteen cannot work in dangerous, nonagricultural jobs. See Chapter 5 for more details on the FLSA.

The FLSA was amended by the **Equal Pay Act of 1963** (see Chapter 5). Employee wage garnishments are regulated under the **Consumer Credit Protection Act (CCPA)**, which protects employees from being fired due to garnishments and limits the amount that can be deducted from an individual's paycheck.

The Employee Retirement Income Security Act (ERISA) regulates employers who offer pension or welfare benefit plans to their employees. The act mandates a wide range of fiduciary, disclosure, and reporting requirements for plan fiduciaries and administrators; these provisions preempt many similar state laws. Under Title IV of ERISA, certain employers and plan administrators must fund an insurance system to protect specific kinds of retirement benefits, with premiums paid to the federal government's **Pension Benefit Guaranty Corporation (PBGC)**.

Employees are entitled to sue for retroactive wage discrimination under the **Lilly Ledbetter Fair Pay Act**, which President Barack Obama signed into law in 2009. This law overturned a previous Supreme Court decision, *Ledbetter v. Goodyear Tire and Rubber Co.* (2007), which limited a person's ability to retroactively file a claim for compensation discrimination. According to the Lilly Ledbetter Fair Pay Act, each paycheck resets the 180-day statute of limitations for filing a lawsuit in regard to pay.

Since the Lilly Ledbetter Fair Pay Act was passed, employees who started five, ten, or twenty years ago can file complaints of discrimination based on their starting wages or other related instances that happened earlier in their careers. It is therefore important that employers keep records of pay decisions.

Health, Welfare, and Workplace Safety

The **Patient Protection and Affordable Care Act (PPACA)** requires certain employers to

- offer affordable health insurance that provides minimum value to their full-time employees (and their dependents),
- communicate about health care marketplaces to employees, and
- provide a standardized summary of coverage to employees (among other requirements).

The PPACA also requires insurers to cover preexisting conditions and to cover all insurance applicants.

The **Consolidated Omnibus Budget Reconciliation Act (COBRA)** grants employees the right to keep the group health insurance that they would otherwise lose after they separate from their employers. The **Health Insurance Portability and Accountability Act of 1996 (HIPAA)**, provides opportunities for people to, among other things, retain (or obtain) health insurance during qualifying events. These acts are discussed in greater detail in Chapter 5.

Helpful Hint:

The US Department of Health and Human Services (DHHS) can provide the most current information on the PPACA.

The **Family and Medical Leave Act (FMLA)**, also discussed in Chapter 5, provides up to twelve weeks of job-protected, unpaid leave during any twelve-month period to eligible, covered employees. It is used for the following reasons:

- the birth and care of the eligible employee's child, or placement for adoption or foster care of a child with the employee
- care of an immediate family member (spouse, child, parent) who has a serious health condition
- care of the employee's own serious health condition

Eligibility for employees includes being employed by an organization with at least fifty individuals in a 75-mile radius and having worked at the organization for at least twelve months and a minimum of 1,250 hours within the previous year.

The law also requires that the employee's group health benefits be maintained during the leave. It was amended in 2008 to provide protections specifically for military families. Please see Table 5.2. in Chapter 5 for additional details about this amendment.

The **Occupational Safety and Health Act** also regulates the safety and health of employees; it is administered by the **Occupational Safety and Health Administration (OSHA)**, which may conduct inspections and investigations. Employers covered by the act must comply with the regulations and the safety and health standards established by OSHA.

Employers must also provide their employees with a work environment that is free from recognized, serious hazards. OSHA violations range from de minimus (the least serious) to willful (the most serious):

- A **de minimus violation** is a technical violation that has no direct impact on health or safety.
- A **willful violation** is an intentional violation, or one that shows disregard for employee health or safety.

Some states operate under an **OSHA state plan** whereby the state, rather than the federal OSHA, protects employees and works to prevent work-related injuries, illnesses, and deaths. These plans must be at least as effective as the federal OSHA and monitored by them.

Practice Questions

7. Which law governs the number of hours that children may work?
   A) FMLA
   B) ADEA
   C) FLSA
   D) IRCA

8. If a nonexempt employee is off for Memorial Day but works ten hours a day the rest of the week, how many hours of overtime pay is she entitled to under the FLSA?
   A) zero
   B) eight
   C) forty
   D) forty-eight

9. The FMLA requires that an organization have at least how many employees in order to provide job-protected leave to qualified employees?
   A) 10
   B) 25
   C) 50
   D) 100

Special Requirements for Government Contractors

Companies that receive government contracts, grants, or financial aid must adhere to certain guidelines when it comes to wages, benefits, and safety and health standards:

- The **Davis-Bacon Act** requires the payment of prevailing wages and benefits to employees of contractors working on federal government construction projects.
- The **McNamara-O'Hara Service Contract Act** establishes wage rates and other work standards for employees of contractors providing services to the federal government.
- The **Walsh-Healey Public Contracts Act** requires the payment of minimum wages and other work standards by contractors providing materials and goods to the federal government.

Government contractors are also required to comply with federal affirmative action and equal opportunity laws, executive orders, and regulations. The **Office of Federal Contract Compliance Programs (OFCCP)** administers and enforces these laws. See Chapter 3 (Talent Acquisition and Planning the Workforce) for more information on affirmative action and the OFCCP.

Finally, the **Drug-Free Workplace Act** of 1988 requires large federal contractors and grantees to have a drug-free workplace policy in place. At a minimum, these policies must prohibit the use, distribution, and manufacturing of controlled substances in the workplace. The act was designed to encourage a safe, drug-free workforce.

Industry-Specific Laws and Regulations

Several federal laws and regulations affect employers in the construction, agricultural, and mining industries:

- OSHA is in charge of specific safety and health regulations for employers in the construction industry.
- The Migrant and Seasonal Agricultural Workers Protection Act (MSPA) of 1983 regulates the employment of agricultural workers.
- The **Fair Labor Standards Act (FLSA)** exempts agricultural workers from overtime premium pay but requires minimum wage for workers employed on larger farms. It also prohibits children under age sixteen from working during school hours and in certain jobs deemed too dangerous.
- The **Federal Mine Safety and Health Act of 1977 (MSHA/Mine Act)** mandates the safety and health standards of miners and the training of miners, levies penalties for violations, and allows inspectors to close dangerous mines.

Other Federal Laws and Protections

Under the **Uniformed Services Employment and Reemployment Rights Act (USERRA)**, certain employees who serve in the armed forces have a right to reemployment with their preservice employers; it also applies to service members in the reserves or National Guard.

The **Employee Polygraph Protection Act** prohibits most employers from using polygraphs (lie detectors) on employees. The law permits polygraph tests only in limited circumstances and prohibits employers from discharging, disciplining, or discriminating against employees or candidates for refusing to take the test. This act does not apply to federal, state, or local governments or to organizations that are contracted through the federal government to provide security.

Mass layoffs or plant closings may be subject to the **Worker Adjustment and Retraining Notification (WARN) Act**. WARN requires that employees receive at least a sixty-day warning of impending mass layoffs or plant closings. The WARN Act applies to businesses with over 100 employees who are laying off 33 percent of the workforce and at least fifty employees total.

Finally, many labor, public safety, and environmental laws protect whistleblowers—employees who make good-faith complaints about violations of the law committed by their employers. Penalties for violating these protections can include job reinstatement and payment of back wages. OSHA generally enforces whistleblower protections. Whistleblower protections are discussed in greater detail later in this chapter.

Practice Questions

10. Which of the following laws allows certain employers to establish drug-testing policies?
    A) the Occupational Safety and Health Act
    B) the Drug-Free Workplace Act
    C) the Worker Adjustment and Retraining Notification Act
    D) the Drug Testing Act

11. What is the main purpose of the Davis-Bacon Act of 1931?
    A) It requires federal contractors to implement affirmative action plans.
    B) It prohibits discrimination on the basis of age for those over fifty.
    C) It requires certain federal contractors to pay a prevailing wage to employees.
    D) It requires the payment of overtime to nonexempt employees.

12. An applicant applying for which of the following positions may be required to take a polygraph test?
    A) a teacher working with small children
    B) a cashier at a grocery store
    C) an agent at an insurance company
    D) a police officer in a rural area

Global Employee and Labor Relations

Global Employee Relations

Many organizations operate in a global environment where employment issues, employment laws, and business practices can vary dramatically from country to country. In order to help organizations run smoothly, HR professionals who work with multinational companies must have global perspectives and solid grasps of international employment issues. For multinational employers, there are unique employee relations issues to manage.

For example, employees abroad may have unique health and safety issues due to the following:

- political or economic conditions
- regulations
- the physical environments in which they work

The employer must also comply with the laws of the countries in which it operates, which adds another level of complexity to managing global employee relations.

Employment laws around the globe can vary greatly from country to country and region to region. It is therefore critical, when operating on a worldwide basis, that the local employment laws are understood and properly executed. For instance, in some parts of the world, employees operate under contracts, and at-will employment is not recognized, whereas other countries may require paid leave or housing. Assuming employment laws will be the same from country to country can lead to both liability issues and employee morale issues.

Recruitment, selection, and onboarding should be addressed on a global level to enhance company-wide collaboration. Not only does the organization need to understand local laws and other workplace norms, but items such as negotiating salary may be also be dictated by the government or trade unions. Additionally, HR and management should consider whether to hire local talent instead of moving people from other locations. Benefits may be different, and expectations may be dictated by laws or rules. Legal compliance must be a top priority when conducting business globally.

Global Health and Safety

Addressing safety and health issues is an important HR function. Employees working abroad may not enjoy the same quality of health care or environmental safety as those working in the United States. HR practitioners must develop policies and employment benefits to support these employees. For example, companies may offer private insurance plans or funds for medical assistance to protect the health of employees; however, policies must comply with the host country's laws and should be generally accepted business practices in that country.

Depending on where they operate, international organizations may also have to address kidnapping, harassment, extortion, and other violence in regions experiencing political unrest. These dangers can occur either on or near the worksite or in residential areas. To protect employees who are working in dangerous areas, many firms provide bodyguards, change travel routes to make it difficult for criminals to track an individual, and provide safety training for family members of employees. Some companies may secure the grounds of their facilities with fences, barricades, armed guards, metal detectors, and/or surveillance devices. Others may take steps to minimize the visibility of the company.

To ensure the safety of expatriates (i.e., foreign nationals working abroad), the company may provide emergency protective services through an organization that can refer the ill or injured employee to adequate medical care if available locally, dispatch physicians, or transport employees to safety via aircraft. Additional safeguards may include in-country legal counsel or emergency cash for medical expenses or travel home.

Cultural Differences in the Workplace

Cultural norms in a country or region influence how people act and interact with one another. When employing international workers, an organization should be clear about its expectations for *all* of its workers, regardless of geography. At the same time, in order to sustain successful operations in a country, an employer should understand the norms, values, and attitudes of the workers there.

If the organization's values contrast with the local culture, conflict may arise if the situation is not properly managed. Providing flexibility for certain cultural practices and helping employees assimilate into the organization can alleviate tensions.

Cultural differences among international employees may include different attitudes toward work. HR practitioners and management must recognize these differences and understand how they affect intracompany relations. HR practitioners can play key roles in facilitating open dialogues and providing learning opportunities for both US and non-US employees to work together more effectively. Examples include workshops and facilitated group discussions.

Facilitated group discussions aim to create an inclusive workplace environment by using discussion as a tool for active learning. Participants are typically placed in manageable-sized groups where they can interact and engage with each other on topics introduced by a **facilitator**, or leader. Group members are encouraged to reflect on what both they and their peers in the group bring to the table. Group discussions also allow participants to consider obstacles to their own communication and reception of others' ideas by identifying behaviors with which they are comfortable as well as those they find challenging. To maximize the effectiveness of group discussions, facilitators should follow a few basic guidelines:

- **Promote an inclusive environment** by encouraging self-awareness and awareness of others' opinions.
- **Ensure that discussions are positive and constructive** by establishing ground rules (e.g., avoiding blanket statements/stereotyping) and outlining the goals of the discussion.
- **Encourage participation** by asking follow-up questions, motivating group members who are shy, and admitting when there are gaps in understanding (and trying to bridge those gaps).

In contrast to group discussions, where ideas and opinions are typically exchanged, **workshops** are designed to be learning experiences that are more collaborative in nature. Workshops are usually led by experts in a particular field or domain and typically have focused goals that can include learning a new skill, teambuilding, or professional development.

Global Labor Relations

As mentioned earlier in this chapter, **labor relations** concern the unionized environment. **Labor unions** are organized groups of workers—usually within the same industry or field—that aim to protect the rights and benefits of workers and achieve more employee rights in the workplace. The term ***trade unions*** is used in Europe to describe organized groups of workers. The impact and nature of labor unions vary worldwide: in some locales, unions are weak or do not exist at all; elsewhere, unions are extremely strong and may be closely aligned with political parties (e.g., in Europe). In other places, such as the US, unions have experienced a decline in influence and membership over time. There are two main types of union structures in the US:

- **Independent unions** are those which are free from outside influence and affect workers' rights in a single company. These types of unions are also called **local unions** and represent the rarest union structure.

- **National unions** represent workplaces across the country. They tend to have a stronger record of achieving workers' rights and usually enjoy strong financial backing and, in some cases, political influence.

These differences also affect how collective bargaining occurs:

- **Independent unions** directly bargain with employers about working conditions and wages.
- **Industry-wide bargaining** or **regional bargaining** typically takes place with numerous employers within the same industry or region.

Global union federations are composed of national trade unions that protect the interests of workers within certain industries worldwide. Examples include Education International, headquartered in Brussels (Belgium), and the International Federation of Musicians, which is headquartered in Paris (France).

Some countries require companies to have union representatives on their boards of directors (a practice called **codetermination**). It is important for multinational organizations to understand the norms of a country and be prepared to work with organized labor where it is present and in the manner that is customary for that country or region.

Practice Questions

13. Which term BEST describes an American who is working for an American company in Germany?
    A) host country national
    B) external immigrant
    C) expatriate
    D) undocumented workers

14. Which of the following HR responsibilities is MOST likely to differ from country to country?
    A) job analysis
    B) training and development
    C) compensation and benefits
    D) personnel records

Safety and Health

Organizations have a responsibility to protect the safety, health, and well-being of their employees. Ensuring safety and health is humanitarian in nature and is therefore a moral obligation. Employers are also legally obligated to ensure employee safety and health. They must follow specific guidelines under these laws and face certain penalties and fines if they do not. Taking the necessary precautions can also reduce costs the business may incur, including those related to medical care, sick leave, disability benefits, and lost productivity.

Workplace Hazards

Depending on the nature of the business and where it conducts its operations, there are a number of health and safety hazards as well as risks that employees may face. A **workplace hazard** is something that can cause harm if it is not mitigated or eliminated. It is the role of HR professionals or safety professionals to identify hazards and assess risks that affect employees for the moral, legal, and financial reasons described previously.

In general, there are three categories of workplace hazards; these are described in Table 7.1:

- physical
- health
- psychosocial

Some industries may be more prone to certain hazards than others. For example, the construction industry may have many physical hazards, whereas the financial industry may have many psychosocial hazards.

Table 7.1. Workplace Hazards
Physical Hazards
▪ heavy machinery ▪ slippery surfaces ▪ hot temperatures or surfaces ▪ confined spaces ▪ extreme heights
Health Hazards
▪ chemical exposure ▪ bacteria ▪ mold ▪ blood-borne pathogens and other communicable diseases ▪ acids ▪ vapors ▪ fire and explosions ▪ repetitive trauma and ergonomics
Psychosocial Hazards
▪ job insecurity ▪ poor work-life balance ▪ high demands ▪ long work hours ▪ unfair working conditions

> **Helpful Hint:**
>
> Safety rules and procedures should be regularly evaluated, with management and employee input, for their effectiveness.

HR, along with a safety officer in some organizations, can take measures to mitigate workplace hazards:

- HR professionals should develop methods and procedures to manage hazards that can cause injury to workers and facilities.
- Workspaces, equipment, procedures, and services should periodically be evaluated for safety.
- Employees should be actively included in developing safe working practices.
- Resources should be allocated to train employees on safety and to enforce safety rules.

The Occupational Safety and Health Administration (OSHA) has three levels of hazard mitigation or control that cannot be eliminated from the workplace:

- The first level includes **engineering** controls—the redesign of a machine or work area to remove the exposure to the employee. Engineering controls might mean installing guards, railings, or barriers.
- The next level of hazard mitigation is **administrative controls**—job rotation or safety procedures that limit an employee's exposure.
- The final level is the use of **personal protective equipment (PPE)**. PPE should only be used when engineering or administrative controls are not possible in eliminating the hazard.

Effective safety officers, who might also have the role of HR, must be well-versed in those laws and regulations that govern employee health and safety, such as the Occupational Safety and Health Act, as well as industry standards on best practices. They must be able to design operational procedures and recordkeeping systems for clarity and accountability. They should also be able to identify and implement the safety equipment and resources necessary to protect employees as they conduct their jobs.

Practice Question

15. What are OSHA's three levels of hazard mitigation?
    A) train employees, test employees, protect employees
    B) engineering controls, administrative controls, PPE
    C) physical, health, psychosocial
    D) policies, protection, restriction

Business Continuity

Organizations should be prepared for disasters like hurricanes, fires, terrorist attacks, pandemics, and other catastrophic events. HR practitioners are valuable partners in business continuity planning through the development of policies and procedures. Furthermore, they manage employee aspects of business continuity, including staffing plans, medical emergencies, PPE acquisition, the allocation of resources, and other concerns. The planning and execution of business continuity processes are organized into four phases, as illustrated in Figure 7.1.

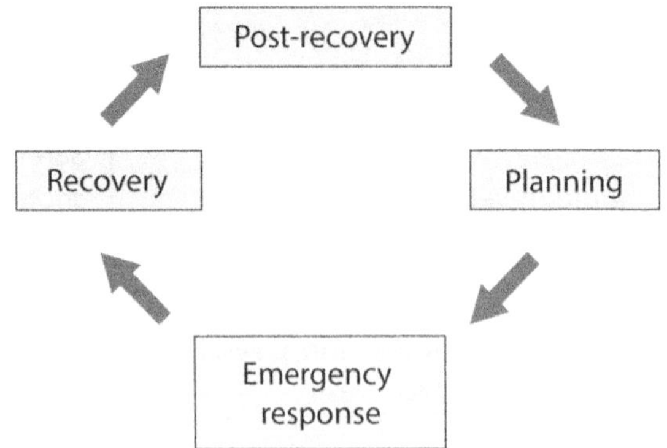

Figure 7.1. The Phases of Business Continuity

Planning Phase

During the **planning phase**, HR practitioners help the organization develop clear goals, procedures, and expectations that are then communicated to employees. These policies are usually included in the employee handbook, but they can also be contained in a stand-alone business continuity plan; employees are trained and retrained on a periodic basis. The policies and procedures should outline important information the employees need to know, including the following:

- how the business will continue operations in the event of disaster
- the employee's role in maintaining contact with the employer
- how employees should handle certain hazards, such as fire or power outages
- how the organization will notify employees of changes to business operations or safety procedures during a disaster

Additionally, the business should develop a more detailed **business continuity plan** that outlines asset recovery, employee mobilization, operations continuity, and compensation. The recovery plan should address all of the logistics necessary to mitigate losses to the business; some of these include the following:

- Who is responsible for notifying authorities?
- How will first responders obtain access to the facilities?
- How will employees be evacuated?
- What will the company do to help employees find medical attention and safety if necessary?
- Where will employees work? Where will they stay? How will the company keep track of where employees are?
- How will employees be paid?
- What resources do employees need to continue doing their jobs (e.g., mobile workstations or PPE), and how will the company provide these resources?
- How will the company's data, files, and information be protected to prevent disaster and recover from disaster? Are backup copies maintained remotely?

Did You Know?

During the planning phase, HR professionals can use business analysis tools like the PESTLE analysis and the SWOT analysis. See Chapter 8 for details on these tools.

HR professionals play key roles in ensuring that the organization is ready to handle disasters and manage employees' whereabouts, safety, and business operations. Employees should understand their roles as well and be trained periodically.

Recovery

During the **recovery period**, the organization must adapt to operating differently for a period of time. For example, employees may need to work remotely, certain services or production may be put on hold, or hours of operation may change. The HR department plays a critical role during this phase by working with managers to deploy and track staff and resources to keep the business operational. HR may notify employees of their roles, hours, and expectations of work during the recovery period. HR may also hire temporary staff if needed.

In addition, the HR department may respond to employees' immediate concerns and notify management of problems. HR can help fulfill employees' immediate needs by deploying emergency food, shelter, cash, or goods if the employee is required to be away from home and the normal worksite. Furthermore, if employees are ill or injured, HR can notify family members and keep them informed. Having these needs met will help able-bodied employees keep the business running as smoothly as possible despite changes in conditions.

Post-Recovery

Once the recovery period has ended and the company is ready to resume normal operations, HR's role is to notify employees and help them transition back. In the **post-recovery period**, if the surrounding area has been severely damaged, HR must respond to employees' needs for time off to find a new home, recover from injuries, or resolve personal and family matters.

During this period, it is important for the organization to remain flexible with employees and recognize their efforts to balance their personal and work responsibilities. Recognizing employees for their resilience and dedication to helping the organization succeed will keep morale higher. If employees feel that their needs are respected and that they are appreciated by the organization, they are more likely to remain loyal to the organization.

HR plays an important role during the planning and execution of business continuity procedures. If these processes are overlooked, the long-term success of the business and the well-being of employees may suffer. Involving HR, management, and employees in each step of the process, and keeping communication open and clear will better position the organization to survive disaster and protect its employees and assets.

Practice Questions

16. What tool might an HR practitioner use during the planning phase to determine which types of natural disasters could impact an organization?
    A) KPIs monitoring
    B) a PESTLE analysis
    C) a SWOT analysis
    D) Porter's Five Forces

17. How could HR determine which resources employees would need to continue working in case of an emergency and how to provide those resources?
    A) the Hersey-Blanchard model
    B) SMART goals
    C) a SWOT analysis
    D) French and Raven's Five Forms of Power

Privacy and Confidentiality

Privacy is the right to be unobserved. Managing an organization's safety and security can prompt privacy concerns. The organization needs to carefully monitor and protect its assets, but employees desire a degree of privacy in their daily activities. To manage risk, organizations may take measures like monitoring computer usage, conducting background checks of employees, and tracking people who enter and exit facilities.

In general, employees in the United States should have no broad expectation of privacy because the employer has a right to monitor and protect its assets; however, federal and state laws do protect the privacy of employees—to an extent. When implementing certain measures, the organization must understand whether the activity is lawful. It must also weigh how effectively each practice achieves a specific business need.

Did You Know?

The **Fair Credit Reporting Act (FCRA)** requires employers to obtain written permission from applicants before conducting credit checks.

Protected Information

Confidential information is private, or secret, information. While employees should not expect too much personal privacy in the workplace, there are certain forms of personal employee information that should be kept confidential or protected.

As a rule, only personally identifiable information, such as a person's name or Social Security number, is afforded special protection by data privacy laws. In some cases, a combination of information (e.g., birth date, address, and gender) can be used to identify an individual and is therefore considered **protected information**. Federal and state laws that govern the usage and sharing of personally identifiable information include the following:

- The **Health Insurance Portability and Accountability Act (HIPAA)** protects health-related information with covered entities, such as insurance plans.

- The **Genetic Information Nondiscrimination Act (GINA)** protects and restricts the usage of employees' genetic information.
- The **Fair Credit Reporting Act (FCRA)** restricts the ways in which consumer data, such as credit reports, may be used for employment purposes.

Many US states have their own laws concerning data security and notifications of breaches, and organizations should be aware of all data security laws in the states in which they operate. Companies also have a legal responsibility to protect not only employee information but also that of job applicants, independent contractors, and customers. Companies that operate internationally should also be aware of the laws of each country in which they operate and implement security mechanisms to comply as legally required.

Even if there is no law that specifically requires the protection of certain data, it is still a best practice for the organization to ensure that all personal information, whether protected or not protected by law, is safe. Keeping active employees' data secure and discarding data that is no longer needed (as allowed by recordkeeping laws and regulations) can help mitigate an organization's risk. Employers can also protect data by only disclosing it to parties on a need-to-know basis, with the explicit authorization of the employee, or by virtue of a court order.

Data should be provided using the most secure means possible, such as encrypted email, and there should be specific procedures in place to manage a data breach. Because HR professionals regularly work with personal data, it is important that they maintain confidentiality to the greatest extent possible and take careful measures not to compromise the security of data.

Workplace Monitoring and Searches

It is common for employers to monitor the computer, email, web, and phone usage of employees for quality control and security. They may also implement drug and alcohol testing to ensure the safety of employees and to prevent accidents or injuries.

Though some federal contractors and grantees may be required to provide a drug-free workplace, most private employers do not have any obligation to create drug and alcohol policies or procedures. Employers are, however, legally required to provide a safe workplace, so it is important to assess which roles require employees to be free of drug or alcohol impairment. Such roles may include those that involve operating mechanical equipment, driving industrial trucks and vehicles, or dealing with critical data. When creating a drug and alcohol policy, it is important to consider laws such as the ADA, HIPAA, or the FMLA to ensure employees' rights are not infringed upon. Interactive conversations, privacy, and other like issues should be built into a drug and alcohol policy in order to incorporate and meet the requirements of these many laws and regulations.

Beyond drug and alcohol testing, as a best practice and to comply with various privacy laws, the organization should notify employees (typically in a handbook) that they should have no expectation of privacy when on the premises or when using company resources and of the specific ways in which the company may monitor employees.

Companies should contact a qualified attorney to understand the legal limits of employee surveillance, drug testing, and personal searches. For example, companies may not put cameras in restrooms, but they may use cameras to monitor a cash register. Employers may also be limited in conduct of personal searches and may not force employees to submit to a search; however, they may rightfully terminate employees who refuse.

Clear policies that are applied consistently to all employees will help the organization set expectations and manage risk. If employees understand what is expected of them as well as the consequences for noncompliance, and if they understand that the rules are enforced universally, the organization can protect itself against claims of unfair treatment or discrimination while promoting a safe workplace.

Practice Questions

18. The Fair Credit Reporting Act requires an employer to do which of the following?
    A) obtain written authorization from an applicant before conducting a credit check
    B) use credit checks to verify an applicant's eligibility to work
    C) conduct a credit check secretly
    D) provide verbal notification that a credit check will be completed on a prospective employee

19. Which of the following may an employer legally do in the workplace?
    A) force all employees to submit to personal searches
    B) place cameras anywhere in the workplace
    C) terminate any employee for drug or alcohol use
    D) monitor employees' company computer usage

Workplace Policies

Employee Handbook

Managers and HR may refer to company policies when resolving disputes, disciplining employees, or addressing grievances. Policies should be outlined in the employee handbook, which should be available to all employees.

An **employee handbook**, also referred to as an **employee manual**, is a document that outlines the organization's policies and procedures that affect all employees. It can provide both employment and practical information like company rules, performance expectations, and office operations. A written employee handbook provides employees with clear guidance, explains organizational expectations, and fosters a culture in which problems are addressed fairly and consistently. It also outlines the employee rights as well as the organization's legal obligations as an employer.

The **psychological contract** refers to the unwritten, informal expectations that exist between employees and the organizations where they work. Examples might include the expectation that an employee will get a raise every year or attend an annual professional conference.

Sections and Policies in Handbooks

Employee handbooks are important tools for maintaining sound employee relations through the consistent and fair treatment of employees; they also provide clear, written expectations. Handbooks and written policies are key methods to documenting expectations and practices, such as fair hiring and equal employment opportunity. They should contain the following types of information:

- **General Employment Information:** An employee handbook should provide an overview of the business and its general employment policies, including employment eligibility, job classifications, employee records, probationary periods, performance reviews, termination procedures, company transfers, and union information, if applicable.

- **Antidiscrimination Policies:** The handbook should contain information about the company's compliance with equal opportunity, anti-harassment, nondiscrimination, and disability laws; it should also include procedures for complaints and grievances.
- **Standards of Conduct:** This information clarifies expectations of employee conduct, including dress code and workplace behavior.
- **Conflicts of Interest:** These describe situations where a professional task or judgment could be influenced by a nonprofessional task or judgment, such as making a decision based on whether the employee could gain a financial windfall by doing so.
- **Competing Interest Statements:** Competing interest statements help protect the company's trade secrets and proprietary information.
- **Payroll Procedures:** This type of information outlines pay schedules, timekeeping requirements, overtime pay, salary increases, bonuses, and deductions for taxes and benefit premiums.
- **Work Schedules:** The handbook should explain work hours and schedules, attendance policies, punctuality, and how to report absences.
- **Safety and Security:** This section explains an employee's rights and obligations in ensuring a safe and secure workplace; it provides instructions on reporting accidents, injuries, and safety hazards. It also provides guidance on securing files, computers, and other company resources.
- **Use of Computers and Technology:** This section explains the appropriate use of company-provided hardware and software, steps to keep data secure, and how to handle personal information. Typically, it reminds employees that the company owns the technology and may monitor and regulate its use.
- **Employee Benefits:** This section outlines any benefit programs and eligibility requirements, including all benefits that are required by law.
- **Time-Off Policies:** This section explains employee entitlement to vacation time, sick time, paid holidays, family and medical leave, jury duty, military leave, and voting; policies and compliance with the law should be clearly documented.
- **Expenses:** Information in this section explains the types of expenses that the company will reimburse as well as the steps employees must take to claim any reimbursements.

Many handbooks also contain specific language that invokes the doctrine of employment-at-will. An **employment-at-will statement** specifies that an employee or employer may terminate the employment relationship—with or without reason—and with or without notice. In an at-will employment situation (which is the case in many states), there is no expectation of employment either indefinitely or for a specified duration.

As part of the onboarding process, new employees usually sign an acknowledgment form stating they have read and understand the information in the handbook. The company may need to update the handbook to reflect new policies, practices, and laws. Revisions should be communicated and distributed to employees and may require a new signed acknowledgment. Additionally, there may be different versions of the employee handbook for certain business units, subsidiaries, or locations. It is important to ensure that all versions are kept up to date.

Handbooks can be useful tools in situations when corrective action, including termination of employment, needs to be taken with an employee. When disciplining or terminating employees, it is helpful to refer to the specific policy or policies being violated. Doing so not only makes it clear to the employee that corrective action has been taken for an objective reason (e.g., violating an established policy), it also provides a reference that enables the company to better defend itself in litigation or complaints to governmental agencies. For this reason, a qualified employment attorney should review the company's handbook for compliance with the law and provide counsel as needed.

Practice Questions

20. Which of the following BEST describes the term *psychological contract*?
    A) a quid pro quo agreement between a manager and her subordinates
    B) unwritten expectations between employees and their employers
    C) a phase of progressive discipline
    D) an employee balancing his own needs with those of his employer

21. Which of the following is NOT typically included in an employee handbook?
    A) conflicts of interest
    B) policies concerning the use of technology
    C) policies for submitting reimbursement paperwork
    D) an employee directory

Resolving Employee Concerns

Resolving Grievances

A major activity for HR professionals in employee relations is managing and resolving employee complaints and grievances. **Complaints** describe when employees voice dissatisfaction or concern; they are generally less serious or severe than **grievances**, which are formal complaints that imply a violation of a policy (or policies). Complaints and grievances both require timely and thoughtful action.

When an employee submits a grievance about work conditions or supervision, HR may actively investigate the situation, interview witnesses, and make recommendations for appropriate action. Management or HR may need to interpret a policy when situations are not expressly documented. They may then recommend or take action based on the facts and whether any policies apply to the situation.

In serious situations, such as sexual harassment or discrimination, employees are typically reminded of their grievance and appeal rights, as well as any whistleblower protections (discussed later in this section). These situations are often documented in the employee's file or another record repository for future reference or required government reporting.

Resolving Complaints

Employee complaints are concerns or problems employees raise with human resources or management. Complaints may be minor, concerning issues like office supplies or coffee, or major, like a boss's management style. Some complaints are quickly and easily resolved by management or HR; other complaints require more time, effort, and patience. Employee complaints can provide HR and management with useful information:

- They alert management to a problem before it grows out of control.
- They give management a chance to respond and display commitment to addressing employee concerns.

When managers or HR professionals are presented with a complaint, they should listen carefully and openly to identify the concern behind the complaint. Asking pointed questions to gather facts will help to determine a proper plan of action. If other employees share the concern, obtaining their perspectives will help to detect widespread problems. During this process, it is important to acknowledge the problem and clarify the action being taken. If action is not being taken on the complaint, it is appropriate to explain why. Demonstrating follow-through is essential to maintaining employee trust.

Employee complaints are inevitable, but methods exist to reduce them. HR professionals can encourage managers to give ongoing feedback on performance and to set clear expectations for roles. Employees can be encouraged to provide input on their work and on specific topics.

Not every employee is going to be satisfied with every action taken in an organization, but it is important not to penalize legitimate complainants—such an action could silence a valuable source of information. On the other hand, if an employee makes petty complaints on a regular basis, it is essential to have a frank conversation as to how these complaints are harming the organization's morale (if they are) and explain that the manner of the complaints is unacceptable.

Alternative Dispute Resolution

Alternative dispute resolution (ADR) refers to a number of tools that can be used to avoid litigation. ADRs can be any procedure or determination method that the parties have agreed on. The most common forms of ADR are arbitration and mediation:

- In **arbitration**, a neutral third party hears the evidence and decides on the outcome. (Arbitration is discussed above in union contexts but may also be used in nonunion contexts.)
- **Mediation** also uses a third party, but rather than making a final decision, the mediator helps negotiate the issue. In mediation, a decision or outcome is not reached unless both of the parties agree.

Grievances

When employees believe that a company policy, collective bargaining agreement, or law has been violated, they may make a formal complaint called a **grievance**. Grievances require immediate attention. A prompt response that results in a quick resolution of the grievance will improve employee morale and productivity, and can potentially prevent costly legal action.

It is imperative to take all grievances seriously, even if they may not seem valid. Grievance submission will follow either company protocol or bargaining unit contract language regarding to whom the grievance should be submitted, the timing around the grievance, and how the resolution should be decided. HR can evaluate the validity of a grievance by obtaining all relevant facts, as follows:

- Actively listen to the person with the grievance. Ask follow-up questions and get concrete examples, dates, times, witnesses, and other alleged facts.

- Consult with an employment attorney or union steward. It is important to take careful steps when validating a grievance. In unionized environments, the collective bargaining agreement may outline specific steps.
- Interview potential witnesses, as appropriate, to get their perspectives on the situation.
- Provide an update to the person who submitted the grievance. If it seems that there is a problem that needs further investigation or action, specify what will be done. If the grievance does not seem valid, explain what was done up to this point, and why no further action will be taken.
- If the grievance is valid, take action to rectify the situation.

The following steps should be taken when deciding to act on grievances:

- If the organization has a collective bargaining agreement, follow the guidelines within the agreement (and with the assistance of a union steward) for handling grievances; otherwise, refer to the employee handbook if there is a specific policy or procedure outlined in the collective bargaining agreement.
- Complainants and their supervisors should try to resolve the problem through discussion, which may be facilitated by HR.
- If no resolution is met, the next higher level of management may speak with the employee, without repercussions. Again, this may also be facilitated by HR.
- During any part of this process, HR may take a more active approach as a mediator. In some cases, however, a third-party arbitrator (outside of the organization) may be used.

There are steps an organization can take to minimize its risk of employee grievances. It is important to maintain a dialogue with employees and be open to feedback. A system should exist for employees to file legitimate complaints before they become bigger and unmanageable. Having a clear policy on submitting grievances, and detailing how the employer will handle grievances, will promote open communication. When employees complain, it is important not to retaliate. While not every complaint may be acted on, it is important to acknowledge the concerns and feelings of employees and to clearly communicate what action will—or will not—be taken and why.

Whistleblower Protection

Under the **Sarbanes-Oxley Act**, violations of securities laws or breaches of fiduciary duties must be reported to the chief legal officer or CEO of the organization. An organization's legal team (in-house or external counsel) must also report these violations to the organization's board of directors audit committee. The Sarbanes–Oxley Act provides protections for people who, in good faith, report suspected or witnessed wrongdoing. These people are called **whistleblowers**: they report violations, assist those who report violations, and help with investigations.

Whistleblower protections are regulated by the US Department of Labor and OSHA. Under OSHA regulations, an employer is prohibited from taking adverse actions against whistleblowers. Adverse actions include the following:

- terminating employment
- reducing pay

- disciplining
- intimidating
- coercing
- retaliating in any other way

Publicly traded companies are required by Sarbanes-Oxley to establish confidential whistleblower complaints and to maintain those records according to the rules established in the law. Organizations that are not publicly traded (and therefore not subject to Sarbanes-Oxley) may elect, at their own will, to establish whistleblower policies and procedures in order to maintain an ethical workplace.

Practice Questions

22. What is the MAIN purpose of a grievance procedure?
    A) to resolve conflict
    B) to empower employees to go on strike
    C) to terminate employees
    D) to provide progressive discipline

23. If an employee files a grievance, who typically handles it first?
    A) the employee's supervisor
    B) the company president or CEO
    C) a third party or arbitrator
    D) the union steward

Employee Discipline and Terminations

Most employees strive to do well at their jobs; unfortunately, sometimes employees do not meet the expectations of the job, or they exhibit unacceptable behaviors. In such cases, most managers use **progressive discipline**, a series of steps that offers the employee opportunities to improve. If the employee does not improve during one step, she will progress to the next step, which is considered more severe and moves the employee closer to termination.

Managers or departments may have their own specific procedures and expectations aligned with those of the organization and clearly communicated to the employee. When employees perform poorly or behave unacceptably, the manager will identify the issues, counsel the employee, and discuss a plan to correct the problem. The following are common examples of poor performance that require counseling or discipline:

- tardiness (chronic lateness)
- absenteeism (failure to be at work during the scheduled time)
- poor performance
- general misconduct (unprofessional behavior)

By proactively identifying issues and being responsive to complaints or problems, organizations can stop or reduce disruptive behavior.

The Steps of Progressive Discipline

The number and details of each step in a progressive discipline program vary from employer to employer. Some employers, especially those subject to collective bargaining agreements, must strictly follow the order of each step in progressive discipline. Other employers reserve the right to use any or all steps necessary to address a particular issue. For example, an employee who does not follow the company's dress code may get a verbal warning, but physical violence toward another employee will likely result in immediate termination.

Taking the steps of progressive discipline is generally useful for repetitive, nonserious offenses (e.g., tardiness) or when there is no indication that the employee will improve. Figure 7.2. outlines the typical steps found in a progressive discipline procedure.

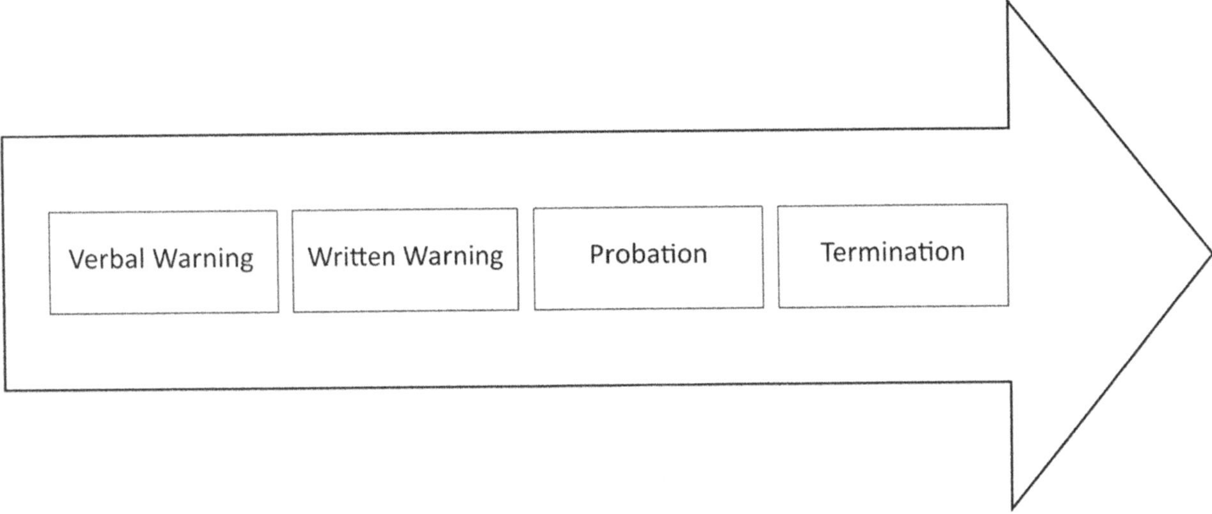

Figure 7.2. A Typical Progressive Discipline Procedure

A **verbal warning** is the least serious consequence of poor behavior. It involves a conversation between a supervisor and an employee during which the inappropriate behavior is identified and expectations for improvement are made clear.

A **written warning** is appropriate when the employee ignores a verbal warning about a specified behavior or does not show improvement. The written warning, or "write-up," documents the incident, explains why the behavior is inappropriate (and references applicable company policies), explains what changes are expected, and describes the consequences of the continued behavior. Typically, an employee is asked to sign a copy to acknowledge receipt of the written warning, although a signature may not necessarily mean the employee agrees with the contents of the write-up.

A **performance improvement plan** places the employee on probation and requires specific actions to be taken in order to meet the supervisor's expectations. The employee is required to follow the plan and show improvement as a condition of continued employment.

A **suspension** is often the final step before termination. A suspension lasts a certain duration and may be paid or unpaid. Suspensions are accompanied by a document that outlines the terms of the suspension, specific steps to correct the issue, and the consequences for not improving. Employees who successfully complete a suspension typically receive one last chance to demonstrate improvement.

Involuntary termination of employment, known as firing, is the final step in the progressive discipline process. It happens when behavioral problems are continual or the employee commits a serious offense, such as theft or violence. A firing is usually immediate, but it should not come as a surprise if the employer has clearly conveyed expectations and provided ongoing feedback to the employee.

There are other steps for progressive discipline that may be used, including demotions, temporary pay cuts, reassignments, and required training. Whichever methods are used, they should fit the behavior and resolve the problem rather than simply provide a route toward termination. Being open and frank during each step of the process can help the employee improve, which benefits both the employee and the company as a whole.

Practice Question

24. Which of the following BEST describes progressive discipline?
    A) It is a "zero tolerance" policy.
    B) It is a system of discrimination in disciplining employees.
    C) It is a series of increasingly serious disciplinary actions.
    D) It is required under the FLSA.

Answer Key

1. C: Option C is the only answer that does not describe a task that would fall solely under the umbrella of employee relations since it describes an activity that an HR professional would take in anticipation of interacting with an employee bargaining unit. The other answer options all describe activities that are specific to the relationship between management and employees only, with no mention of any union-related components to those tasks.

2. C: The National Labor Relations Act (NLRA), or Wagner Act, was enacted in 1935.

3. A: Collective bargaining is key to labor relations. A labor union's greatest strength is therefore in its bargaining power.

4. B: Generally, if a company wants to change the terms of a collective bargaining agreement while it is in effect, it must give sixty days' notice.

5. B: Union shop security clauses are used when workers are required to join a union.

6. D: Right-to-work laws prohibit or limit union agreements that require employees' membership or payment of union dues or fees as a condition of employment; in other words, they prohibit or limit union shops.

7. C: The Fair Labor Standards Act (FLSA) mandates standards for the employment of minors as well as the payment of regular wages and overtime.

8. A: Nonexempt employees are not entitled to overtime pay under the FLSA.

9. C: Companies with fifty or more employees in a 75-mile radius qualify for this Family and Medical Leave Act (FMLA) provision.

10. B: According to the Drug-Free Workplace Act, recipients of federal grants and some federal contractors must provide a drug-free workplace.

11. C: The Davis-Bacon Act of 1931 requires the payment of prevailing wages and benefits to employees of contractors working on federal government construction projects.

12. D: The Employee Polygraph Protection Act does not apply to federal, state, or local governments or to organizations contracted through the federal government to provide security.

13. C: An expatriate is an individual who works in a country that is not his home country.

14. C: HR responsibilities differ among countries, especially when it comes to compensation and benefits.

15. B: The Occupational Safety and Health Administration's three levels of hazard mitigation or control are engineering controls, administrative controls, and personal protective equipment (PPE).

16. B: A PESTLE analysis shows how external factors (Political, Economic, Social, Technological, Legal, and Environmental) may impact an organization. For instance, environmental factors like hurricanes or wildfires might impact an organization's day-to-day operations. A PESTLE analysis would reveal those specific factors.

17. C: A SWOT analysis examines internal Strengths and Weaknesses and external Opportunities and Threats. In the planning phase, HR could outline resources (e.g., existing facilities, workstations, budgets, and technical skills) under "strengths" and then determine what is still needed for employees who might need to work from home in case of a pandemic or natural disaster. For example, the organization might have a shortage of laptop computers with cameras, a shortage of remote workstations, or no budget for remote working programs that require a monthly subscription. Those could go under "weaknesses," and HR could plan accordingly to resolve those shortcomings.

18. A: According to the Fair Credit Reporting Act, employers must have written authorization from an applicant before conducting a credit check.

19. D: Employers may legally monitor the employees' use of company computers.

20. B: The term *psychological contract* refers to the unwritten, informal expectations that exist between employees and the organizations where they work. Examples might include the expectation that an employee will get a raise every year or attend an annual professional conference.

21. D: Employee handbooks are designed to provide employees with clear, written expectations about the workplace and its practices, such as fair hiring and equal employment opportunity. The information they contain should document these expectations and practices and include information about conflicts of interest, the use of technology, and reimbursement policies. An employee directory (option D) is not a part of an employee handbook.

22. A: The main purpose of a grievance procedure is to resolve a conflict or dispute.

23. A: Not all employees are union members. Typically, a grievance is first addressed by an employee's supervisor. Depending on the situation, the grievance may progress higher in the organization, or to arbitration.

24. C: Progressive discipline can best be described as a series of steps that offer the employee opportunities to improve.

Chapter 8 – Information Management in Human Resources

Interpreting and Understanding Data and Metrics

There are numerous systems, tools, and technological advances designed to streamline and maximize the human resources data that HR professionals rely on to keep staffing and operations running smoothly. In order to leverage these tools to the benefit of an organization, HR professionals must understand the importance of these systems, how to best use them, and how to analyze the data they provide.

Data Gathering and Analysis

Several techniques and methods exist for gathering data. It is therefore important to understand the different data collection methods in order to choose the best techniques to obtain the information needed.

Surveys are a quick, easy, and cost-effective method of gathering data. A **survey** involves collecting information from a sample of a targeted group. Surveys can be done by questionnaire or interview. Data collected through the surveys is then used to track and determine information about a situation.

Similar to surveys, **focus groups** obtain information from individuals who represent a sample of a broader group. A focus group typically comprises six to twelve people who participate in a discussion led by a facilitator. It is important that a focus group be led by a trained individual who knows how to pose questions in a manner that does not lead or influence the responses of group members.

The design of both surveys and focus groups is critical in order to obtain objective information. The distortion of information is a risk if employees feel that their pay or position may be in jeopardy.

Measurement error refers to all of the variations that impact a participant's performance. These variations might include conditions (e.g., quietness of the room, behavior of the facilitator or survey administrator) or the emotional state of the participant.

Though evidence-based decision-making and the use of HR data have obvious benefits, they still pose risks to the organization. Even advanced technology, like artificial intelligence (AI), may be prone to inaccuracy and unreliable predictions. Additionally, personal data must be protected and only shared appropriately. Breaches in a company's systems or unsecured databases may lead to private information being shared. It is therefore critical that businesses have policies in place concerning recordkeeping and how to protect employee information.

When collecting data, completing an **environmental scan** can provide insight into future planning by determining how external and internal factors could impact the business and personnel. Examples of environmental factors include the following:

- internal organizational metrics
- economic trends

- competition for employees
- political and legal trends
- technological trends
- social trends
- geographic trends (e.g., the opening and closing of plants or offices in an area)

Another practice in human resources analytics is benchmarking. **Benchmarking** involves an analyst comparing such items as HR policies, practices, wages, and benefits with those of another organization. Benchmarking can also take place in larger organizations with multiple locations or divisions. Benchmarks and benchmark data are then used to measure HR initiatives in relation to competitors and other relevant businesses. By using benchmarking, HR can ensure best practices in its initiatives and programs.

In general, data and metrics offer ways that the HR professional can measure the successes and outcomes of initiatives. Using data and metrics strategies allows HR professionals to measure the impact of an initiative upon an organization by analyzing trends within the data, which results in an objective evaluation.

HR professionals should understand basic statistical methods, including descriptive statistics, correlations, and measurements such as reliability and validity:

- **Descriptive statistics** are brief, meaningful descriptions (i.e., basic summaries) of data sets.
  - These statistics may include the distribution and spread of information (e.g., the range of wage data), or they might provide information about the mean or average, such as an average wage for a position.
  - A summary of the data might include items such as the range, quartiles, deviation, and variance.
- **Correlation** explains the relationship between two items or variables.
  - For example, an HR practitioner might question whether there is a correlation between gender and wages.
  - Correlation can be determined through tools like regression analysis (a process that can help form estimates about relationships between dependent and independent variables) or scatterplots.

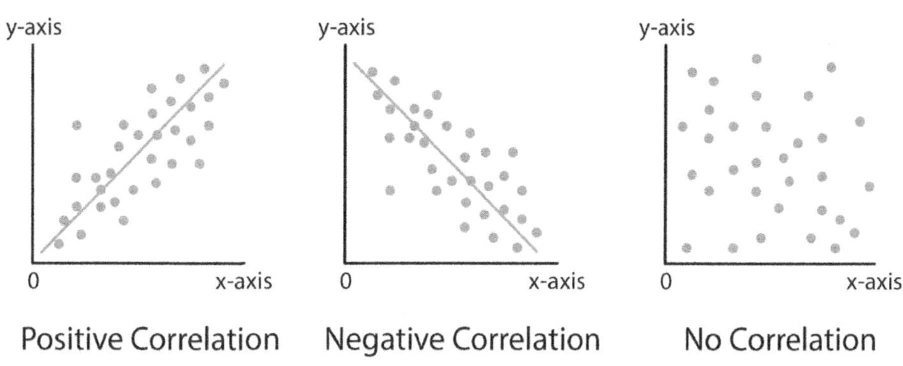

Figure 8.1. Scatterplots Showing Correlation

It is also important to understand if data is reliable and valid:

- **Reliability** describes the consistency of the measurement.
  - For example, for a performance scoring system to be reliable, it must measure employees in the same manner; by doing this, employees are measured consistently even though their individual scores may be different.
- **Validity**, on the other hand, refers to what is being measured and whether it is relevant.
  - In the example of a performance review, if an employee's performance on a nonwork-related issue is being measured, that item is not valid; it may be a reliable measurement, but it is neither accurate nor relevant to the actual review.

When analyzing data, it is important to spot misleading or flawed data. Looking at validity and reliability is one way to do this, but it is also important to consider how the data is presented. For instance, for data presented as a graph, a PHR professional might consider the following:

- What is the scale of the graph?
- Is it sized in a particular way to make a topic look more impactful than it actually is?
- What is the actual size of the data?
- Is a 25 percent increase due to the addition of five people to a twenty-person company or 5,000 people to a 20,000-person company?
- Is the data complete, or does it only have specific periods of times or items included?

> **Helpful Hint:**
>
> Think of the concept of reliability the same as you would a person who is reliable. A reliable person behaves as expected every time. A reliable assessment instrument does too.

It is important to never accept data at face value but to instead objectively interpret it to ensure a full understanding of the information.

HR professionals ensure objectivity by using metrics and data. This allows the HR professional to make decisions based on facts—not emotions, opinions, or perceptions. Objectivity also allows HR professionals to build a business case for decisions, goals, and strategies.

HR Metrics

HR metrics show important trends and information regarding an organization's personnel. This information helps decision-makers improve the organization and meet the needs of employees. There are several metrics that can be tracked and analyzed by HR professionals; these are described in Table 8.1.

Table 8.1. Common HR Metrics	
Metric	**Calculation**
Cost per hire	recruitment costs --- (compensation cost + benefits cost)
Average time to fill a position	sum of days to fill all jobs in a period --- total jobs filled in the period
Absence rate	number of days absent in month for all employees --- (average number of employees during a month × number of workdays)
Benefit costs per employee	total cost of employee benefit or program --- total employees
Benefit utilization rate	total number of employees using a benefit --- total number of employees eligible to use a benefit

Organizations can track and measure other calculations, depending on the organization's needs. When deciding which metrics to analyze and track, the following factors should be considered:

- Which metrics are important to organizational leaders and the strategic plan?
- What data must be obtained to calculate these metrics, and from what sources should they be obtained?
- How will data be analyzed, and against what sources will data be benchmarked?
- How can the analysis be presented for use in planning, development, and problem-solving?

Practice Question

1. A group of employees all fill out a survey with the exact same answers, which is a surprising result. HR finds out later that the room in which the survey was administered was very hot; the AC was out of order, and employees were uncomfortable and eager to leave the room quickly. What can be said about this data?
   A) The data likely has a measurement error.
   B) The survey given was unreliable.
   C) The survey is not valid.
   D) The survey could be used as an initial screening for a new product.

Business Analysis

HR professionals use business analysis tools to maintain business and competitive awareness. **Statistical models** analyze data to uncover trends affecting the organization. For example, as discussed earlier, an environmental scan analyzes external and internal conditions that impact an organization. Another valuable tool is the SWOT analysis, developed by business and management consultant Albert Humphrey at the Stanford Research Institute in the 1960s.

A **SWOT analysis** looks at an organization's internal **s**trengths and **w**eaknesses, and external **o**pportunities and **t**hreats, which can reveal important factors to consider before making a decision. In order to visualize the internal and external landscapes, these factors are broken down into four quadrants, as seen in Figure 8.2.

Opportunities and threats are always external and cannot be controlled; however, they can be planned for. Strengths and weaknesses are internal and can be controlled; in addition, strengths and opportunities can help overcome weaknesses and threats.

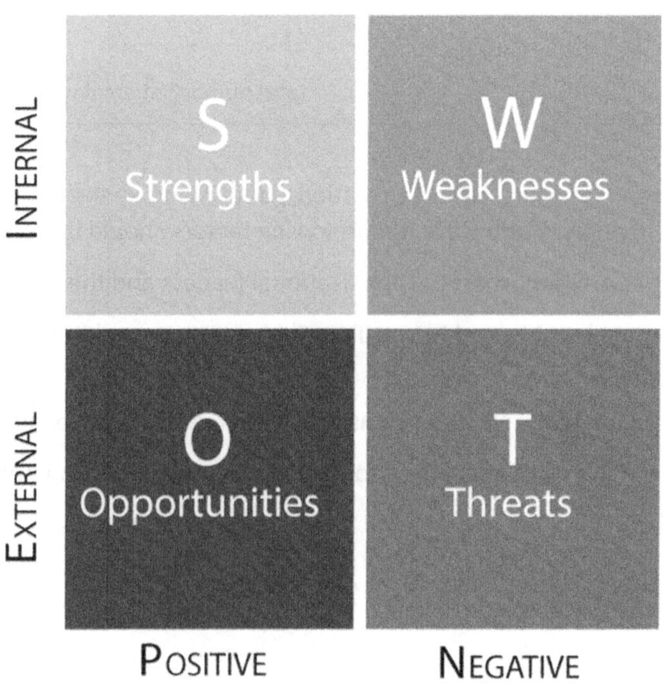

Figure 8.2. SWOT Analysis

Human resource professionals use business analysis tools to track outcomes, costs, and the ROI of HR initiatives and programs. HR dashboards track and monitor key performance indicators (KPIs).

> **Helpful Hint:**
>
> Conduct a SWOT analysis before setting objectives. The SWOT analysis will show if an objective is realistic and achievable.

KPIs should be relevant to the business and impact profitability. For instance, an organization that hires only a few people a year might choose to monitor and manage the costs of training efforts or benefit programs; however, if an organization hires a large number of employees due to growth or turnover, KPIs such as time to hire or cost of hire would be strategically important. Through KPIs, HR speaks the language of business by showing the results of programs through data and dollars. KPIs are used not only for measuring the success of past programs but also for developing and planning for the future.

A **human resources information system (HRIS)** is an electronic platform used for data entry, tracking, and reporting human resources information. The system maintains important static information about employees, such as addresses, Social Security numbers, tax withholding information, job and pay information, and benefit elections. The HRIS can typically produce static reports, such as employee lists, as well as analytical reports like turnover, head count, and other information that is useful for planning purposes. HRIS vendors package their systems with various capabilities, and some are more robust than others. An HRIS will typically provide an organization with the following:

- the ability to manage all employee information and records
- the ability to track applicants
- reporting capabilities on HR metrics
- the ability to post HR documents (e.g., employee handbooks, procedures, and forms)
- benefits administration
- integration with payroll or other HR management systems

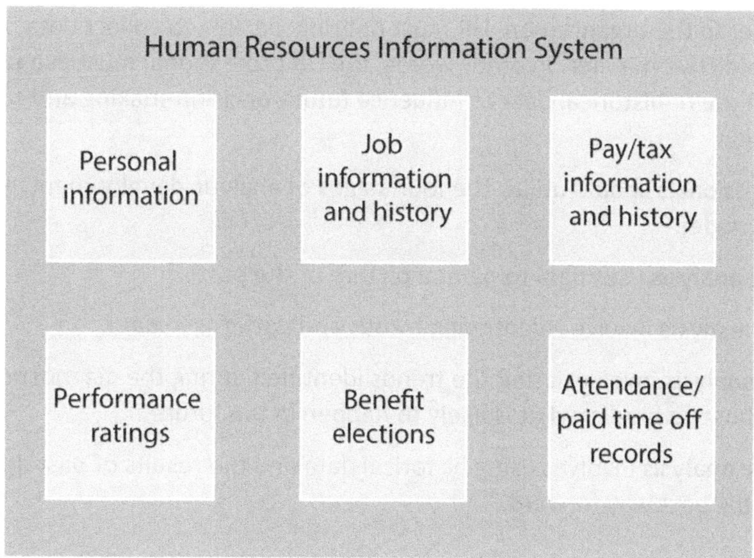

Figure 8.3. Information Collected in HRIS

The HRIS should provide data the company needs to track and analyze applicants, employees, and former employees. Some systems allow employees to update their own basic information (e.g., address changes or tax withholdings) and benefit enrollments. HR staff can then focus on strategic functions rather than administrative data entry. Some more robust HRIS systems also allow organizations to conduct performance reviews within the system to allow for easy dissemination, collection, and tracking. The data collected in an HRIS can be used to make employment decisions, such as merit increases, promotions, and restructuring. Managers can also access information to effectively support the success of their direct reports.

HRIS systems are often integrated with other HR functional systems, such as applicant trackers or learning management systems:

- With an **applicant tracking system (ATS)**, the employer can post jobs and collect candidate profiles within one system. An ATS typically allows for candidate assessments and the sharing of candidates with the hiring manager.
- A **learning management system (LMS)**, like the ATS, is a platform with one location for the creation, distribution, and record retention of training and development within the organization.

Using these systems allows for a seamless integration of static employee information along with a common platform to access and store information.

HR professionals also use an HRIS to maintain all personnel records, including employee names, addresses, emergency contacts, job and pay information, performance ratings, leaves of absence, benefit elections, and more. They also provide reports to leaders and managers to support personnel decisions or to monitor employee metrics (e.g., turnover). HRIS functions may be managed by an HRIS specialist, a departmental assistant, an HR generalist, or another specialist.

Critical Evaluation and Predictive Analytics

Critical evaluation is key to the HR function. **Critical evaluation** means the HR professional understands how to analyze data and implement it to further the organization's objectives.

As a strategic partner to the organization, HR must not only be able to collect data but also analyze and use the data in a predictive manner. In other words, the HR professional must use **predictive analysis**, which describes the use of historical data to influence future decision-making and scenario planning within an organization.

To do this, HR professionals should utilize the four stages of analytic development, which form the **analytics maturity model:**

1. **Descriptive analysis** uses data to paint a picture of the past.
2. **Diagnostic analysis** involves identifying trends and patterns in data.
3. **Predictive analysis** involves using the trends identified during the diagnostic analysis stage and using those to *predict* what is likely to happen in the future.
4. **Prescriptive analysis** involves using historical data and the results of past decisions to determine the best way forward.

Strategic Alignment

In addition to being a business partner, HR is also a strategic partner to the organization. HR must align the strategic initiatives of the HR function with those of the organization. In **strategic alignment**, HR balances the strategies of the business with the needs of employees and the requirements of laws and legislation. More than ever, organizational culture and employee morale are strategically important to the success of the business. Strategic alignment from the HR perspective incorporates five critical components:

1. workforce planning
2. organizational capability assessment
3. organizational development and structure
4. diversity and inclusion
5. change management

Human resource professionals are no longer seen as members of personnel departments that process paperwork; rather, HR is considered a component of the organization's broader decision-making process. Areas like employee compensation, talent acquisition, training and development, and organizational design must support the direction and mission of the business as a whole. To make decisions, HR uses analytics and business intelligence tools, such as SWOT analysis (discussed earlier in this chapter) and PESTLE (discussed in the next section).

HR also plays a critical role in achieving key organizational initiatives by leading organizational design and change management programs. HR professionals formulate, implement, and monitor the people side of the business by using analytics to measure the success and return on investment (ROI) of programs and initiatives. Leadership looks to HR for the systems and processes that will ensure the strategic HR goals and metrics are met and will support the organization as it works toward its mission and vision.

Business and Competitive Awareness

As a business partner, HR must learn and understand the organization's business operations, functions, products, and services. It is not enough that HR understands only the HR function and the laws and rules that surround it. To be a strategic partner, HR must understand the core business of the organization and the forces that impact it.

Regularly monitoring and responding to the external environment is critical to the organization's success. HR professionals must remain keenly aware of changes in the external environment and respond strategically by implementing HR solutions. External forces include the economy, consumer demand, laws and regulations, technology, and the labor force. Being proactive and adapting to these changes keeps an organization strong.

HR professionals use many tools to assess and analyze such forces. The PESTLE analysis allows HR professionals to conduct situational analysis before implementing a strategy or plan. The **PESTLE analysis** shows how the following external factors may impact an organization:

- Political factors include government stability, policies, foreign relations, taxes, and so forth.
- Economic factors include inflation, interest rates, unemployment, trade, and other issues.
- Social factors include culture, age distribution, public health, population growth, and so on.
- Technological factors include innovation, automation, awareness of and access to technology.
- Legal factors include consumer protection laws, antitrust laws, copyright laws, and other laws.
- Environmental factors include climate change, weather events, and the risk of natural disasters.

Another tool is Porter's Five Forces. In his 1979 article "How Competitive Forces Shape Strategy," Harvard Business School professor Michael E. Porter describes five forces to better understand an industry and ensure an organization stays competitive and relevant. These forces shape industries and show their strengths and weaknesses. Human resources must, along with other functions within the organization, access these forces to proactively develop strategic initiatives. **Porter's Five Forces** include the following:

1. competition (rivalry)
2. the potential threat of new entrants to an industry
3. the power of suppliers
4. the power of consumers
5. the threat of substitute products

Competition, or competitive rivalry, refers to competition within an industry. Profit hinges on competition—even dominant companies in an industry face competition. All companies must be alert to the potential threat of new entrants to an industry. New entrants (i.e., new competition) could take away from profits. For example, millions of people went to Blockbuster Video every weekend to rent movies until Netflix pioneered a new model of video rentals.

Still, new entrants to an industry face barriers to entry. Porter discusses six barriers to entry:

1. economies of scale
2. product differentiation
3. capital requirements
4. cost disadvantages relative to size
5. access to distribution channels
6. government policy

The power of suppliers and the power of consumers (or buyers) refers to the bargaining power of both:

- **Suppliers** are powerful (i.e., have strong bargaining power) when they control a product by reducing supply or raising prices. In 1973, for example, the Organization of the Petroleum Exporting Countries (OPEC) placed an embargo on the United States by refusing to export oil, resulting in a gas shortage.
- Consumers are powerful when they demand higher quality or service. Consumer shift in demand can also force down prices. For example, there are usually discounts on Halloween candy in November and Easter candy the week after the holiday.

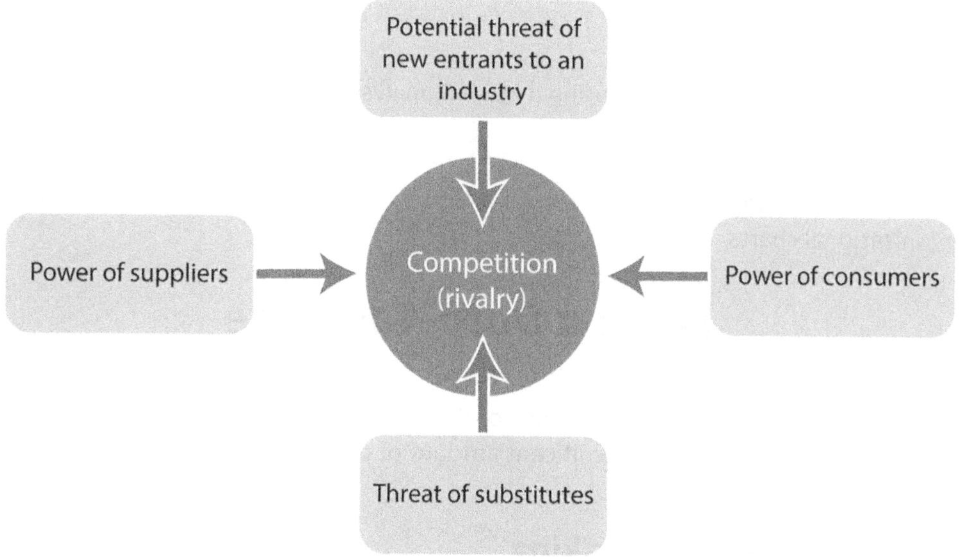

Figure 8.5. Porter's Five Forces

Finally, companies must address the threat of substitute products (or services). **Substitute products** take away market share and threaten profits. For example, Apple produces the iPhone but must contend with Samsung's Android.

How do business and economic considerations affect HR? When the economy is strong, consumers can afford more products and services. Companies thrive if they meet the demands of consumers, and companies often expand their staff to meet that demand. On the other hand, when the economy is stagnant or in decline, consumers buy fewer products and services; consequently, companies may have to reduce production costs or lay off employees to offset the loss of profits.

Consumer demand can affect economic conditions for companies as demand for specific products increases or decreases. Over time, consumers develop new tastes, attitudes, and behaviors: what may have been popular with consumers a decade ago may not be popular today. Therefore, to meet consumer demand, companies refine their existing products and services and develop new ones. This process also affects staffing practices.

Still, organizations must look beyond economics. Local, state, and federal governments and agencies constantly implement new laws and regulations, which inform how a company compensates and treats employees and how it operates. Depending on where the company conducts business, it may have to follow rules in different locations and keep up with the changing legal landscape in each place.

It is strategically advantageous for any organization to follow developments in technology. The organization may benefit from new technology that streamlines operations and increases efficiency.

Finally, an organization should try to attract the most qualified people to fulfill its goals and remain a desirable place to work. The talent and skills of individuals within the workforce are critical to the success of all organizations.

Practice Questions

2. Which of the following factors is considered in an environmental scan?
   A) competition
   B) succession plan
   C) staffing metrics
   D) compensation analysis

3. Which of the following is examined during a PESTLE analysis?
   A) turnover rate
   B) economic factors
   C) employee complaints
   D) organizational charts

Being a Data Advocate

Senior-level HR professionals understand the use of data to not only speak the language of business but to also predict future needs. There is a significant amount of data that can drive and inform decision-making.

Evidence-Based Decision-Making

Evidence-based decision-making involves making decisions around actual evidence, data, and root-cause analysis instead of using gut feelings or intuition. By using an evidence-based approach to decision-making, decisions are based on facts rather than assumptions. In regard to employee development, training, and performance management, facts—not feelings—must drive the design and implementation of programs. For example, the description of the ADDIE model in Chapter 4 also examines the importance during the assessment phase of determining the actual needs of both the organization and the individuals who work for it.

When making decisions, HR professionals should be cautious of the following rater errors that could cloud their judgments:

- The **halo effect** is when the interviewer allows one positive characteristic of a candidate to overly influence her decision.
- The **similar-to-me effect** happens when the rater allows characteristics he shares with the employee to impact the rating.
- The **recency effect** occurs when the rater gives greater importance to recent events than to the overall performance of the employee or candidate.
- The **horns effect** happens when the rater allows one negative characteristic to influence the entire rating.

- **Central tendency errors** occur when a manager gives most or all employees a rating that falls in the middle of the scale.

Through evidence-based decision-making, HR is able to report key findings to leadership, recommend courses of action, and measure the return on investment.

Applicant Tracking Systems

An **applicant tracking system (ATS)** is a program that automates the application and recruitment processes. An ATS allows job seekers to find and apply for jobs by electronically submitting an application with a resume and cover letter attached. Data is collected from internal applications through the ATS interface. The ATS interface may also be linked to the company website or internet job boards in order to attract external applicants. Recruiters can post jobs, search through applications, track candidate progress, and communicate with applicants through the ATS.

The main function of an ATS is to provide a central location and database to support the company's recruiting activities. The ATS helps recruiters maintain resumes and applications and stay compliant with federal and state employment and document retention laws.

Securing Data

Just as a home needs to be secure from intruders, an organization also has security needs. A data breach, for example, can lead to key information being leaked to competitors and can harm the organization financially. An intruder breaking into the company's headquarters can steal important records, potentially resulting in financial or other losses. Protecting the physical security of the organization's employees, facilities, infrastructure, and resources is vital to its survival. An organization should carefully plan its security strategy.

The following essential steps are used to develop an organizational security policy:

- Develop security policies and procedures that are well documented and accessible to all employees.
    - This documentation shows the organization's commitment to security and clarifies procedures to management, which enforces security concerns on a day-to-day basis.
- Maintain a physically secure environment.
    - If the business is at risk of theft, robberies, violence, or other crimes, it is important to secure entries and to install surveillance equipment, metal detectors, and other devices to monitor the premises and prevent security breaches.
    - The organization should also have policies and procedures regarding employees' handling of company equipment, including computers. The policies should clearly indicate what steps the employee should take when company property is lost or stolen so that the organization can respond appropriately and mitigate the effects of the loss.
- Restrict information only to those who need to know it.
    - Employees should have access only to the files, records, and information necessary to conduct their jobs; in particular, access to sensitive information should be

limited to those who need it to perform a certain function or who are in a position to make decisions related to that information.

    - Additionally, the company should have a policy requiring employees to protect the confidentiality of any sensitive or proprietary information to which they have access.
    - In some industries, it is important to have employees complete a noncompete and/or confidentiality agreement to ensure specific information is kept confidential even after an employee leaves the company.
- Protect data from loss, theft, or intrusion.
    - Viruses, malware, and cyberattacks threaten an organization's technological infrastructure.
    - The organization should install the appropriate firewalls, antivirus software, and network monitoring software necessary to protect its infrastructure from attacks.
    - Employees should be required to maintain strong computer and network passwords, which should be changed regularly.
    - The organization should have "acceptable use" policies restricting employees from accessing suspicious websites; these aim to minimize inadvertent downloads that can be harmful to the organization's computer or even the entire network.
    - Installing web-filtering software on the network can help prevent inadvertent downloads.
    - Training on how to detect cyber threats (e.g., phishing attempts in emails) and on what steps to take in case of malware and cyberattacks is critical; many attacks happen through individual employee emails and similar sources.
- Protect financial assets from loss or theft.
    - If the company interacts with the general public and employees have access to certain cash reserves, protocols should be in place to monitor the flow of money and require employees to balance cash at the end of their shifts.
    - The company should also protect any reserves it has on site by using a safe.
    - The company should limit the funds it keeps on the premises to only the amount necessary to conduct daily business.
- Train employees on security practices and hold them accountable.
    - Poor training often leads to security breaches, and thorough training conducted periodically will keep employees aware of and invested in the security of the business; this is especially true in regard to cybersecurity, whereby threats are transnational and organizations of any size are at risk.

Finally, it is important to consider how privacy and data regulations vary among countries. For instance, companies with employees in European Union countries must follow the **EU Data Protection Directive**, which restricts how personal information can be collected, stored, and shared. The EU also restricts the sharing of data with countries that do not have rigorous security standards.

Practice Question

4. Why should an organization develop written security policies and procedures?
   A) to outline policies and procedures to customers and clients
   B) to ensure policies and procedures are compliant with congressional regulations
   C) to clarify procedures to employees and show the organization is serious about security
   D) to keep policies and procedures on a "need-to-know" basis

Answer Key

1. A: If employees were uncomfortable and wanted to leave quickly, it is unlikely they took the time to answer survey questions carefully and thoughtfully. The data therefore likely contains a measurement error. Measurement error refers to the factors, such as test conditions, that impact the test results.

2. A: An organization's competition is an external factor in its operating environment. Competition would be examined in an environmental scan.

3. B: A PESTLE analysis studies political, economic, social, technological, legal, and environmental factors. Economic factors like interest rates, unemployment, and more would be considered during a PESTLE analysis.

4. C: Documented security policies and procedures that are accessible to employees show the organization's commitment to security and clarify procedures to management. Written policies facilitate the enforcement of security concerns on a day-to-day basis.

PHR Practice Test #1

1. Strategic HR management includes which of the following activities?
   A) planning
   B) developing objectives
   C) aligning resources
   D) all of the above

2. Which of the following is NOT a criteria for evaluating training programs?
   A) synthesis
   B) reactions
   C) learning
   D) behavior

3. An employer has the right to do which of the following?
   A) forbid employees from discussing union membership or activities
   B) terminate two nonunion employees for discussing the conditions of their job
   C) describe a union's strike history and the economic consequences of strikes
   D) give preferential treatment to one union over another

4. Which of the following is an important activity in strategic planning?
   A) external scan
   B) internal scan
   C) SWOT analysis
   D) all of the above

5. Which theory states that people are motivated by outcomes?
   A) equity theory
   B) expectancy theory
   C) Alderfer's ERG theory
   D) motivation-hygiene theory

6. An election has just been held in a bargaining unit. Of the employees who voted, 85 percent voted for the union; however, only 55 percent of those who voted are actually dues-paying members of the union. Which employees does the union represent?
   A) only the dues-paying members
   B) all who voted for the union
   C) all who voted for or against the union
   D) all employees in the bargaining unit

7. An organization's mission statement includes which of the following?
   A) a statement of purpose
   B) a strategic plan
   C) a staffing model
   D) all of the above

8. Which of the following is NOT a benefit of training?
   A) reduced profits
   B) reduction in errors
   C) reduction in turnover
   D) improved productivity

9. Which law governs collective bargaining for federal employees?
   A) the National Labor Relations Act
   B) the Affordable Care Act
   C) the Civil Service Reform Act
   D) the Taft-Hartley Act

10. Which type of learning curve gradually increases in pace with larger increments?
   A) S-shaped learning curve
   B) positively accelerating learning curve
   C) negatively accelerating learning curve
   D) plateau

11. Which of the following strategies is associated with workforce expansion?
   A) outsourcing
   B) demotions
   C) management training
   D) job rotations

12. What is the PRIMARY purpose of an HR audit?
   A) to provide information to the federal government
   B) to determine how many HR staff are needed
   C) to evaluate the effectiveness of the HR function
   D) to determine which HRIS system to use

13. Which of the following is NOT part of behavioral-based training?
   A) diversity training
   B) internships
   C) case studies/incidents
   D) business games

14. Which OSHA violation is the LEAST-serious?
   A) serious
   B) willful
   C) de minimus
   D) nonqualified

15. Which types of employees CANNOT be represented by a union under the NLRA?
   A) supervisors, confidential employees, and managers
   B) seasonal employees, managers, and supervisors
   C) supervisors and key employees
   D) managers, supervisors, and non-US citizens

16. A consistent wage despite the number of hours worked is called what?
    A) salary
    B) bonus
    C) variable pay
    D) base pay

17. At a company with a global reach, when does the centralized approach to compensation work best?
    A) when the company wants to pay the same wages to US and international employees
    B) when international employees have a lower standard of living than US employees
    C) when there are few international employees
    D) when inflation is low

18. The Family and Medical Leave Act (FMLA) requires employers to do which of the following?
    A) provide affordable health insurance to employees and their dependents
    B) provide employees with up to twelve weeks of paid leave for surgeries and sickness
    C) provide workers' compensation insurance to employees who are injured on the job
    D) give employees up to twelve weeks of unpaid leave to care for themselves or a family member with a serious health condition

19. What does at-will employment mean?
    A) The employee is guaranteed a job only for a specified amount of time.
    B) The employee or employer may terminate the relationship at any time.
    C) Employees may only be fired for serious offenses.
    D) Employees must have an employment contract with the employer.

20. Which agency is responsible for enforcing federal laws regarding safety on the job?
    A) the Internal Revenue Service
    B) the Department of Commerce
    C) the Occupational Safety and Health Administration
    D) the US Citizenship and Immigration Service

21. Which of the following federal laws applies to most employers?
    A) the Rehabilitation Act of 1973
    B) the Vietnam Era Veterans' Readjustment Assistance Act
    C) the Age Discrimination in Employment Act
    D) affirmative action

22. A company wants to restructure a department. Which task would HR likely NOT conduct?
    A) developing a project plan for handling the restructuring
    B) designing new products and services
    C) writing job descriptions for the new or refined positions
    D) assessing the skills and competencies of staff

23. How long must employers keep records of occupational illnesses, injuries, and incidents?
    A) one year
    B) five years
    C) ten years
    D) indefinitely

24. An employee removes his safety glasses because they are uncomfortable. He then gets a chemical in his eye and requires medical treatment. This is an example of which of the following?
   A) unsafe act
   B) unfair treatment
   C) organizational risk
   D) unsafe work environment

25. ERISA was designed to protect employee rights in which area?
   A) retirement plans
   B) unemployment compensation
   C) workers' compensation
   D) recruitment and hiring

26. Which of the following is NOT a type of retirement plan?
   A) defined-contribution plan
   B) defined-benefit plan
   C) defined retirement age plan
   D) profit-sharing plan

27. Which of the following is an example of pay for performance?
   A) variable pay
   B) piecework
   C) gainsharing
   D) all of the above

28. Which job might apply to the Title VII rule that allows an employer to discriminate on the basis of race, color, sex, religion, or national origin if any of these are a "bona fide occupational qualification"?
   A) teacher
   B) doctor
   C) actor
   D) police officer

29. When must the OSHA Form 300 be completed?
   A) when an employee dies due to a work- related illness or injury
   B) when a work-related injury leads to missed days
   C) when a work-related injury requires medical care beyond first aid
   D) all of the above

30. Which of the following activities is typical of the transactional leader?
   A) They allow workers to be autonomous.
   B) They get involved when standards are not met.
   C) They micromanage employees.
   D) They set unrealistic expectations.

31. Which of the following is a method of comparing the relative performance of employees?
   A) structuring
   B) pay for performance
   C) ranking
   D) performance improvement plan

32. An organization wants to improve its proportion of employees who identify as members of the LGBTQ community. Which of the following outreach plans is BEST designed to encourage LGBTQ candidates to apply for an open position?
    A) Change the organization's graphics on social media to celebrate Pride Month each June.
    B) Require each internal promotion to include one LGBTQ candidate on the shortlist of applicants.
    C) Profile an LGBTQ employee and their partner while advertising the organization's workplace culture.
    D) Advertise the open position as only accepting applicants who identify as LGBTQ.

33. Which of the following elements is part of a company's compensation philosophy?
    A) fixed and variable pay
    B) pay in relation to the market
    C) pay for the job
    D) all of the above

34. Which of the following would be considered a bona fide occupational qualification for firefighters?
    A) Applicants must be at least five feet and five inches tall.
    B) Applicants must be able to handle extreme temperatures.
    C) Applicants must be US citizens.
    D) Applicants must have a bachelor's degree.

35. Which of the following is NOT part of job analysis?
    A) selecting jobs to analyze
    B) collecting data from incumbents
    C) writing job descriptions
    D) designing jobs

36. Which law protects employees who are covered by private pension programs?
    A) the Employee Retirement Income Security Act
    B) the Fair Credit Reporting Act
    C) the Tax Reform Act of 1986
    D) the Retirement Act

37. How much time does an employee have to file a complaint of discrimination with the EEOC?
    A) 30 days
    B) 90 days
    C) 180 days
    D) 365 days

38. An employee born in 1968 is part of which generation?
    A) Baby Boomers
    B) Millennials
    C) Silent Generation
    D) Generation X

39. Which of the following is NOT a requirement of the Americans with Disabilities Act (ADA)?
    A) Newly built public facilities must be accessible to people with disabilities.
    B) Buildings financed with public funds must be accessible to people with disabilities.
    C) Employers may ask applicants to disclose their disabilities to determine if an accommodation will need to be made.
    D) Employers with more than fifteen employees are required to provide reasonable accommodations to employees with disabilities.

40. Which of the following is NOT an important feature of new hire onboarding?
    A) determining job satisfaction
    B) training staff on company policies and procedures
    C) providing a tour of the facilities
    D) integrating new employees into the organizational culture

41. Which learning domains influence behavior?
    A) skills
    B) attitude
    C) knowledge
    D) all of the above

42. What occurs when an apparently neutral employment policy has a disproportionately negative effect on a protected group?
    A) disparate treatment
    B) disparate impact
    C) discriminatory practice
    D) personal bias

43. What is an interview process called in which identical questions are asked of each candidate?
    A) structured
    B) unstructured
    C) EEO requirement
    D) open-ended

44. Which type of compensation is an annual bonus?
    A) time-based
    B) direct
    C) indirect
    D) equitable

45. According to Herzberg's theory, which of the following is a motivation factor?
    A) personal growth
    B) relationships with coworkers
    C) job security
    D) work environment

46. Which of the following is a funding model of insurance?
   A) self-funded
   B) fully insured
   C) both A and B
   D) none of the above

47. Which of the following is NOT an example of a wellness program?
   A) a smoking cessation program
   B) profit sharing
   C) a weight loss program
   D) an employee assistance program

48. Which restructuring practice broadens job scope by expanding the tasks required of it?
   A) job rotation
   B) job elimination
   C) delegation
   D) job enlargements

49. What is a payment given to employees who are laid off through no fault of their own?
   A) life insurance
   B) unemployment compensation
   C) temporary pay
   D) variable pay

50. What is an appropriate first response by employers to sexual harassment complaints?
   A) to report the complaint to law enforcement
   B) to announce the complaint to all employees
   C) to investigate the complaints
   D) to call a meeting to discuss sexual harassment in the workplace

51. Which law prohibits mandatory retirement based on an employee's age?
   A) the Americans with Disabilities Act
   B) the Genetic Information Nondiscrimination Act
   C) the Age Discrimination in Employment Act
   D) the Fair Labor Standards Act

52. Someone who is paid below the established pay range of a job is considered to be which of the following?
   A) green-circled
   B) red-circled
   C) eligible for a raise
   D) discriminated against

53. When does salary compression occur?
   A) when employees are paid below the market rate
   B) when employees in the same job receive the same salary
   C) when the starting salaries for new hires outpace year-to-year raises for existing staff
   D) when international workers earn less than others due to the cost of living

54. Which of the following is true under ADEA?
   A) A company may not set a retirement age.
   B) A company may discontinue pension accruals for employees over age sixty-two.
   C) An employer may terminate an employee over age forty for poor performance.
   D) It is against the law to require employees to be over the age of eighteen.

55. A company wants to understand the attitudes of employees in a short amount of time. Which method would be MOST appropriate?
   A) observation
   B) in-person interview
   C) questionnaire
   D) social media scan

56. Which of the following laws protects people with physical or mental limitations from discrimination?
   A) FMLA
   B) ADA
   C) ADEA
   D) ERISA

57. Which of the following is considered indirect compensation?
   A) the use of a company cell phone
   B) short-term disability insurance
   C) 401(k) matching contributions
   D) all of the above

58. The term *quid pro quo* refers to which of the following?
   A) sexual harassment
   B) workplace accommodations
   C) orientation
   D) whistleblowing

59. Which term is used to describe a workweek in which a full week's work is completed in fewer days?
   A) a compressed workweek
   B) telecommuting
   C) job sharing
   D) work-life balance

60. Which of the following is NOT an internal recruitment activity?
   A) employee referrals
   B) job posting on a website
   C) job rotation
   D) promoting from within

61. If the state's minimum wage is higher than the federal minimum wage, what is the MINIMUM amount that employers are required to pay employees?
   A) state minimum wage
   B) federal minimum wage
   C) average of state and federal minimum wages
   D) none of the above

62. Right-to-work laws allow states to do which of the following?
   A) ensure all citizens retain their jobs
   B) require binding arbitration for disputes
   C) require union membership at any company
   D) prohibit compulsory union membership

63. Collective bargaining, through which unions negotiate pay and working conditions that are similar to those that exist within the industry, is referred to as which of the following?
   A) multiple bargaining
   B) parallel bargaining
   C) coordinated bargaining
   D) market bargaining

64. Which of the following can occur directly from employee complaints?
   A) Employees can be reassigned to other departments.
   B) Managers can be suspended or fired.
   C) The company can identify areas where improvements may be needed.
   D) Management can hire more staff.

65. One measurement that can be used to evaluate the recruitment process is the comparison between the number of applicants per stage of hire and the number that moves onto the next stage of hire. What is this metric called?
   A) yield ratio
   B) recruitment costs
   C) selection ratio
   D) acceptance rate

66. An employee with HIV/AIDS who can perform essential functions of her job and is not a threat to the safety of other employees is protected by which law?
   A) EEOC
   B) FLSA
   C) ADA
   D) ADEA

67. Which of the following is an informal process of dispute resolution used by the EEOC?
   A) employment at will
   B) conciliation
   C) mandated benefits
   D) reconciliation

68. Which of the following does NOT usually affect recruitment planning?
   A) government regulations
   B) demographics of the workforce
   C) available labor pool
   D) location of the organization

69. Which of the following is a compensation philosophy that determines the value of the person's job in the organization and in the market?
   A) market-based pay
   B) pay for the person
   C) pay for the job
   D) equitable pay

70. As part of the hiring process, a scenario is set up in which candidates must make decisions about a customer concern. This is an example of which type of testing?
   A) physical abilities test
   B) cognitive abilities test
   C) situational judgment test
   D) work sample test

71. Which of the following is NOT a characteristic of independent contractors?
   A) They can work off-site.
   B) They have flexibility to set their own work schedules.
   C) They have an indefinite relationship with the employer.
   D) They must use their own work tools.

72. Which of the following BEST describes mentoring?
   A) providing feedback to a subordinate regarding her performance on the job
   B) a professional relationship between two people that involves advice and support
   C) training a classroom of new hires on a product or service
   D) shadowing a person to learn his job

73. A manager at a restaurant hires only young women as servers. What is this an example of?
   A) disparate treatment
   B) adverse impact
   C) harassment
   D) fair employment practice

74. How long do employers have to verify an employee's eligibility to work in the US?
   A) one day
   B) three days
   C) seven days
   D) fourteen days

75. What should be completed before writing a job description?
   A) candidate interview
   B) job analysis
   C) downsizing
   D) restructuring

76. A forced distribution method of rating employees does which of the following?
   A) It rates employees across a standard distribution.
   B) It ranks employees in order of productivity.
   C) It distributes 360 surveys to the employee's peers.
   D) It makes the employee rate himself or herself.

77. Which of the following is true about nondiscrimination laws?
    A) Federal laws supersede state laws.
    B) Employers must follow the law that provides the greatest employee protection.
    C) State laws supersede federal laws.
    D) The Bill of Rights supersedes federal and state laws.

78. Which question should an employer NOT ask its applicants?
    A) Are you able to perform the essential functions of the job with or without reasonable accommodation?
    B) Are you able to work on Sundays?
    C) Are you a US citizen?
    D) Are you over eighteen years old?

79. Workers' compensation is regulated by which body?
    A) state government
    B) the Department of Labor
    C) the OFCCP
    D) the NLRB

80. The ADEA prohibits discrimination against which age groups?
    A) people over age eighteen
    B) people between the ages of twenty-one and sixty-five
    C) people between the ages of forty and sixty-five
    D) people over age forty

81. Which of the following questions may an employer ask an applicant?
    A) Do you speak English fluently?
    B) What race are you?
    C) Are you married?
    D) Do you have a disability?

82. What did the *McDonnell-Douglas Corp. v. Green* case establish?
    A) adverse impact
    B) unfair employment practices
    C) disparate treatment
    D) pregnancy nondiscrimination

83. Whose needs does career planning focuses on?
    A) employees
    B) managers
    C) the organization
    D) owners

84. Which concept recognizes that employee productivity is directly related to job satisfaction?
    A) HR management
    B) strategic planning
    C) human relations
    D) performance management

85. Who does NOT typically appraise an employee's performance in a 360-degree performance appraisal system?
   A) peers
   B) subordinates
   C) current supervisor
   D) clients

86. Which of the following terms refers to an audit of the services and costs billed by health care providers?
   A) claims analysis
   B) utilization review
   C) performance guarantee
   D) pay for performance

87. Carl supervises a team of accountants in Michigan. He is hot-tempered, screams at individuals, and blows up over the smallest errors. He micromanages and rides employees when they are given assignments. When he is in a particularly bad mood, he likes to choose one person on which to focus his negative attention. The team is always on edge because they do not know when they might be the focus of Carl's rants. What is this an example of?
   A) bullying
   B) illegal harassment
   C) wage and hour violation
   D) nepotism

88. When settling a labor contract, what is the process called when two parties cannot come to an agreement and use a third party to make a final decision?
   A) conciliation
   B) arbitration
   C) pacification
   D) ratification

89. The human resources manager has created a document listing all of the requisite education, skills, and abilities needed to perform a specific role. What is this document called?
   A) job description
   B) job specification
   C) job analysis
   D) job requisition

90. When creating an offer of employment, which of the following is inappropriate to include?
   A) job details
   B) pay-related items
   C) employee benefits summary
   D) permanent or temporary status

91. Your payroll clerk has been performing well. She currently enters time and attendance and is interested in taking on more responsibilities, so you add verification and payroll run to her duties. This is an example of which type of job redesign?

A) job enlargement
B) job enrichment
C) job rotation
D) task significance

92. An organization that is reducing the number of hours employees are working, initiating a hiring freeze, and offering a voluntary separation program may be implementing strategies to manage which of the following?

A) a talent shortage
B) a redesign of work
C) a merger or acquisition
D) a talent surplus

93. An employee who is paid a fixed amount but also qualifies for overtime pay falls into which classification?

A) salaried
B) hourly
C) salaried nonexempt
D) exempt

94. Which of the following offers the advantage of flexibility in staffing levels and access to subject-matter experts?

A) a professional employer organization
B) a recruitment agency
C) independent contractors
D) employee referrals

95. Cost of testing, background checks, relocation, and signing bonuses are examples of expenses that could be included when computing which of the following?

A) yield ratio
B) costs of recruiting
C) acceptance costs
D) selection ratio

96. Which of the following cases first recognized a hostile work environment as sexual discrimination under Title VII?

A) *Burlington Industries Inc. v. Ellerth*
B) *Green v. Brennan*
C) *Meritor Savings Bank v. Vinson*
D) *Griggs v. Duke Power Co.*

97. Which of the following describes when a firm contracts with an organization to support terminated employees in their job searches during a layoff?
   A) job elimination
   B) downsizing assistance
   C) outplacement services
   D) temporary services

98. A human resources department is assessing its performance compared to other divisions and organizations. What is this is an example of?
   A) benchmarking
   B) balanced scorecard
   C) human resources audit
   D) human resources metrics

99. The Pregnancy Discrimination Act requires employers of fifteen or more people to do which of the following?
   A) offer family and medical leave
   B) treat maternity as any other leave
   C) offer six weeks of paid leave
   D) designate a space for nursing mothers

100. An organization may use separation costs, replacement costs, and training costs to measure which of the following?
   A) turnover costs
   B) recruitment costs
   C) absenteeism costs
   D) job satisfaction

101. Anthony works in a high-stress job that requires a significant amount of creativity. His organization has offered to give him three months off with pay so that he can travel and rejuvenate. What is this type of benefit called?
   A) PTO
   B) vacation
   C) sabbatical
   D) leave of absence

102. Craig was a good performer all year, but in the last few weeks he has missed a significant amount of time to tend to his aging mother. His supervisor gave him a poor rating because of this change in behavior. This is an example of which type of rater error?
   A) varying standards
   B) sampling error
   C) recency effect
   D) central tendency

103. What is the set of shared values and beliefs that govern an organization?
   A) psychological contract
   B) organizational culture
   C) vision statement
   D) organizational convention

104. An employee is fired two days after filing a discrimination complaint with his manager. It appears that which of the following may have occurred?
   A) disparate treatment
   B) disparate impact
   C) harassment
   D) retaliation

105. An interview is scheduled during the week before Easter. The hiring manager is making small talk with the candidate and asks what Easter traditions their family celebrates. Which type of discrimination could occur as a result of this question?
   A) gender
   B) age
   C) religion
   D) disability

106. When deciding on a relocation area, it is important to look at the pool of candidates in that area. What is this local candidate supply called?
   A) the labor market
   B) the applicant pool
   C) the unemployment rate
   D) the outsourcing market

107. Which type of organization does NOT have to complete the EEO-1 annual reporting form?
   A) private employers with 100 or more employees
   B) state and local governments
   C) federal contractors with fifty or more employees and $50,000 or more in contracts
   D) financial institutions that hold government funds or bonds and have fifty or more employees

108. Which of the following is an advantage of using a questionnaire during a job analysis?
   A) It is widely used and accepted.
   B) Information on a large number of jobs can be collected.
   C) It allows for clarification and verification.
   D) It can simultaneously measure literacy.

109. Which of the following agencies ensures that federal contractors use nondiscriminatory practices?
   A) the EEOC
   B) the OFCCP
   C) the NLRB
   D) the DOL

110. If the director of HR asks how many candidates are in the applicant pool, which number should be given?
   A) the total number of individuals who are available for selection
   B) the total number of individuals who have been evaluated for selection
   C) the total number of individuals selected for a final interview
   D) the total number of hires versus applicants

111. Which type of organization supplies its own workforce to an employer?
   A) an employment-leasing organization
   B) a professional employer organization
   C) a recruitment agency
   D) an outsourcing firm

112. Interns sometimes complain that they are not fully utilized during their time at an organization. Which step could an organization take to offer a successful internship experience?
   A) pay reasonable rates that are lower than what full-time employees earn
   B) take advantage of the help and finish off mundane projects
   C) plan ahead of time and decide what the company really needs
   D) do not bore interns with new-hire paperwork

113. In testing, the term *validity* refers to what?
   A) consistency of the test between applicants
   B) the extent to which the test measures what it intends to measure
   C) the measurement of personality characteristics
   D) the fit of the right person to the culture of the organization

114. A former employee has submitted a claim with the EEOC and received a "right to sue" letter. What does this mean?
   A) The EEOC acknowledges their complaint submission.
   B) The complaint will be moving into mediation.
   C) The complainant has a right to sue in federal court.
   D) The EEOC has determined it has jurisdiction.

115. A physical abilities test was designed internally, but the supervisor administered the test before it could be validated. Which act could the organization be violating unintentionally?
   A) FLSA
   B) ADA
   C) OSHA
   D) the Immigration Reform and Control Act

Answer Explanations #1

1. D: Strategic HR management includes planning, developing objectives, and aligning resources.

2. A: Synthesis refers to the combination of multiple sources or ideas. It does not measure or evaluate training outcomes. Reactions, learning, and behavior are all outcomes or criteria that can be evaluated.

3. C: An employer cannot restrain or coerce employees who are exercising their rights under the National Labor Relations Act (NLRA). Employers do, however, have the right to correct untrue statements, discuss their own experiences with the union, and compare the pay and benefits of the company to those of union facilities.

4. D: It is important to include all three activities. Assessing both the external and internal factors influencing the organization and using assessment tools such as the SWOT analysis are necessary when conducting strategic planning.

5. B: Vroom's expectancy theory states that employees will act or behave in specific ways when they believe their efforts will lead to positive outcomes. Expectancy theory includes an individual's effort, performance, and outcomes.

6. D: In right-to-work states, an employee cannot be forced to become a full-dues-paying member of a union; however, the union still has a legal duty to represent nonmember employees in the bargaining unit.

7. A: A mission statement is the company's statement of its purpose.

8. A: Training can lead to a reduction in errors and turnover, along with improved productivity. These all help increase profits.

9. C: Title VII of the Civil Service Reform Act of 1978 recognizes the right of federal employees to engage in collective bargaining.

10. B: The positively accelerating learning curve represents the learner's increasing pace over time.

11. C: Management training is associated with workforce expansion to ensure the needed skills as the organization grows.

12. C: HR audits are internal audits that measure the effectiveness of the function and identify strategies for improvement. Determining the number of staff or the type of HRIS system might be an outcome of the audit, but these are not the primary purposes.

13. B: Behavioral-based training focuses on impacting behavior with the goal of changing overall behavior. Internships provide real-world experiences to gain skills for future jobs or roles.

14. C: A de minimus violation is a technical violation that has no direct impact on health or safety and falls into the category of least-serious class of violation.

15. C: The NLRA excludes several occupations from union representation including agricultural laborer, domestic service employees, supervisors, and key employees.

16. A: Salary simply refers to an employee receiving regular payments. Salaried employees can be exempt or nonexempt from the Fair Labor Standards Act (FLSA).

17. C: A centralized approach creates a standard compensation system that may be difficult to implement in an organization with a large global presence.

18. D: The FMLA requires employers of a certain size to provide leave, but it does not require that this leave be paid.

19. B: At-will employees are those who work without a contract or agreement that establishes any set length of employment. The employee or employer may terminate the relationship at any time.

20. C: The Occupational Safety and Health Administration (OSHA) was established in 1970 by the Occupational Safety and Health Act to enforce federal laws regarding safety on the job.

21. C: The Age Discrimination in Employment Act (ADEA) applies to any employer with twenty or more employees. Both the Vietnam Era Veterans' Readjustment Assistance Act and affirmative action apply to federal contractors and subcontractors. The Rehabilitation Act applies to federal agencies.

22. B: Product and service design are not typical HR functions. Customer service, research and development, or operations would usually handle these tasks.

23. B: OSHA dictates that illness, injury, and incident records must be kept for a minimum of five years.

24. A: When an employee fails to follow safety rules, no matter the reason, it is considered an unsafe act.

25. A: The Employee Retirement Income Security Act of 1974 (ERISA) is a federal law that establishes minimum standards for retirement, health, and welfare benefit plans.

26. C: Defined-contribution, defined-benefit, and profit-sharing plans are all forms of employee retirement plans.

27. D: All three of these compensation programs reward employees, either individually or as a group, for productivity or performance.

28. C: The law does allow a bona fide occupational qualification (BFOQ) to be used when there is a work-related reason, such as hiring a particular actor for a specific role.

29. D: The OSHA Form 300 is a detailed log of all work-related injuries and illnesses whether recordable or not. This form is different from the 300A, which is a public summary that counts only recordable work-related injuries and illnesses.

30. B: Transactional leaders reward or punish based on an outcome to influence an employee's behavior. This type of leader typically becomes involved when standards are not met because an outcome is not reached.

31. C: A ranking system compares employees based on their performances. Employees are ranked against other employees within their departments or the organization.

32. C: Option C is correct because this plan emphasizes the employee's inclusion within the organization as an equal member of the employee team. A likely consequence is that prospective LGBTQ candidates will feel welcome to apply for the position. Option A is incorrect because Pride Month is celebrated by most major organizations; it is therefore unlikely that this plan will be effective in helping the organization stand out from among its peers. Option B is incorrect because, while this plan is likely to improve the company's DEI metrics, it is unlikely to increase the quantity of external diverse candidates who apply to the position. Option D is incorrect because this plan makes the mistake of discriminating against candidates of a certain background. Encouraging diversity is different from restricting applicants.

33. D: A compensation philosophy should include all of these elements.

34. B: A bona fide occupational qualification (BFOQ) must be related to the individual's ability to perform the role. In this case height, citizenship, and education do not limit performance.

35. D: Designing jobs is a task that uses job analysis; it is not part of the job analysis process.

36. A: The Employee Retirement Income Security Act (ERISA) of 1974 is a federal law that establishes minimum standards for retirement and health and welfare benefit plans.

37. C: An employee has 180 days to file a complaint from the day the discrimination took place.

38. D: People born between 1965 and 1980 are considered part of Generation X.

39. C: As part of the interactive process to determine reasonable accommodations, the employer may review accommodation requests from a health care provider. The employer may also ask the employee for documentation about the disability.

40. A: Training, facility tours, and integration all should be included in the onboarding process. Job satisfaction cannot be determined before the job has even begun.

41. D: An employee's behavior—the way an employee acts or conducts themself—is influenced by that person's skills, attitude, and knowledge.

42. B: Disparate impact is a result of unintentional discrimination that can arise from a seemingly neutral policy.

43. A: In a structured interview, established questions are asked of each candidate.

44. B: Direct compensation refers to monetary compensation for time worked or results obtained.

45. A: Herzberg's motivators include personal growth as well as achievement, recognition, the work itself, responsibility, and advancement.

46. C: Both the self-funded and fully insured models are used by organizations.

47. B: Profit sharing is an example of a variable compensation program.

48. D: Job enlargement means adding tasks to an existing job.

49. B: Unemployment compensation is paid to individuals who have lost their jobs through no faults of their own.

50. C: The employer should investigate the complaints. A policy and regular training plan should be in place to address accusations of sexual harassment. This policy should include an investigation procedure that should be carried out if a complaint is received. Law enforcement may or may not need to be involved, depending on the complaint.

51. C: The Age Discrimination in Employment Act (ADEA) prohibits age discrimination against individuals who are aged forty years or older.

52. A: A green-circled employee is one who has been identified as being compensated below the minimum of the pay range and who is tagged for wage adjustments in order to ensure that the employee is brought into the grade over an established period of time.

53. C: Salary compression happens when a more senior employee is paid relatively the same as a new hire with less experience.

54. C: The Age Discrimination in Employment Act (ADEA) prohibits age discrimination against individuals who are aged forty years or older; however, it does not prohibit an employer from terminating an employee for performance or other job-related issues.

55. C: A questionnaire can most accurately gather data in a short time frame from a large number of individuals. The other options would take more time or be less accurate.

56. B: The Americans with Disabilities Act (ADA) protects individuals with disabilities, including physical or mental, from discrimination based on those disabilities within the workplace.

57. D: Indirect compensation refers to expenditures the company makes on behalf of an individual. These include benefits and nonmonetary rewards.

58. A: Quid pro quo refers to harassment—often sexual—in which an employee does some sort of favor for another employee with the expectation of something in return. For example, a job outcome might be tied directly to unwelcomed sexual advances.

59. A: In a compressed workweek, an employee works the traditional number of hours in fewer than the traditional number of days (e.g., four ten- hour days instead of five eight-hour days).

60. B: Website job postings notify the external candidate pool about a job and attract talent from outside the organization.

61. A: Employers are required to pay the higher of the minimum wages when the state and federal minimum wages differ.

62. D: One feature of right-to-work states is that compulsory union membership is prohibited.

63. B: Parallel bargaining is collective bargaining in which unions negotiate pay and/or working conditions within an industry or region.

64. C: An employee complaint may indirectly lead to termination, reassignment, or increased hiring; however, only employee opinion directly identifies areas of concern or improvement.

65. A: The yield ratio is the ratio of applicants at one stage of hiring versus the number that moves on to the next stage.

66. C: The Americans with Disabilities Act (ADA) protects employees with actual and perceived disabilities. The employee's diagnosis may not affect her ability to do her job in any way; however, she is protected by the ADA from what others may perceive to be a disability should they be aware of her diagnosis.

67. B: Conciliation is informal and voluntary. Each party must agree to the resolution. According to the EEOC, no party—including the EEOC—can be forced to accept certain terms.

68. B: Recruitment planning focuses on obtaining and interviewing candidates.

69. A: A market-based pay philosophy is one whereby external pay is used to establish internal pay structures.

70. C: A situational judgment test asks candidates to make decisions or judgments about how they would handle certain situations.

71. C: An independent contractor works under contract with an organization that defines the nature and scope of the job to perform, which typically includes a time frame to complete the job.

72. B: Mentorship describes a relationship between two people in which one person with professional experience provides advice and support to the other person, who typically is more junior in the field.

73. A: Disparate treatment is a form of discrimination whereby an employee with a protected characteristic under Title VII is treated differently from other employees.

74. B: The US Citizenship and Immigration Services (USCIS) gives an employer three days to verify an employee's work eligibility.

75. B: Job analysis is the process of identifying the knowledge, skills, abilities (KSAs), tasks, responsibilities, and other requirements of a job. This information is then used to write the job description.

76. B: A forced distribution method creates a normal distribution curve of employees' performance, including productivity.

77. B: Employers must always follow the law that gives the employee the greatest protection.

78. C: This question is prohibited only if there is a bona fide occupational qualification (BFOQ). An employer should instead ask if the candidate is eligible to work in the United States.

79. A: Workers' compensation is regulated by the state.

80. D: The Age Discrimination in Employment Act (ADEA) prohibits age discrimination against individuals who are aged forty years or older.

81. A: An employer may ask if an employee speaks fluent English if it is required to perform the role.

82. C: *McDonnell-Douglas Corp. v. Green* established that disparate treatment is unlawful discrimination under Title VII of the Civil Rights Act.

83. A: In career planning, employees determine their career goals, and the organization supports their growth to achieve those goals.

84. C: The term *human relations* describes the relationship between how people are treated and how they perform and are satisfied with their jobs.

85. D: Typically, 360-degree reviews focus participation on individuals who work directly with the employee.

86. B: A utilization review compares the services performed and the cost of care.

87. A: This is bullying. Although Carl's behavior is unacceptable, this type of bullying is not considered illegal harassment because it is not focused on a specific protected class.

88. B: Arbitration uses a neutral third party to make a decision when there is an impasse.

89. B: A job specification is a list of the knowledge, skills, and abilities (KSAs) required for a job. Job specifications are determined during the job analysis and are often included on the job description.

90. D: Avoid using the term *permanent* regarding employment status in the offer letter, as this could imply an employment contract and become an issue if the employee is terminated in the future.

91. B: Job enrichment happens when more responsibilities are added within a specific role, increasing the depth of that role.

92. D: During a talent surplus, employers must consider a number of options, including freezing hiring and limiting the number of hires and hours worked, reducing compensation, and introducing a voluntary separation program. All of these measures are designed to control labor costs.

93. C: Employees who do not meet certain exemption criteria are not exempted from the Fair Labor Standards Act (FLSA). Even if they are paid on a salaried (i.e., fixed) basis, these individuals must be paid time and a half for working forty or more hours in a workweek.

94. C: An organization can achieve flexibility in staffing levels by using independent contractors during busy seasons or for specific projects. Additionally, using independent contractors allows the organization to work with individuals who are subject-matter experts in certain areas.

95. B: The cost of recruiting is computed by dividing recruitment expenses by the number of hires.

96. C: The 1986 case of *Meritor Savings Bank v. Vinson* was the first to show that the courts view a hostile work environment as discrimination under Title VII. It also established that the term *voluntary* does not mean "welcomed" when the initiator is in a position of authority.

97. C: Outplacement services provide support such as interviewing workshops or career counseling for displaced workers.

98. A: Benchmarking is one approach used to assess HR effectiveness by comparing specific measures against those measures in other organizations.

99. B: The Pregnancy Discrimination Act of 1978 requires that, in companies employing fifteen or more employees, maternity leave be treated the same as other leaves (e.g., medical or personal).

100. A: When measuring turnover costs, an employer may look at the costs of separation, replacement, and training along with other hidden costs such as employee morale, productivity impact, or customer satisfaction.

101. C: A sabbatical is a benefit that allows employees to be paid to leave work for a significant amount of time (e.g., three months) for job development or rejuvenation.

102. C: The recency effect occurs when the rater gives greater importance to recent events than to the overall performance.

103. B: The organization's culture is the shared values and beliefs that set norms and govern actions.

104. D: Retaliation occurs when an employer takes punitive action against an employee for an action, such as filing a claim.

105. C: Though the hiring manager may have had good intentions, this line of questioning could lead to information about religion and religious affiliation; it may also lead to information involving other protected information, such as familial status or national origin. During the interview process, it is best to avoid questions about religious holidays.

106. A: The labor market refers to the pool of individuals an organization attracts as applicants or employees.

107. B: State and local governments are not required to submit the EEO-1 report.

108. B: Using a questionnaire allows a large amount of job-related information to be collected quickly and cost-effectively.

109. B: The Office of Federal Contract Compliance Programs (OFCCP) is charged with ensuring that federal contractors and subcontractors are using nondiscriminatory practices.

110. B: The applicant pool is the total number of individuals who are actually being evaluated for selection.

111. B: A professional employer organization (PEO) supplies its own workforce to an employer.

112. C: One of the most important steps an organization can take to ensure an intern's success is to spend time planning the organizational needs and creating meaningful work for the intern.

113. B: Preemployment tests must be both valid and reliable. This means they need to measure job-related skills and abilities and do so consistently between candidates. Validity relates to what the test is measuring, and reliability relates to consistency among applicants.

114. C: A "right to sue" letter is issued to the complainant if the employer rejects conciliation or the charge itself. The complainant then has ninety days to file a suit in federal court.

115. B: This test might violate the Americans with Disabilities Act (ADA). Any test should be valid and reliable. In particular, a physical abilities test should be administered after the job offer and should focus on specific job-required measures in order to avoid disability discrimination.

PHR Practice Test #2

1. Which of the following terms refers to the process new employees undergo to learn about the organization, their role, and their coworkers?
   A) onboarding
   B) job shadowing
   C) coaching
   D) on-the-job training

2. What does it mean when an organization is described as an "open shop"?
   A) There is a union, but employees are not required to join it.
   B) There is an open floor plan for collaboration.
   C) Visitors and family are welcome to come and go within the building.
   D) There is an open-door policy whereby employees can stop by their supervisors' offices at any time.

3. An organization is hiring a new human resources manager, and it has been decided that several individuals will be interviewing the candidate at the same time. What type of interview is this?
   A) structured interview
   B) panel interview
   C) realistic job preview
   D) nondirective interview

4. Which of the following calculations is MOST often used to measure the cost of recruitment for a specific role?
   A) the total number recruited divided by the total number hired
   B) the number of recruits hired divided by advertising expenses
   C) total recruiting costs divided by the number of hired employees
   D) the total number of candidates divided by recruitment expenses

5. Which type of interview involves asking the candidate to give specific examples of how she handled past problems or tasks?
   A) biographical interview
   B) behavioral interview
   C) structured interview
   D) cognitive interview

6. Your hiring manager's top candidate won an Olympic gold medal in skating. This accomplishment seems to be clouding the manager's judgment. Which type of interviewing error is this?
   A) snap judgment
   B) stereotyping
   C) cultural noise
   D) halo effect

7. A manufacturing organization wants to increase production-level employees' pay for mastering new equipment and processes. Which of the following types of compensation would BEST meet this goal?
   A) compensable factors
   B) skill-based pay
   C) incentive pay
   D) pay-for-performance

8. What is the MOST common type of training in any organization?
   A) external training
   B) cross-training
   C) on-the-job training
   D) cooperative training

9. A human resources manager has been asked to conduct a job analysis for an accounting position. Which job analysis method is MOST appropriate?
   A) observation and diary/log
   B) interview and observation
   C) interview and diary/log
   D) diary/log and web review

10. Which of the following is NOT a recognized method of base wage adjustment?
   A) cost-of-living adjustment
   B) seniority adjustment
   C) merit adjustment
   D) hardship allowances

11. Under the Fair Labor Standards Act, which job type could be considered exempt if it meets minimum wage requirements?
   A) salaried
   B) hourly
   C) outside sales
   D) inside sales

12. The HR manager just completed a wage assessment and noticed that Kelli is paid significantly above the range and the market. Which step might the HR manager take?
   A) green-circle Kelli
   B) red-circle Kelli
   C) set up a job rotation for Kelli
   D) make a contrast adjustment for Kelli

13. An organization works with an independent contractor; however, the HR professional is concerned that this individual should actually be classified as an employee. Which of the following causes the HR professional to question the classification?
   A) The individual supplies their own tools.
   B) The organization is the only one this person works with.
   C) The individual sets his own hours.
   D) The individual has a second person working with him.

14. Which of the following BEST describes a pay grade?
    A) when employees receive increases based on performance or a "grade"
    B) when the employer uses market data to determine the value of a job
    C) when jobs are grouped by relative value within an organization and assigned a wage range
    D) when an organization provides a retirement program

15. Which of the following should NOT be included in the "personal information" section of an employment application?
    A) name
    B) address
    C) date of birth
    D) phone number

16. Which of the following would be a job specification for an accounting role?
    A) laptop computer
    B) bachelor's degree in accounting
    C) quarter-end reporting
    D) supervises three individuals

17. An employer felt extreme pressure to hire since production was suffering. A person who stopped by to inquire about employment was therefore hired on the spot; no references or background checks were done. Later, this person was violent in the workplace and injured another employee. It was discovered that the new hire has a criminal record that includes felony assault. What is this an example of?
    A) halo error
    B) nondirective interview process
    C) negligent hiring
    D) poor advertising

18. Employees were complaining about boredom and muscle fatigue, so management developed a schedule to move them from one work center to the next throughout the day. What is this method of job redesign called?
    A) job enlargement
    B) job enrichment
    C) job rotation
    D) task significance

19. The term *turnover* describes the number of—and reasons for—employees leaving an organization. Which of the following is NOT a type of turnover?
    A) involuntary
    B) voluntary
    C) controlled
    D) no fault

20. When designing training for the adult learner, which design idea should be considered?
    A) Adult learners need to know why they are learning something.
    B) Adult learners have more time to focus on training because they are done with formal schooling.
    C) Adult learners do not like to spend time practicing, so reinforcement is not needed.
    D) Adult learners respond better to lectures than to hands-on training.

21. Which of the following question types should a human resources manager encourage a hiring manager to use during an interview?
   A) "yes" and "no" questions
   B) leading questions
   C) situational questions
   D) personal questions

22. Which of the following refers to a survey conducted when an employee leaves an organization?
   A) termination questionnaire
   B) attitude survey
   C) exit interview
   D) retention evaluation

23. An employer can take steps to prevent unionization; however, there are specific actions that are considered illegal under the NLRB and other requirements. Which of the following actions would be considered LEGAL?
   A) explaining to employees that the plant will close down if the union is voted in
   B) telling employees the disadvantages of having a union
   C) surveying employees to determine how they will vote
   D) asking for information or attending union organization meetings

24. To which of the following does Title VII of the Civil Rights Act NOT apply?
   A) private employers of ten or fewer employees
   B) state and local governments
   C) private employment agencies
   D) educational institutions

25. A firm completes a study of its workforce and discovers that racial underrepresentation exists throughout its internal population. Which of the following steps might the firm take to correct this issue?
   A) ask employees to mention open roles on their social media sites
   B) institute an employee referral program
   C) initiate an anonymous application procedure
   D) employ personality testing to assess cultural fit in an unbiased manner

26. Which of the following refers to the failure to report to work per the job schedule or to stay at work through a shift?
   A) turnover
   B) tardiness
   C) job dissatisfaction
   D) absenteeism

27. The HR manager would like to clarify job expectations and key performance indicators. Which tool should the manager create?
   A) job specifications
   B) job analysis
   C) performance standards
   D) work sample

28. An employer can legally justify difference in pay under the Equal Pay Act if which the following is true?
   A) The difference is attributed to seniority and market rates.
   B) The difference is attributed to quality of work and the natural progression of previous wages.
   C) The difference is attributed to performance and seniority.
   D) The difference is attributed to internal equity within a specific department.

29. What is the perceived fairness of a process called?
   A) distributive justice
   B) equality
   C) procedural justice
   D) external equity

30. Which of the following evaluates the relative value of one job against all jobs in a single organization?
   A) compensable factors
   B) job analysis
   C) compensation surveys
   D) internal consistency

31. There are many laws that protect workers' rights when it comes to pay and pay discrimination. Which of the following laws is NOT designed to provide this type of protection?
   A) Equal Pay Act of 1963
   B) Title VII of the Civil Rights Act of 1964
   C) Age Discrimination in Employment Act of 1967
   D) Consolidated Omnibus Budget Reconciliation Act of 1984

32. Sally and Bill are both managers at a local manufacturer. They have been dating for about a year and appear to be getting along quite well; however, their supervisor has noted that they have been spending a significant time away from their desks at the same time, and this is impacting the organization's overall performance. What might this be an example of?
   A) hostile work environment
   B) nepotism
   C) inadvisable dating in the workplace
   D) quid pro quo

33. A company's guideline indicates that employees must be at least 5'7" and 200 pounds to drive a piece of equipment. This guideline has been in place for several years for the safety of the crew; however, there are no official guidelines that this type of restriction is needed. For which reason might this situation potentially be illegal?
   A) disparate treatment
   B) OSHA regulation deviation
   C) disparate impact
   D) restrictive covenant

34. An organization has recently made productivity improvements by eliminating layers, changing reporting relationships, and downsizing certain departments. What is this type of initiative called?
    A) redesigning work
    B) aligning human capital activities
    C) organizational restructuring
    D) waste elimination coordination

35. The hiring manager is sharing her list of interview questions with HR so that the HR professional can note which ones might be discriminatory. Which of the following questions is most likely NOT discriminatory?
    A) Did you graduate from high school?
    B) Where did you go to high school?
    C) What year did you graduate?
    D) What is the origin of your last name?

36. An organization that just established a flexible-hours policy, increased the number of jobs with a telecommuting option, and scheduled compressed workweeks may be trying to do what?
    A) help employees balance work-life issues
    B) find cost reduction in wages
    C) comply with OSHA regulations
    D) manage pay compression

37. Which of the following BEST defines federal regulations?
    A) sound, well-documented policies
    B) acts of Congress at the federal level
    C) laws based on judicial decisions that emerge from court cases
    D) directives that have the force of law enacted by federal agencies

38. An organization is considering a merger. Which activities should the HR manager conduct before the deal has closed and before integration has started?
    A) addressing key HR processes
    B) recognizing cultural differences
    C) identifying conflicts
    D) optimizing the workforce

39. Though Juan was born and raised in Michigan, he is of Mexican descent. His coworkers have nicknamed him "Speedy Gonzales" because, they say, he is the fastest person on the line. They also make jokes about him being an alien and constantly ask him "how" he got to the States. On Cinco de Mayo, they placed Mexican flags all over his locker. In the break room they constantly make comments about his food, asking why he did not bring tacos or burritos for lunch. Though Juan thought this treatment was funny at first, he now dreads going to work and his productivity is starting to fall due to stress. What is this situation an example of?
    A) quid pro quo
    B) diversification breakdown
    C) hostile work environment
    D) affirmative action

40. Which of the following would be considered a reasonable accommodation under the Americans with Disabilities Act (ADA)?
   A) purchase of a wheelchair
   B) screen-reading software
   C) monitoring employee medications
   D) providing hearing aids

41. A supervisor states that he does not want to hire anyone with an Italian background. This is an example of discrimination based on which protected class?
   A) race
   B) religion
   C) national origin
   D) color

42. During union negotiations, the two sides have failed to reach an agreement. In order to put pressure on the company, the employees refuse to work. Additionally, they have begun to picket and carry signs. What is this demonstration called?
   A) unfair labor practice strike
   B) wildcat strike
   C) jurisdictional strike
   D) economic strike

43. Which of the following requires federal contractors and subcontractors to implement affirmative action in order to eliminate discrimination?
   A) Title VII
   B) Executive Order 11246 as amended by 11375
   C) the Congressional Accountability Act
   D) Executive Order 11478

44. Which process is designed to measure individual performance, coach and develop employees, and reward and recognize performance?
   A) performance management
   B) pay-for-performance
   C) predictive validity
   D) psychological contract

45. Kendra has taken a role overseas with her organization. This is a two-year role after which she will return to her home country. While working abroad, what is Kendra considered?
   A) an expatriate
   B) reassigned
   C) repatriated
   D) on sabbatical

46. An employer with more than fifty employees fires a woman after finding out her spouse has schizophrenia. Which two of the following acts might the employer have violated?
   A) ADA and ADEA
   B) ADEA and Title VII
   C) ADA and FMLA
   D) FMLA and FLSA

47. Under the Americans with Disabilities Act (ADA) an employer cannot discriminate against an individual who is “regarded as disabled.” Which of the following is an example of “regarded as disabled”?
   A) an individual who has been disfigured from a severe burn but has no restrictions
   B) an individual who uses a wheelchair but is able to perform the essential functions of the job
   C) an individual who has a spouse with a significant disability that limits essential life functions
   D) an individual who is recovering from an addiction but is able to be present at work

48. An organization identifies a deficiency regarding diversity within its workforce and implements an initiative to recruit persons of a specific protected class. This is an example of which of the following?
   A) equal employment
   B) disparate treatment
   C) affirmative action
   D) accommodation

49. During an interview, the hiring manager realizes that he graduated from the same high school as the candidate. He asks what year the candidate graduated to see if they share any common friends. What type of discrimination could occur as a result of this question?
   A) familial status
   B) citizenship
   C) age
   D) disability

50. When performing a job analysis, what does the initial stage of the planning process include?
   A) review and compile data
   B) review existing job documents
   C) identify the objective of the job analysis
   D) update the job descriptions

51. When creating an employment application, which of the following is NOT advisable to include?
   A) an at-will employment statement
   B) notification of employment testing
   C) request for permission to contact references
   D) space for an employee’s Social Security number

52. Which of the following BEST describes the psychological contract?
   A) elements included in the offer letter upon entry into a workplace
   B) unwritten expectations between an employer and employee
   C) a supported bias to sustain a specific culture
   D) an agreement with an employee assistance program to offer services

53. When determining the essential functions of a job, which of the following is NOT acceptable to use in the analysis?
   A) the amount of time spent performing the function
   B) the number of employees available who can perform the function
   C) the highly specialized nature of the function
   D) the fact that the function is included in the job description

54. Which term refers to the section of a job description that indicates an employee is hired at at-will status and allows an employer to change employee duties?
   A) identification
   B) summary
   C) functions and duties
   D) disclaimer

55. During a strategic planning session, the human resources manager obtained data about internal metrics such as head count, cost of recruitment, and yield ratio, along with external information including market pay and unemployment rates. What is this process called?
   A) wage analysis
   B) environmental scanning
   C) human resources planning
   D) PESTLE analysis

56. Which of the following is the BEST example of a BFOQ?
   A) a manufacturing facility that requires an individual to be able to lift their 30-pound products
   B) a marketing agency that requires a personality test as part of the interview process
   C) a construction company that requires fall protection use
   D) an Italian restaurant that hires only female servers

57. An HR professional performs a job analysis by going out to the factory floor to watch the different operations. What is this type of analysis called?
   A) interviewing
   B) questionnaire
   C) observation
   D) functional job analysis

58. When verifying eligibility to work in the United States, which document is NOT acceptable to use?
   A) driver's license
   B) US passport
   C) foreign birth certificate
   D) Social Security card

59. During a union organization campaign at a hospital, an HR professional teaches managers the TIPS rule. This is an easy acronym to help the managers remember what they can and cannot say. What does TIPS stand for?
   A) training independence in personnel situations
   B) threats, interrogation, promises, and surveillance
   C) timing, induction, presence, and sympathy
   D) treat individuals with preferred security

60. Which benefit is mandatory for an organization with twenty-five people?
   A) retirement
   B) workers' compensation
   C) health care
   D) relocation

61. What is the name of the overarching process that organizations use to create and deliver products or services?
   A) production management
   B) value chain
   C) vertical integration
   D) process mapping

62. A manager who uses goal setting and focuses on the development of the team is applying which type of leadership style?
   A) affiliative
   B) pacesetting
   C) coaching
   D) democratic

63. An enterprise resource planning (ERP) system may include which of the following components?
   A) a human resources information system (HRIS)
   B) a logistics benefit calculator
   C) a production activation manager
   D) a quantum data processor (QDP)

64. A business that works to identify the strengths, weaknesses, opportunities, and threats of an organization in order to assess risks is using which decision-making tool?
   A) SOAR analysis
   B) force-field analysis
   C) SWOT analysis
   D) multiple-criteria decision analysis (MCDA)

65. Which of the following financial statements provides a measurement of a business's financial position by looking at its assets, liabilities, and equity?
   A) income statement
   B) profit and loss statement
   C) balance sheet
   D) cash flow statement

66. Which employers are required to file an EEO-1 report, which includes the hiring rates of individuals based on race and gender?
   A) federal contractors with contracts over $100,000
   B) all employers
   C) employers with more than one hundred employees
   D) federal subcontractors with more than fifty employees

67. Which term describes a candidate who is not currently looking for employment but might be interested in a move when contacted?
   A) a passive candidate
   B) a sourced candidate
   C) an employee referral
   D) an external candidate

68. Which of the following is NOT part of the onboarding process?
   A) a tour of the facility
   B) new-hire paperwork
   C) retention interview
   D) on-the-job training

69. The ADDIE model, used to design training programs, stands for which of the following?
   A) adapting, developing, deployment, integration, and evaluation
   B) achievement, discipline, development, investigation, and effectiveness
   C) analysis, design, development, implementation, and evaluation
   D) analysis, data, dynamic, intervention, and effective

70. What does the term *SMART goal* mean?
   A) The goal aligns with the company's values and is "smart" as to how this happens.
   B) The goal is data-driven, realistic, and includes a deadline for completion.
   C) The goal is small, manageable, actionable, relevant, and timely.
   D) The goal is created in partnership with the employee.

71. There are six steps in the succession planning process. An organization soliciting feedback from leadership and analyzing employee satisfaction is in which step of the process?
   A) analyzing gaps in future workforce needs
   B) implementing succession-planning strategies
   C) identifying the talent pool
   D) monitoring and evaluating

72. When performing wage analysis, which of the following will help determine the wage level that is held by the most people?
   A) median
   B) mean
   C) mode
   D) frequency

73. An organization offers a traditional company-provided pension plan. This is an example of which type of retirement plan?
   A) ERISA
   B) defined contribution plan
   C) defined benefit plan
   D) profit-sharing program

74. Which of the following is NOT a mandated benefit?
   A) Social Security
   B) military leave
   C) life insurance
   D) unemployment

75. Which term describes an employee who is excepted from the FLSA?
    A) nonexempt
    B) exempt
    C) salaried
    D) hourly

76. An employee moves through many stages, including attraction, recruitment, onboarding, development, retention, and then separation or termination. Which model describes all of these stages?
    A) employment stages
    B) total rewards
    C) employee life cycle
    D) career management

77. In Maslow's hierarchy of needs, which stage describes individuals' need for confidence, achievement, and respect of others?
    A) safety and security
    B) love and belonging
    C) self-actualization
    D) self-esteem

78. During the change management process, once the change has been made, efforts shift to making the change part of the regular operations. What is this step called?
    A) moving
    B) refreezing
    C) unfreezing
    D) incorporation

79. Which of the following is a good practice to ensure pay equity within the workplace?
    A) variable compensation programs
    B) pay grades or bands
    C) merit adjustments
    D) seniority adjustments

80. The Hazard Communication Standard requires an employer to do which of the following?
    A) train employees on guarding usage
    B) provide safety data sheets
    C) address concerns over adequate oxygen content
    D) protect from potentially infectious materials

81. Which section of an employee handbook clarifies expectations of employee behavior, including dress code and workplace comportment?
    A) safety and security
    B) general employment information
    C) standards of conduct
    D) termination procedures

82. Arbitration and mediation are examples of which of the following?
   A) complaint procedures
   B) grievances
   C) negotiations
   D) alternative dispute resolution

83. Which of the following guarantees any employee the right to have representation during an investigation interview?
   A) NLRB
   B) Weingarten Rights
   C) Wagner Act
   D) Taft-Hartley Act

84. Which term describes instant, immediate feedback?
   A) informal feedback
   B) constructive criticism
   C) verbal warning
   D) management by walking around

85. According to the FLSA, a nonexempt employee must be paid overtime for over forty hours worked within which of the following?
   A) one pay period
   B) one paycheck
   C) one pay week
   D) one pay statement

86. Which of the following is the third phase of the organizational/product life cycle?
   A) renewal
   B) growth
   C) decline
   D) maturity

87. In Hofstede's cultural dimensions theory, which of the following describes the achievement culture versus the ascription culture?
   A) an individual gaining status through knowledge and skills versus gaining status based on position
   B) the extent to which uncertainty and risk are accepted
   C) the extent to which inequality in power is accepted
   D) where rules are consistent for all versus rules that are based on relationships

88. When ensuring strategic alignment with a business's strategies, which of the following is one of the five critical components that should be analyzed?
   A) organizational development and structure
   B) dress code in relationship to cultural goals
   C) payroll processing cycles
   D) external forces

89. Which 2002 law addresses unethical practices in public corporations and enforces penalties for violations?
   A) the Business and Ethics Act (BEA)
   B) the Sarbanes-Oxley Act
   C) the Robison-Waller Act
   D) the Fair Labor Standards Act (FLSA)

90. When designing a survey, which of the following should HR be mindful of?
   A) that the survey is valid and measures the desired outcome
   B) that employees like to share their opinions and would therefore appreciate a longer survey
   C) to use company letterhead to ensure the validity of the survey
   D) to limit the number of participants to ensure valid data analysis

91. Which of the following is a potential negative consequence of an employee referral program?
   A) The retention rate is higher.
   B) The lack of diversity is a risk.
   C) New hires may be more expensive.
   D) Candidate qualifications may be lower.

92. An employer using the online system to ensure that a new hire is eligible to legally work in the United States is using which of the following systems?
   A) Form I-9
   B) 300 Log
   C) E-Verify
   D) ICHAT

93. What is the name of the analysis that looks at the gap between expectation and performance for training design?
   A) ADDIE
   B) training needs assessment
   C) development plan
   D) learning management system

94. Which term describes the process that employees follow to progress through their careers?
   A) career planning
   B) career management
   C) career development
   D) apprenticeship

95. For a succession plan to be viable, which of the following must be true?
   A) There must be a talent surplus.
   B) The organization must have over one hundred employees.
   C) The executive team and leadership must support the plan.
   D) A company vision must have been developed.

96. A manufacturer uses a bonus system whereby employees can earn more money if they produce above a targeted amount of product. This is an example of which of the following?

A) overtime
B) deferred compensation
C) indirect compensation
D) variable pay

97. An employee injured on the job who received income while unable to work is using which of the following?

A) a retirement plan
B) disability insurance
C) unemployment insurance
D) workers' compensation insurance

98. If an employer provides a qualified high-deductible plan, which benefit can be paired with this insurance?

A) flexible spending account
B) health reimbursement account
C) health savings account
D) prescription drug plan

99. An ice cream parlor hires workers who are under the age of sixteen. According to the FLSA, what is this employer required to do?

A) verify employees' driver's licenses before allowing minors to deliver orders
B) limit the workday to no more than three hours on a school day
C) verify work authorization
D) pay minimum wage for the first ninety days

100. How many stages are in the employee life cycle model?

A) four
B) ten
C) six
D) unlimited

101. Which of the following is NOT a recommended practice to increase employee engagement?

A) job enrichment
B) learning and development
C) applicant tracking system
D) performance and career management

102. Which kind of culture is collaborative, team-focused, and promotes active participation by employees?

A) learning
B) high-performance
C) participative
D) authoritarian

103. Which one of the following is a benefit of a diverse workforce?
   A) reduced cost
   B) improved creativity and innovation
   C) better communication
   D) reduced development needs

104. Which of the following is the required log through which covered employees must track work-related injuries and illnesses?
   A) Form 301
   B) Form 300A
   C) Form 300
   D) accident report

105. Verbal warnings, written warnings, suspensions, and terminations can be steps within which type of program?
   A) grievance
   B) progressive discipline
   C) alternative dispute resolution
   D) at-will employment

106. Which act allows employers to monitor oral and electronic communications if there is a legitimate business reason?
   A) ECPA
   B) FLSA
   C) HIPAA
   D) USERRA

107. When two or more employees—union or nonunion—use social media as a platform to discuss the need to increase wages, this concerted activity is protected by which of the following?
   A) OFCCP
   B) NLRB
   C) OSHA
   D) DOL

108. A supervisor considers an employee's actions only in the few weeks leading up to the appraisal rather than during the entire appraisal period. Which type of error is this?
   A) halo effect
   B) recency
   C) leniency
   D) bias

109. Which act provides employment protection for people who are pregnant, including requiring certain health plans to provide the same level of coverage for pregnancy as for other conditions?
   A) PDA
   B) EPPA
   C) PPACA
   D) ADA

110. What did the Lilly Ledbetter Fair Pay Act of 2009 do?
  A) It established the right to sue for unfair labor practices.
  B) It created the 180-day statute of limitations reset for each paycheck.
  C) It established equal pay for equal work regardless of gender.
  D) It created a woman's right to sue for a hostile work environment.

111. Businesses use a PESTLE analysis to determine which factors might influence their organizational strategies. Which of the following are included in the PESTLE model?
  A) political, employment, labor market
  B) social, technological, environmental
  C) sustainability, production, legal
  D) economic, labor market, sustainability

112. A team that is producing well and has established unwritten rules about working together is in which phase of group development?
  A) norming
  B) storming
  C) performing
  D) forming

113. Which type of corporation is organized to provide liability protection for the company while offering a simplified tax status?
  A) partnership
  B) corporation
  C) limited liability company
  D) sole proprietorship

114. Which of the following is true about an organization that creates an ethical work environment?
  A) Cameras are used to ensure the safety of employees.
  B) There are frequent injuries, but all are investigated and resolved.
  C) Policies are implemented in a fair and equitable manner.
  D) Employee searches are conducted to ensure firearms do not enter the workplace.

115. Which costs should be included in the cost-per-hire calculation?
  A) the number of qualified candidates
  B) onboarding and training
  C) third-party agency fees
  D) payroll processing costs

Answer Explanations #2

1. A: Onboarding is the process of helping new hires integrate into their new work environments, learn their jobs, and transition into their roles.

2. A: An open shop is one in which workers are not required to join the union that is representing them, nor are they required to pay union dues.

3. B: A panel interview is when multiple people interview the candidate at the same time.

4. C: Total recruiting costs divided by number hired will reveal the cost per hire.

5. B: A behavioral interview involves asking candidates to describe in depth how they reacted to or handled certain situations.

6. D: The halo effect happens when interviewers allow one positive characteristic of a candidate to overly influence their decision.

7. B: Skill-based pay rewards employees for mastering new skills and is typically given to those who perform physical or production work.

8. C: On-the-job training occurs once the individual has taken up the role; it is most common because it directly relates to an employee's role and allows for flexibility.

9. C: An accounting role is difficult to observe; an interview and diary/log are therefore most appropriate. Web resources will not provide specific information for the organization. The accounting employee should keep a log of her duties in order to capture items that do not occur on a daily/hourly basis. An interview will allow the HR professional to ask probing questions about the role.

10. D: A hardship allowance is not a base wage adjustment; rather, it is extra compensation given to expatriates for their sacrifices while working abroad.

11. C: Exempt jobs include outside sales, executives, administrative, professional, and computer employees.

12. B: Red-circling happens when an employee's pay is held until, through inflation, the range or market catches up with the employee's salary.

13. B: The IRS has strict guidelines for who may be considered an independent contractor. If the contractor works only with your organization, this may be a red flag to the IRS that this person has been misclassified.

14. C: An organization can group roles based on relative value to create pay grades within an organization.

15. C: Date of birth should not be included on the employee application because it could lead to age-related discrimination.

16. B: Job specifications refer to the knowledge, skills, and abilities (KSAs) required to perform a role. A bachelor's degree in accounting falls into this category.

17. C: Negligent hiring describes when an employer fails to perform a background check that might have revealed a potential issue—in this case, a violent employee with a criminal record.

18. C: Job rotation allows employees to move through a number of different roles in order to reduce boredom and the stress of static work on the body.

19. D: The term *no fault* is typically used in an attendance or disciplinary policy. For instance, a no-fault absence might not count toward a disciplinary process.

20. A: An adult learner usually has limited time and therefore wants to know how the training will impact his work and improve productivity.

21. C: Situational questions can give insight into how candidates handled specific situations in the past and how they may handle similar situations in the future.

22. C: An exit interview is conducted when an employee leaves an organization. The purpose of an exit interview is to gather information about why that person is leaving. This information may help the organization improve HR processes.

23. B: The National Labor Relations Board (NLRB) does not restrict employers from talking about why they oppose the union or discussing its disadvantages; however, the employer cannot threaten or coerce employees.

24. A: Title VII of the Civil Rights Act applies to all private employers with fifteen or more employees.

25. C: Using an anonymous application system in which applicant names or other identifying information are hidden during the initial screening will help focus selection on job-related criteria.

26. D: Absenteeism describes an employee's failure to be at work during the scheduled time.

27. C: A performance standard uses tools such as job analysis or job description to set performance indicators and expectations for a specific role or job.

28. C: The Equal Pay Act permits difference in pay if it is shown to be based on seniority, performance, or quality or quantity of work.

29. C: As employees access processes or procedures, their perceived fairness of these is known as procedural justice.

30. D: Internal consistency uses job analysis, wage data, and job descriptions to analyze the relative value and pay of a role as they relate to other roles in the organization.

31. D: The Consolidated Omnibus Budget Reconciliation Act (COBRA) provides continuation of group health care after loss of coverage due to reduction in hours, loss of employment, or other qualified reasons.

32. C: The relationship appears to be consensual, and the two parties are at the same level within the organization, which indicates it is most likely not a coerced relationship. However, since the relationship is impacting their performance, it is inadvisable and should be addressed.

33. C: Disparate impact happens when an employment policy has an adverse effect on a member of a protected class. In this case, women—who on average might be shorter and weigh less than the requirement—would be affected. There is no bona fide occupational qualification (BFOQ), since the manufacturer has not indicated that this type of restriction is needed for safe operation.

34. C: Organizational restructuring involves improving performance or productivity through analysis, elimination, and change of an organization's layers, head count numbers, and structure.

35. A: When interviewing, it is best to focus on job-related questions. A hiring manager may need to know if a candidate graduated from high school, but the other questions could lead to unlawful inquiries.

36. A: Flexible hours, compressed workweeks, and telecommuting are all ways that employers can support work-life balances for their employees.

37. D: Regulations are specific directives with the same force of law enacted by federal agencies in order to execute acts of Congress.

38. C: Before a merger deal is completed, HR should conduct a risk assessment to identify possible conflicts in order to proactively address any issues. Understanding HR processes and recognizing cultural differences should take place during the actual merger, while optimization of the workforce typically happens after the merger.

39. C: Though there is no evidence that negative employment decisions have been made due to Juan's heritage, the offensive comments and jokes are impacting Juan's workplace, creating an unhealthy environment that affects his performance and, therefore, employment.

40. B: Under the Americans with Disabilities Act (ADA), employers are not required to provide devices or services to support employees on a personal level beyond the workplace. Screen readers, however, might be necessary for some employees to do their jobs; the other devices listed are used outside of work for personal reasons.

41. C: Title VII of the Civil Rights Act prohibits employment discrimination based on national origin. Having an Italian background refers to a person's national origin.

42. D: An economic strike happens when the two sides who are negotiating fail to reach an agreement during the collective bargaining process.

43. B: Executive Orders 11246 and 11375 established the expectation that federal contractors and subcontractors must use affirmative action to reduce historic discrimination.

44. A: Performance management measures an individual's performance, coaches and develops employees, and rewards and recognizes performance.

45. A: An employee who is a citizen of one country but is working in another country is called an expatriate.

46. C: The Americans with Disabilities Act (ADA) protects workers from discrimination for being associated with an individual with a disability, and the Family and Medical Leave Act (FMLA) offers job protection for caregivers.

47. A: Though the individual's disfigurement might cause others to be uncomfortable, this person does not have a physical or mental impairment that substantially limits a major life activity; therefore, the person is not disabled. However, due to others' assumptions or discomfort, this person may experience discrimination because there is a perceived disability.

48. C: Affirmative action plans compensate for historic discrimination against people in certain protected classes.

49. C: Though the hiring manager may have had good intentions, this question could reveal the candidate's age, which might lead to discrimination based on this protected characteristic.

50. C: Before beginning a job analysis, it is important to identify the goal of the process and gain management support.

51. D: Employers should protect an employee's Social Security number and should not include it on any documents, such as an application, that might be shared or left in a public place. Many states have laws protecting employees' Social Security numbers.

52. B: A psychological contract describes the unwritten expectations that exist between employees and the organizations where they are employed.

53. D: Just because a function is included in a job description does not mean it is essential for the role.

54. D: A disclaimer section typically discusses change in duties, performing duties not listed, and the employment relationship.

55. B: An environmental scan involves both an external and internal analysis of conditions that impact an organization. This information is often used during a strategic planning process.

56. A: BFOQ stands for "bona fide occupational qualification." This is a legitimate work-related reason to exclude an otherwise protected class. In the case of the manufacturing company, employees would have to be able to move and manage the product they are producing even though it may eliminate some candidates due to disability or age. Personality testing should not be used during the hiring process, and hiring only female servers in an Italian-themed restaurant is most likely illegal. Fall protection is an OSHA regulation.

57. C: The observation method is used for jobs that include tasks that can be easily watched, such as physical actions. This method is often used in an industrial setting and may include work sampling or a log.

58. C: A birth certificate issued by a foreign government is not an acceptable document for verifying work eligibility in the United States.

59. B: TIPS stands for threats, interrogation, promises, and surveillance. The National Labor Relations Board (NLRB) prohibits all of these behaviors during a union organization campaign.

60. B: Any organization with at least one employee must have workers' compensation insurance.

61. B: The term *value chain* describes and encompasses the process that creates goods and services and delivers them to the market.

62. C: A leader who uses a coaching style focuses on the team and its development, and works to align individual goals with those of the department and organization.

63. A: An enterprise resource planning (ERP) system may house many functions, including a human resources information system (HRIS), a customer relationship management (CRM) system, manufacturing resource planning (MRP), financial resource management (FRM), and supply chain management (SCM).

64. C: A business that works to identify these factors to assess risks is using a strengths, weaknesses, opportunities, and threats (SWOT) analysis.

65. C: A balance sheet is a snapshot in time of the company's assets, liabilities, and equity.

66. C: Employers with more than one hundred employees are required to make workforce data available to the US Equal Employment Opportunity Commission (EEOC) via the EEO-1 report.

67. A: A passive candidate is one who is not currently seeking new employment but would be open to the opportunity if it presented itself.

68. C: Retention interviews are conducted with established employees to reduce turnover and identify issues early.

69. C: ADDIE stands for analysis, design, development, implementation, and evaluation.

70. B: The term *SMART goal* refers to a goal that is specific, measurable, action-orientated, realistic, and time-based.

71. D: The last step in the succession planning process is "monitor and evaluate succession planning efforts," during which feedback is solicited so that changes and future needs can be met.

72. C: The mode represents the most frequently occurring value.

73. C: A defined benefit plan is a company-provided pension program in which employees' pension payments are calculated according to their length of service with the company and their earnings prior to retirement.

74. C: Life insurance is not a mandated benefit. Mandated benefits include Social Security taxes; unemployment insurance; workers' compensation; the Family and Medical Leave Act (FMLA); health insurance at a minimum value (for organizations with more than fifty employees); military leave; and, in some states, disability.

75. B: An exempt employee is exempted or excepted from the Fair Labor Standards Act (FLSA).

76. C: The many stages of employment are collectively known as the employee life cycle.

77. D: Self-esteem is the stage during which individuals are looking for confidence, achievement, and respect.

78. C: Unfreezing is the last stage of the change process whereby the new initiative or change is incorporated into day-to-day operations.

79. B: A well-designed pay grade or band can help ensure pay equity, as employees in a specific role are paid relatively equal amounts within that established range.

80. B: The Hazard Communication Standard, also known as the Right to Know, requires the use of labeling, safety data sheets, training, and a written program concerning hazardous chemicals in the workplace.

81. C: The section of the employee handbook that concerns standards of conduct also clarifies expectations of employee conduct, including items such as dress code and workplace behavior.

82. D: Alternative dispute resolution (ADR) refers to arbitration, mediation, and other tools that can be used to avoid litigation.

83. B: The Weingarten Rights were established in the 1975 *NLRB v. J. Weingarten* case, which determined that an employee's right to representation during an investigation interview was established.

84. A: Informal feedback is given as an action occurs and can include praising, correcting, and coaching.

85. C: A nonexempt employee must be paid for having worked over forty hours in one pay week. If the pay period is greater than forty hours, the overtime must still be calculated weekly.

86. D: The life cycle phases are (1) introduction, (2) growth, (3) maturity, and (4) renewal/no growth/decline.

87. A: In an achievement culture, an individual gains status through knowledge and skills, whereas in an ascription culture, status is based on position or connections.

88. A: When looking at strategic alignment, human resources should consider organizational development and structure, workforce planning, organizational capability assessment, diversity and inclusion, and change management.

89. B: The Sarbanes–Oxley Act of 2002 addresses unethical corporate practices and penalizations for violations.

90. A: When designing a survey, it is important to ensure that the data is valid and measures the desired outcome.

91. B: Employee referral can lead to a lack of diversity in a talent pool because it may reflect the lack of diversity in the organization itself.

92. C: E-Verify is an internet-based system managed by the federal government that allows employers to verify a person's employment eligibility.

93. B: A training needs assessment identifies the gap between the performance and the expectations of an individual, department, or organization.

94. C: The term *career development* describes the process of employees progressing through their careers and moving from role to role.

95. C: A viable succession plan has the support of top leadership to ensure that the plan is valued and followed through.

96. D: Variable pay is compensation that changes directly with performance or results; it includes bonuses, commissions, or performance-sharing incentives.

97. D: Workers' compensation insurance is a mandatory benefit that pays workers when they are injured or become ill during the course of employment.

98. C: A health savings account (HSA) must be legally paired with a qualified high-deductible health plan.

99. C: All employees must show proof of work authorization and complete an I-9 form. Employees who are ages seventeen and under are not allowed to drive on public roads for work. Work hours for fourteen- and fifteen-year-olds are limited, whereas sixteen- or seventeen-year-olds can work unlimited hours in nonhazardous occupations. Employers may pay a lower wage to employees under age twenty during their first ninety days of employment. Employers should always review state laws before making hiring decisions.

100. C: There are six stages in the employee life cycle model: attraction, recruitment, onboarding, development, retention, and separation.

101. C: Practices to increase employee engagement include job enrichment, learning and development, strategic compensation, and performance and career management. Applicant tracking systems (ATSs) are electronic systems created for the collection and management of applications.

102. C: A participative culture is one in which there is collaboration, team focus, and active participation by employees.

103. B: Benefits of a diverse workplace include improved creativity and innovation.

104. C: The Occupational Safety and Health Administration's (OSHA) Form 300 is the required log for work-related injuries and illnesses.

105. B: Progressive discipline programs vary from employer to employer but typically include verbal warnings, written warnings, suspensions, and terminations.

106. A: The Electronic Communications Privacy Act of 1986 (ECPA) allows employers to monitor oral and electronic communications if there is a legitimate business reason.

107. B: Concerted activity for both union and nonunion employees is protected by the National Labor Relations Board (NLRB).

108. B: A recency error happens when a supervisor considers and/or gives more weight only to actions that occur closer to the appraisal session.

109. A: The 1978 Pregnancy Discrimination Act (PDA) prohibits discrimination on the basis of pregnancy, childbirth, or related medical conditions.

110. B: The Lilly Ledbetter Fair Pay Act of 2009 overturned a previous Supreme Court decision that limited a person's ability to retroactively file a claim for compensation discrimination by allowing each paycheck to reset the 180-day statute of limitations for filing a lawsuit regarding pay.

111. B: The PESTLE model involves analyzing political, economic, social, technological, legal, and environmental factors.

112. C: According to Bruce Tuckman's model of group development, the last phase—performing—describes when a team has the least amount of friction because processes have been established.

113. C: A limited liability company (LLC) is a hybrid of a partnership and a corporation. It offers the liability protection of a corporation and the simplified tax implications of a partnership.

114. C: Ethical organizations protect the rights of employees and create safe work environments. These protections include those regarding employee privacy and procedures that are fair and equitable to both the organization and its employees.

115. C: Recruitment costs include items such as advertising, job fairs, travel, third-party agency fees, and recruiters.

ONLINE RESOURCES

Trivium includes online resources with the purchase of this study guide to help you fully prepare for the exam.

Practice Test #3

The 3rd practice test is provided online in an interactive format.

Review Questions

Need more practice? Our review questions use a variety of formats to help you memorize key terms and concepts.

From Stress to Success

Watch "From Stress to Success," a brief but insightful YouTube video that offers the tips, tricks, and secrets experts use to score higher on the exam.

Reviews

Leave a review, send us helpful feedback, or sign up for Trivium promotions—including free books!

Access these materials at: triviumtestprep.com/phr-online-resources

Dear PHR test taker,

Great job completing this study guide. The hard work and effort you put into your test preparation will help you succeed on your upcoming PHR exam. Thank you for letting us be a part of your education journey!

We have other study guides and products that you may find useful. Search for us on Amazon.com or let us know what you are looking for. We offer a wide variety of study guides that cover a multitude of subjects.

If you would like to share your success stories with us, or if you have a suggestion, comment, or concern, please send us an email at support@triviumtestprep.com.

Thanks again for choosing us!
Happy Testing
Trivium Test Prep Team

Made in the USA
Las Vegas, NV
20 September 2024